I0894299

The Popular Frontier

The William F. Cody Series on the History and Culture of the American West

The Popular Frontier

Buffalo Bill's Wild West and Transnational Mass Culture

EDITED BY FRANK CHRISTIANSON

UNIVERSITY OF OKLAHOMA PRESS : NORMAN

BUFFALO BILL
CENTER
OF THE WEST

Buffalo Bill Center of the West sponsorship of The William F. Cody Series on the History and Culture of the American West is generously funded by the Geraldine W. & Robert J. Dellenback Foundation, Inc.

Library of Congress Cataloging-in-Publication Data

Name: Christianson, Frank, editor.

Title: The popular frontier : Buffalo Bill's Wild West and transnational mass culture / edited by Frank Christianson.

Description: Norman : University of Oklahoma Press, 2017. | Series: William F. Cody series on the history and culture of the American west ; 4 | Includes bibliographical references and index.

Identifiers: LCCN 2017010797 | ISBN 978-0-8061-5894-5 (hardback)

Subjects: LCSH: Buffalo Bill's Wild West Show—History. | Wild west shows—Europe—History. | Buffalo Bill, 1846–1917—Travel—Europe. | National characteristics, American. | West (U.S.)—History. | West (U.S.)—Social life and customs. | America—Foreign public opinion, European. | BISAC: HISTORY / United States / 19th Century. | HISTORY / Native American. | HISTORY / United States / State & Local / West (AK, CA, CO, HI, ID, MT, NV, UT, WY). | SOCIAL SCIENCE / Popular Culture.

Classification: LCC GV1821.B8 P66 2017 | DDC 791.8/4—dc23

LC record available at https://lccn.loc.gov/2017010797

The Popular Frontier: Buffalo Bill's Wild West and Transnational Mass Culture is Volume 4 in The William F. Cody Series on the History and Culture of the American West.

The paper in this book meets the guidelines for permanence and durability of the Committee on Production Guidelines for Book Longevity of the Council on Library Resources, Inc. ∞

Copyright © 2017 by the University of Oklahoma Press, Norman, Publishing Division of the University. Manufactured in the U.S.A.

All rights reserved. No part of this publication may be reproduced, stored in a retrieval system, or transmitted, in any form or by any means, electronic, mechanical, photocopying, recording, or otherwise—except as permitted under Section 107 or 108 of the United States Copyright Act—without the prior written permission of the University of Oklahoma Press. To request permission to reproduce selections from this book, write to Permissions, University of Oklahoma Press, 2800 Venture Drive, Norman OK 73069, or email rights.oupress@ou.edu.

1 2 3 4 5 6 7 8 9 10

Contents

Illustrations

Series Editors' Foreword

From his early life to his various professional phases, including the decades of the Wild West tours, William F. Cody, and the Buffalo Bill phenomenon more generally, reflects fundamental currents in American culture during the period from 1850 to 1920. Buffalo Bill's Wild West exhibition exemplified a culture of mass spectacle in the closing decades of the nineteenth century, dramatizing an image of the western frontier just as Americans experienced a growing nostalgia for this mythic place and time.

In addition to scholarship on Cody's life and enterprises, the William F. Cody Series on the History and Culture of the American West fosters interdisciplinary studies such as history, literary criticism, American and transatlantic studies, and art history, engaging the broader phenomena that made the Wild West exhibition possible. The series includes within its purview the post-1850 settlement of the West; the relationship between the American frontier and mass culture; representations of the American Indian in popular media; the export of Western narratives and iconography across the globe; and the social and political uses of key western figures and tropes such as the cowboy and cowgirl, the Indian Wars, and the pioneer.

The Popular Frontier exemplifies the broader aims of this series in both its subject and scope. For many, the frontier symbolized the tradition of

American exceptionalism, and the Wild West demonstrated the success of that message through its remarkable longevity. That success was as much a testament to the careful management of the exhibition's logistics, public relations, and marketing as it was the popular interest in the topic. But for all the care William F. Cody, his business partner Nate Salsbury, and the other collaborators took in publicizing their version of frontier history, they could not control its meaning for the extraordinarily varied audience they encountered as they crossed the Atlantic and crisscrossed Europe during multiple international tours. Beginning in 1887 with the first visit to England, the exhibition would be forever defined, in large measure, by its internationalism.

Each chapter in this collection addresses the interplay of performers and consumers across linguistic and cultural divides. The scholars whose work is assembled here repeatedly show how material particulars evoked symbolic narratives that were, in turn, adapted to the interests and needs of the local population. The variability of this process significantly complicates the story of Americanization in Europe even as it speaks to an early chapter in the history of globalization. The histories offered here fill gaps in a larger story of European-American relations, while also inviting further inquiry into the cultural impact of the Wild West's European tours.

This book, like others in the series, owe much to the support of the Geraldine W. and Robert J. Dellenback Family Foundation. The Papers of William F. Cody lost a passionate friend and ally with the passing of Bob Dellenback in 2016. His intellectual energy and enthusiasm for the documentary history of Buffalo Bill helped shape the project in vital ways over the years, and he will be missed.

Jeremy Johnston
Frank Christianson
Douglas Seefeldt

The Popular Frontier

Prologue

Exceptionalism, Globalism, and Transnationalism: The West, America, and the World across the Centuries

DAVID WROBEL

To state the obvious, the "American West" was a global frontier from the very beginning—a contested space where competing peoples and powers traded, negotiated, intermarried, and fought. By the end of the nineteenth century, indigenous nations had been conquered, and through the continued pressure of settler colonialism and the acquiescence of the nation's courts, their already massively reduced landholdings were being further diminished. Also, by this time the American states, which had only recently been embroiled in civil war and the tumultuous reconstruction years that followed, had emerged as a global power with newly acquired possessions in the Caribbean and Pacific. Throughout the century, American and European observers of the United States' expansion across the continent had readily considered that march of settlement, displacement, and conquest as part of a larger story of imperialism impacting cultures and economies across the globe.

Yet, as the twentieth century—the so-called "American Century"—unfolded, a nation-centric and exceptionalist narrative increasingly obscured the global reality of the region's past. In short, the emergence of the United States as a world power by the start of the century, and as a superpower by the end of World War II, was accompanied by a rhetoric centered on the distinctiveness of the national heritage. That modern envisioning of a quintessentially

American frontier rested on strong nineteenth-century foundations that had emphasized the ready availability of land. But it was not vacant space or free land—as the rhetoric of righteous white possession insisted—nor lands that conveniently presented themselves at just the right moments in the nation's expansionist trajectory; rather, it was land purchased in global markets or conquered by armies and colonists. The profound notion that the continent, from the Atlantic to the Pacific, had been a divinely ordained American space all along, and never really a globally contested one, also undergirded this envisioning of western settlement as the ultimate expression of the unfolding story of American democracy and liberty.

The well-known narrative of the West as the lodestone of national exceptionalism might begin as early as the late eighteenth century with the first of two notable French commentators on America, Hector St. John de Crèvecoeur, who declared that the European on the American continent became "a new man acting upon new principles," and this was because of the availability of "unrented, untaxed lands." The German philosopher Georg W. F. Hegel made a similar point in the early 1820s, noting that "the immeasurable space which [the United States] presents to its inhabitants" guaranteed its freedom from social upheaval, at least until those lands were gone. A decade later, the second storied French observer of American life, Alexis de Tocqueville, in his famous study *Democracy in America* (2 vols., 1835 and 1840), explained that Americans' fortunate inheritance of a sparsely peopled continent was the key to their democratic inclinations, declaring that "the soil of America is opposed to territorial aristocracy." A half century later, in 1888, the Englishman Lord Bryce (later British ambassador to the United States) ventured that the West was "the most distinctly American part of America," and Italian economist Achille Loria joined him in predicting that the closing of the frontier of available western land would precipitate "the chronic problems of old societies and crowded countries," and in warning that "it will be a time of trial for economic institutions."

Likewise, numerous American observers also commented on the role of the frontier in shaping American democracy and on the likely impact of its disappearance. In his influential study *Progress and Poverty* (1880), Henry George credited the vast public domain as "the transmuting force which has turned the thriftless, unambitious European peasant into the self-reliant Western farmer," but he warned that land monopoly was fast becoming the norm and that the nation's democratic future was as a consequence increasingly fragile. Theodore Roosevelt in *The Winning of the West* (4 vols., 1889–1896) pointed to the harsh, heroic lives of the western pioneers "who have shared in this fast vanishing frontier life"; he celebrated their legacy while at the same time lamenting their absence from the American present and the deleterious impact on American manhood that was likely to result. Most famously, or infamously, for scholars of the West, the historian Frederick Jackson Turner in 1893 pointed to the 1890 Census Bureau's official declaration of the frontier's end. He identified the process of western exploration, conquest, and settlement as the wellspring of American democracy, individualism, nationalism, and pragmatism, and he expressed his concern that the very conditions that had made the nation exceptional had now played out, leaving an ominous postfrontier reality in their wake, with all the positive qualities of the American character and social and political life now endangered.[1]

The geographic determinism of those European and American observers across the nineteenth century was augmented by the democratic, demographic, and divine determinism of Manifest Destiny that emerged at midcentury. America's democratic foundations, along with the "yearly multiplying millions" that John L. O'Sullivan emphasized (and which he and other architects of the theory contrasted with the relative handfuls of nomadic Natives) and the will of Providence, too, collectively mandated that the nation should stretch from ocean to ocean. Manifest Destiny offered the tripartite support of a political system, the weight of numbers, and the mandate of the divine creator. This all proved such an alluring and enduring imagining of American exceptionalism that even today the term *empire* graces the chapter titles of most US history textbooks only once the end of the nineteenth century has been reached and the process of extracontinental expansion receives coverage. Thus Manifest Destiny implicitly becomes the working explanation for the acquisition of the West rather than what it in fact was—a justification for the process of imperial expansion that was actually playing out. In this way, America becomes a favored nation merely growing into its own foreordained skin, or an empire for liberty, to use Thomas Jefferson's phrase, rather than one more empire among the several that developed in the nineteenth century, including those of Russia, Britain, France, and later Germany.

The traditional place of Buffalo Bill Cody's Wild West in this powerful narrative of national distinctiveness is well known. After gaining some renown as a stage performer of frontier dramas that highlighted his own experiences as a scout, Cody performed his first outdoor frontier extravaganza in 1883 in

Nebraska. The popularity of his dramatic reconstructions of the old western past had grown so rapidly that a mere four years later, in May 1887, his Wild West achieved one of its crowning glories, playing in London to Prime Minister Gladstone, the Prince of Wales, and the globe's most powerful monarch Queen Victoria. Just a few years later, on December 15, 1890, Indian police on the Standing Rock River Reservation killed the famous Sioux leader Sitting Bull, who had toured with the exhibition in the mid-1880s. Sitting Bull had just returned to the reservation from his exile in Canada, and the US military feared he might leave to participate in the Ghost Dance. Just two weeks later the massacre at Wounded Knee on the Lakota Pine Ridge Reservation marked the symbolic end of indigenous resistance on the western frontier. Sitting Bull's participation in Cody's performances, which showcased the conquest of the frontier, serves as another major milestone marking the end of that era. In this rendering, Native Americans such as Sitting Bull sold out to their conquerors by participating in the reconstructed narrative of their own conquest, and Buffalo Bill sold the story to America's former mother country, prefacing the global commercial onslaught of the American Century. How wild could the West be if it was now being marketed abroad as entertainment, with its victims serving as participants in the carefully choreographed drama?

In this telling of the story, Buffalo Bill's Wild West illuminates the story of the frontier's closing as the great watershed moment in western history. Cody's commodification of conquest marks the end of a process. He may have insisted that he was performing a painstakingly accurate reenactment of recent history—not a "show," but the real thing. Yet the audiences, thrilled as they surely were, knew it was a show, that they were there to be entertained, and that the show's very existence meant that the historical process it featured must now be over. Buffalo Bill Cody and the end of the American frontier is a powerful and compelling narrative, but another telling of the story, the one reflected in the essays contained in this volume, serves as a vital concurrent global narrative and one that American and world audiences were equally familiar with. The two narrative trajectories coexisted, despite their seemingly contradictory nature. The exceptionalist one was fueled not just by the observations of Tocqueville, Bryce, Roosevelt, Turner, and others, but by the popular literary works of James Fennimore Cooper, Washington Irving, and Francis Parkman, and the dramatic paintings of Albert Bierstadt, Thomas Moran, Frederick Remington, and other renowned artists who placed a colorful, mythical West at the center of the story of American exceptionalism.

Generations of American and European immigrant settlers in the West also built up and buttressed the narrative of national frontier distinctiveness through their collective and selective memories of personal hardship and endurance on the old frontier. They shared these memories at old settler and pioneer society meetings and preserved them for posterity in a veritable mass of published reminiscences. Those pioneer reminiscences, starting in the mid-nineteenth century and impactful through the mid-twentieth (and still maintained in parts of the West by organized groups today), gave human life to the social forces that Turner examined, putting flesh on the bones of his arguments about frontier democracy, ruggedness, and self-reliance. The lived experience of old settlers—or better, their memories of it—seemed to legitimize the romantic representations of the western frontier by the artists and popular writers. The narrative of western exceptionalism would prove a remarkably powerful and enduring one.[2]

There was another narrative, however, one that recognized the West for what it was: one dangerous and undeveloped frontier among many across the globe. That concurrent narrative also recognized the nation for what it was: a developing empire that had conquered its western territories much like Russia, to take just one example, had conquered its eastern ones. That story of the globally envisioned West of the nineteenth century might begin also with Tocqueville. By the middle of the twentieth century, over a hundred years after it first appeared, *Democracy in America* had emerged as one of the core texts of American exceptionalism, and its author was widely cited as a prophetic observer who had outlined the contours of the nation's benign national distinctiveness in its representative democracy and presciently alluded to its Cold War tensions with Russia (by then the Soviet Union).

That is the usable part of the Tocquevillian heritage for proponents of American exceptionalism. The unusable part is the road map to successful maintenance of empire that Tocqueville provided in his later *Reports on Algeria* (1847), where he argued that for the French to succeed in crushing the Algerian resistance and shore up their imperial ambitions, they needed to follow the example of the United States' government in addressing the "Indian problem" on its western frontier. Thus, American empire became the model for the French to follow, not American democracy. But that reading of the American heritage did nothing to bolster American exceptionalism, so it was conveniently ignored and *Democracy in America* was enthusiastically seized upon as a foundational text that undergirded the superiority of the

United States' historical trajectory as the nation sought to distinguish itself from its Soviet adversary during the Cold War. American scholars during the early Cold War years frequently contrasted the development of democracy in America—from early settlement and revolution to its position as the selfless defender of freedom and democracy around the world—with the story of the expansionist, totalitarian Soviet Union's direct evolution from the authoritarian tyranny of Ivan the Terrible (Tsar of All the Russias, 1547–1584).

Tocqueville's global positioning, in the *Reports on Algeria,* of the United States' westward expansion was as common in the nineteenth century as the now much better known national exceptionalism counternarrative. Almost a half-century before Buffalo Bill took American Indians to Europe to perform, the artist George Catlin was displaying his famous Indian Gallery at London's Egyptian Hall in 1840—a venue that housed cultural artifacts from Captain James Cook's South Sea voyages. In his lectures in London, Catlin condemned the "exterminating policy of the United States government," which he contended was dooming the Indians to extinction. By 1843 a small group of Ojibway Indians from Canada were serving as a human backdrop to Catlin's lectures. These performers were soon replaced by a small group of Iowas who traveled with Catlin around England, Scotland, and Ireland, and then to Paris in 1845, where his Indian Gallery was displayed in the Louvre and visited by King Louis Philippe.

Catlin's live Indians were there to showcase his core message that they were dying out. Then, tragically, two of the Iowas contracted diseases and died. Another group of Ojibways replaced them, but two of their number also died from disease. Thus, the representatives of a dying race, working in a living history exhibit designed to highlight their fate, were themselves dying. These tragedies brought Catlin's show to an end, and he never exhibited Indians again. He did, however, consider a new ethnographic project, a "Museum of Mankind" that would "perpetuate the looks and manners and history of all the declining and vanishing races of man." Catlin reminded English audiences that "Great Britain has more than thirty colonies in different quarters of the globe, in which the numbers of civilized men are increasing, and the native tribes are wasting away." He declared, "the march of civilization is everywhere, as it is in America, a war of extermination, and that of our own species."[3] Catlin then offered a chillingly macabre proposal that a ship would sail around the world exhibiting his human museum of dying races before they were lost forever. Thankfully, that ship never sailed. Catlin had effectively placed the story of American empire and its devastating impact on indigenous peoples into a larger global context of the terrible human consequences of imperialism and colonialism.

Likewise, the popular and prolific German writer and traveler Friedrich Gerstäcker, in his *Narrative of a Journey Round the World* (1853), emphasized a global context for consideration of American imperialism. There is no small irony in the fact that many of Gerstäcker's published frontier stories were shamelessly appropriated, without attribution, by American dime novelists in the late nineteenth century; thus parts of his work became a foundational source of western frontier myth making, while other parts provided a framework for placing the American frontier into its world context. In *Narrative of a Journey,* Gerstäcker compared the impact of the California Gold Rush on the region's Indian peoples with the consequences of the Australian Gold Rush for that country's aboriginal population, and the nature of Dutch colonialism in Java. Several years later, British explorer Richard Francis Burton was traveling across the frontier to visit the Mormon kingdom in Utah Territory. In the resulting chronicle, *The City of the Saints* (1861), Burton compared the peoples and landscapes of the Great Plains, the Rockies, and the Great Basin with those of the Indian subcontinent, the Middle East, and the African Continent. Burton also contradicted Tocqueville, suggesting that the United States and Britain, in their respective western and eastern empires, could actually learn from the military example of the French in Algeria.

Likewise, George Kennan, an elder relative of the more famous George Frost Kennan (the architect of US Cold War containment policy), in his popular work *Tent Life in Siberia* (1870), compared the landscapes and indigenous peoples of the "frontiers of our western States and Territories" with those of Russia's Siberian hinterlands. Describing the "Wandering Chookchees," "the most powerful tribe in northeastern Siberia," Kennan noted that aside from their dress, "they could hardly have been distinguished from North American Indians—many of them being as tall, athletic, and vigorous specimens of savage manhood as I had ever seen." Kennan emphasized the cultural connections between those indigenous peoples on both frontiers who resisted imperialism—including the Sioux in the West and the Chukchis and Koriaks in Siberia, whom he formally categorized as part of the "North American Indian class."[4]

As the century drew to a close, America's most famous writer Mark Twain (Samuel Clemens) undertook a speaking tour of all the British colonial possessions around the world and provided a scathing critique of that nation's imperialism, and more broadly, the imperial ventures of European nations, in his final travelogue, *Following the Equator* (1897). In Australia he cynically observed that "the white man knew ways of reducing a native population 80 per cent in twenty years." Twain further commented that the Australian aboriginal population was not represented in the country's museums, and then reflected that the same was the case for American Indians in his country. As a result of his global travels Twain became increasingly concerned by the racial injustices in his own country and increasingly critical of America's thrust toward empire in the wake of the war against Spain. His influential voice serves as a fitting bookend to a century of global contextualization of the American West by Europeans and Americans.[5]

That was the nineteenth-century global narrative of empire: a conversation that compared and contrasted imperial systems across the globe, sometimes drawing on the experience of other expansionist powers to offer advice on how best to conquer far-flung frontiers, and other times condemning colonialism's tragic consequences for conquered peoples. The United States' western frontier was very much a part of that conversation, not a region or process apart from it. And Buffalo Bill Cody's Wild West has as central a place in the narrative of the global West as it does in the exceptionalist narrative more commonly known today. As Frank Christianson notes, the Wild West spent a third of the entire period from 1887 to 1906—six years in total—touring central and western Europe. There were eight separate European tours in total, four from 1887 to 1892 and four more from 1902 to 1906. During those tours, Cody's martial extravaganza played in fourteen separate countries, performing in close to five hundred separate venues, and hosting millions of spectators. In London alone in 1887, there were three hundred performances and a total of 2.5 million paying spectators.

By 1893, the show was officially titled "Buffalo Bill's Wild West and Congress of Rough Riders of the World" and featured performers from southern and eastern Europe, central Asia, South America, and the Middle East. Of course, it was primarily a showcasing of the conquest of the American frontier, but a global cast of characters augmented the western performers and essentially placed the West in the world. And audiences would not have been surprised by the presentation of that global context—the stories of the West as a quintessentially American frontier and of the global West had coexisted throughout the nineteenth century. Moreover, as several of this volume's essayists demonstrate, different audiences found varied meanings in the Wild West based on their particular cultural heritages and national needs.

This volume's rich contributions collectively comprise an important addition to a growing body of scholarship on the West in global and transnational contexts. The historiographical foundations of this global West run deep. Herbert Eugene Bolton, while certainly Anglocentric in his thinking, was, nonetheless, in the early twentieth century painting a transnational canvas of social, political, and economic relations. His 1921 study *The Spanish Borderlands* (1921) birthed the now vibrant field of borderlands history. In his 1932 presidential address to the American Historical Association, Bolton called for a more holistic study of European influences stretching across a "Greater America," from the southern cone to northern Canada. Around mid-century, Henry Nash Smith's *Virgin Land: The American West as Symbol and Myth* (1950) emphasized early Anglo exploration of the West as a search for trade routes to the Orient, and Walter Prescott Webb's *The Great Frontier* (1952) placed American frontier settlement into a larger story of the global expansion of North Atlantic capitalism. A few decades later, Howard Lamar and Leonard Thompson's seminal anthology *The Frontier in History: North America and South Africa Compared* (1981); the work of New Western Historians such as Patricia Limerick, Richard White, and Donald Worster (starting in the mid-1980s); and Walter Nugent's work in the 1990s all encouraged the adoption of broad comparative contexts to de-exceptionalize western American history.[6]

In the early twenty-first century such global reenvisioning of the western past has become increasingly evident in scholarship on the region, from Gunther Peck's landmark transnational study of late nineteenth- and early twentieth-century immigrant labor in the West (2000) and David Igler's vital examination of the significance of the Pacific World to the West from the mid-eighteenth to the mid-nineteenth century (2013), to Anne Hyde's pathbreaking examinations of how family structures complicated the relations of nations and empires in the region during the first half of the nineteenth century (2011), and to the wave of new and innovative transnationally conceived work on the United States' northern and southern borderlands that takes us back full circle to Bolton. The excellent contributions of the scholars showcased in the present volume constitute an important set of additions to this globally envisioned West by returning Buffalo Bill Cody's Wild West to the world context within which it operated and was understood a century and more ago, both as a powerful example of transnational mass culture and as a vital part of the conversation about imperial conquest, consequence, and administration.[7]

Notes

1. Crèvecoeur, Hegel, Tocqueville, Bryce, Loria, George, Roosevelt, and Turner are all discussed in Wrobel, *End of American Exceptionalism.*
2. For more on the role of pioneer and old settler societies, and published reminiscences in building the foundations of America's frontier heritage, see Wrobel, *Promised Lands.*
3. Catlin, *Adventures of the Ojibbeway and Ioway,* 1:61–62.
4. Kennan, *Tent Life*, 161, 310n321.
5. The global positioning of the West by Tocqueville, Gerstäcker, Burton, Kennan, Twain, and others is discussed in Wrobel, *Global West, American Frontier.* Kennan is discussed in Wrobel, "Considering Frontiers and Empires."
6. Smith, *Virgin Land*; Webb, *Great Frontier*; Lamar and Thompson, *Frontier in History*; Worster, *Rivers of Empire*; Limerick, *Legacy of Conquest*; White, *"It's Your Misfortune"*; Nugent, "Comparing Wests and Frontiers"; Nugent, *Crossings*; Nugent, *Habits of Empire.*
7. Peck, *Reinventing Free Labor*; Igler, *Great Ocean*; and Hyde, *Empires, Nations, and Families.* See also Limerick's presidential address to the Western History Association, "Going West and Ending Up Global"; and Aron's "Returning the West to the World.". Richard White's *Railroaded* weaves transnational themes seamlessly into his narrative. James Belich places the conquest and settlement of the West into his broader narrative of Anglo settlement worldwide in *Replenishing the Earth.* See also Tyrell, *Transnational Nation.*

Introduction

Americanization Theses

FRANK CHRISTIANSON

Europe is central to the legacy of Buffalo Bill's Wild West. Any study of the Wild West exhibition in Europe is also, at least implicitly, an account of *how* the Wild West became "America's National Entertainment," and how this promotional claim—its meaning shifting based on when and where it appeared—found, or formed, a credulous public on two continents between 1887 and 1906. The essays in this volume address a unique chapter in the history of American nationalism and mass culture at a time when the discourse of exceptionalism was peaking even as European and American economic and cultural foundations were converging. The Wild West show reflects the contradictions and possibilities created by this moment in ways that may seem at first paradoxical but actually express the deeper logic of globalism at the turn of the century.

Buffalo Bill's Wild West exhibition grew out of William Cody's life as a plainsman and his stage experience as an actor in western melodramas. The touring production found success beginning in 1884 and spent the next three years traveling primarily throughout the eastern and Midwestern United States. These initial years were formative in several ways. During this period, the playbill evolved to include most of the performances that would play to domestic and foreign audiences over the entire life of the show, including exhibitions of horsemanship, marksmanship, and dramatic reenactments of frontier conflicts.[1] The first few years also brought together the team of individuals that made the show both profitable and sustainable over the next two decades. They included Nate Salsbury, Cody's managing partner, John Burke, his publicity agent, and Annie Oakley, one of the Wild West's most enduringly popular performers. The 1885–86 season also boasted the addition of Sitting Bull to the cast, significantly elevating the exhibition's public profile. By 1886, through the combination of personnel and staging, the "central pieces" of the show, as Louis Warren describes them, consisted of "the frontier scenes of mobility and the domestic scenes of fixity" that would prove central to the Wild West's long-term appeal.[2]

Given how foundational the first three years of the exhibition were, the account of them by John Burke, Cody's first biographer, is all the more notable. After detailing the initial development of Cody's pageant of "border life," Burke states, "After several times swinging around the circle in this country, the Wild West crossed the ocean in a steam ship chartered to carry the vast aggregation, and landed upon the shores of England."[3] The minimal attention Burke gives the early years parallels other contemporaneous accounts of the Wild West's history and reflects a concerted interest in emphasizing the *international* character of the exhibition above all else.

In fact, Cody's own 1879 autobiography concluded with the announcement that he would take his stage play, *The Knights of the Plains,* to England the following year. He was echoing ambitions he had expressed as early as 1872, at the beginning of his stage acting career, to perform for English audiences. Although his autobiography appeared before Cody had conceived of the Wild West exhibition, he was planning to export a protoversion in the form of his western melodrama. He claimed to have been "urged to do so by [his] many friends abroad."[4] Cody would invoke these unnamed friends once again in an addendum to the second edition of his autobiography, which appeared in 1888, six months after the Wild West's first tour to Britain. Titled "The Wild West in England," this triumphal account of the 1887 London season claimed that the inaugural European venture was inspired by the "repeated suggestions of prominent persons of America, and particularly by urgent invitations extended by distinguished Englishmen."[5] The prominent persons included Mark Twain and British actor Henry Irving, as well as the principals behind the American Exhibition.

Cody's accounts of domestic and foreign inducements for the Wild West's international tour reflect the interplay of perspectives informing American nationalist discourse in the late nineteenth century. Claiming the Wild West was *called forth* by Americans and Europeans alike, Cody suggests its cultural work went beyond the immediate motive of commercial opportunism. The essays in this volume address the nature of that work in conceptual and material terms, with studies of the transnational forces that shaped Cody's exhibition and enabled its success, as well as examinations of the *inter*national impact of the exhibition as it toured specific European countries, including Britain, France, Germany, Italy, and Spain. The very fact of the Wild West's success raises questions about the nature of its appeal across disparate cultures. Why, for instance, did German audiences express a singular interest in the Native American performers, the Show Indians, among the various spectacles of frontier life on offer? How and why did the Wild West's version of frontier nationalism play into the hands of Italian fascists a generation after the show toured southern Europe? As a whole, these essays confront the challenge Warren identifies in his landmark cultural biography, *Buffalo Bill's America,* in which he observes that a "full accounting of the show's meaning for its diverse European audiences would require a book in itself."[6] In at least extending, if not offering, the *full* account of the Wild West's Europe, these essays explain how the exhibition contributed simultaneously to the project of American national self-definition and European views of and uses for the frontier mythology it popularized.

Buffalo Bill International

Given Cody's early ambitions to take a stage show, and subsequently an arena exhibition, abroad, it is surprising only that it took as long as it did to find the right means. By 1887 the Wild West exhibition had been touring for four years. Although originally conceived as an international exhibition, Cody and his partner, Nate Salsbury, had opted for a more conservative beginning and found success touring throughout the United States. Indeed, after early difficulties with financing and logistics, they had honed their operation into a well-managed and financially solvent enterprise. Those initial years of domestic touring served as an apprenticeship, preparing them for the high risk and higher degree of difficulty of the transatlantic tour. When Englishman John Whitley invited them in 1886 to collaborate with the American Exhibition he was organizing for the following year, they were prepared to accept the offer with confidence in their prospects. They were rewarded beyond their expectations with a five-month summer season in London that shattered previous results in attendance and gate receipts. Both Cody's and Salsbury's accounts of the first European tours suggest that with each success a new horizon of possibility opened up for the showmen. The achievement documented in "The Wild West in England" led directly to the 1889 Exhibition Universelle in Paris, and its success, in turn, launched an extended tour that would keep the Wild West in Europe until it was drawn home in 1893 by the irresistible prospect of the Chicago World's Fair. In 1892, show posters proclaimed the Wild West had traveled over 63,000 miles during its second tour of Europe. Between 1887 and 1906, the Wild West performed in fourteen countries across western and central Europe. The combined overseas tours took place cumulatively over six years, during which the Wild West performed in over 450 different locations and traveled more than 200,000 miles.

The unprecedented exposure (both direct and indirect) to millions of Europeans of this pageant of nationalism makes Buffalo Bill's Wild West a uniquely productive site for examining how culture shapes the ways and means of national affiliation in relation to broader political, social, and economic processes. A study of the transatlantic Wild West affords a perspective on nineteenth-century American nationalism that understands the nation, in Thomas Bender's terms, as a "partially bounded historical entity imbricated in structures and processes that connect to every part of the world."[7] This unfixing of a bounded category of nationness can account for a broader transnational context, while also making the internal mechanisms of national affinity more legible. Indeed, these two objectives are not so much parallel as they are causally related, an *internalized* conception of the nation drawing on an awareness of an outside in the form of a national counterpart. Rituals of allegiance on a national scale, from the 4th of July to the national anthem, readily demonstrate this truism. Thus, it should not be surprising that the very moment of most intense national consolidation—postbellum America—correlated with a process of increasing *inter*nationalism. As Thomas Peyser has suggested, the former was not a precondition of the latter. To the degree that the Wild West exhibition expresses nationalist sentiments, it exemplifies what Peyser, referring to literary culture of the same period, has called "the mutually constitutive relation between nation and globe."[8] Buffalo Bill's Wild West shows us how transnational influences actually motivated expressions of nationalist sentiment and speaks to the ambiguities at the heart of what has come to be called the Americanization thesis. The late nineteenth-century sense of globality represents for Peyser an "important shift in terms of the exceptionalist tradition" that recalls David Wrobel's broader framing in the prologue to this book of the "global West" as a contested space.[9] Examining how Cody and his partners constructed their mythmaking machine and why it met with the success it did enables us to confront the suggestion, made by John Carlos Rowe, that "a single nationalist mythology no longer prevails" insofar as our understanding of "just what constitutes the cultural border of the United States" has become increasingly obscure.[10] Rowe was trying to imagine American Studies as a field that represented more intentionally a postnational environment. But Rowe himself would express perhaps the most realistic version of this aim when, acknowledging the persistence of an "irreducible array of discourses" associated with nationalism, he called for a scholarship that was "less insular and parochial, and more internationalist and comparative."[11] While this somewhat generalized expectation may sound less ambitious than the term "postnationalist" portends, Rowe, writing in 2000, seems prescient now in his account of the continuing potency of nationalist nativisms.

The culture that produced the Wild West exhibition may offer some parallels with the current moment of economic and cultural nativism. But then as now, the extradomestic claims nationalist rhetoric makes can be contradictory and even paradoxical. The Wild West's transatlantic circuit speaks to these dimensions of national self-consciousness in ways that both characterize the nineteenth century and anticipate the twentieth. In her study of antebellum American Anglophile culture, Elisa Tamarkin offers a formulation that might just as readily describe the role of the Wild West once it had traveled abroad. Tamarkin encourages us to consider how nationalism, "as a form of feeling, an ideology, and a set of practices, works every bit as serious[ly] at bringing some aspects of the outside in, as it does at keeping others out."[12] To explain how these appropriations informed perceptions of American character, Tamarkin describes the ways British culture was translated within a range of American subcultures. After its early European tours, the Wild West was certainly animated by a related impulse as it internationalized its format with additional features such as the Rough Riders of the World. This principle encourages us to think about what the Wild West exhibition brought back from its travels abroad and what it came to signify for Americans precisely because of its transnational history.

Americanizing Abroad

Historian Frederick Jackson Turner's effort to capitalize on the 1890 US census and its declaration of a formal end to the American frontier was a milestone in the discourse of Americanization. Turner distinguished the American frontier from European borderlands as the site of a peculiar form of social evolution, one uniquely amenable to the formation of democratic institutions. Like Turner's histories, the Wild West exhibition combined triumphalism and nostalgia in a potent mixture that drew on a more and more commonly held view of an anachronistic frontier life. But Cody's exhibition would continue to reimagine the relationship between the provincial frontier and its global stage as a function of its movement within and without the United States. The Wild West's success as a tradition that elicited nationalist sentiment mirrored (and rivaled) the Chicago World's Fair during the summer of 1893. The Wild West's triumphant run in Chicago capped back-to-back extended European tours, and both the exhibition and the mass marketing that accompanied it revealed a very different brand of nationalism than was originally conceived when the show began in 1883. In fact, the bookends of the Wild West in London in 1887 and Chicago in 1893 suggest the degree to which globalism was shaping American national culture during this period.

Turner's model in "The Significance of the Frontier in American History" points to one form of Americanization that emerged in the late eighteenth century and saw many variations over the next century. It describes one of many schemas for the process of American *naturalization* with its account of the frontiersman who sheds the trappings of European civilization through a remaking encounter with nature. The Wild West exhibition also represented this internal form of Americanization with its "Drama of Civilization": a story of Anglo-Saxon conquest in various versions that sensationalized and sentimentalized the doctrine of Manifest Destiny.

With the exporting of that drama, however, the Wild West entered a different domain. The history of the Wild West's European tours has been understood within a broader thesis on the changing state of late nineteenth-century American nationalism. One common narrative describes it as the first wave of Americanization in Europe, the preface to the "American Century," and as a key chapter in the related account of an emergent global mass culture. While these issues inform the current project as well, this collective examination of the Wild West's documentary record tries to look beyond the abundant prima facie forms of nationalism—which invariably function as exhibits for the standard Americanization thesis. Previous studies tend toward the descriptive in identifying examples but stop short of demonstrating *how* they extend or complicate established narratives of American influence. Although the general concept of Americanization helps account for the advent of a new epoch in American internationalism, it also tends to reductively portray a relentless expansion of American-style capitalism with its templates for industrial standardization and mass entertainment. The various figurations of America's economic and cultural conquests/empires/colonizations render the subject nations in generic terms that can belie the complex interplay of international cultural relations at work in phenomena such as the Wild West tour. Americanization can look very different in Europe than it does in South America, for instance. It also varies meaningfully among European nations. Even when writers of the period employed the term, as British journalist William T. Stead did at the turn of the century, they were frequently ambivalent about its meaning for their home cultures.[13]

In his account of the rise of newspaper culture in Britain and the United States, Joel Wiener points out that both the terms *Americanization* and *transatlantic* entered popular parlance at approximately the same time in the 1870s and '80s. In fact, the first substantive use of "Americanization" with regard to the British press appeared in the very year the Wild West exhibition first arrived in Britain.[14] Wiener's study demonstrates that the primary medium for the dissemination of these related concepts was, in fact, the newspaper. Wiener details how the transatlantic Anglophone-newspaper trade transformed the reading habits of American and British consumers from the mid- to late nineteenth century by catering to individual tastes with increasing particularity.[15] What the British called New Journalism and Americans called yellow journalism emphasized "human-interest, visual matter, typographical boldness, and rapid, speedy news coverage" in ways that appealed to an increasingly broad and diverse readership.[16] The rise of cheap print is an important context for most of the essays in this volume. As the primary platform for mass culture, cheap print was central to the Wild West's success by serving as an extension of the exhibition's own marketing innovations. The direct marketing generated by Cody's publicity team could actually include planted features in newspapers, even as it sought to influence the indirect content produced by reporters. The breadth of newspaper coverage, in all its forms, points to an audience of millions more outside the showground and thus also supports claims of a cultural impact that go far beyond the numbers of actual attendees at Wild West performances.

Stead's 1902 *Americanization of the World* was subtitled "The Trend of the Twentieth Century" and offered a portrait of American political and commercial systems that were quite literally irresistible. Stead concludes his study by presenting his fellow Britons with a "momentous choice" between "merging" with the United States to become an "integral part of the greatest of all World-Powers" or accepting "ultimate status as an English-speaking Belgium."[17] Citing prominent voices such as Teddy Roosevelt, Andrew Carnegie, and Walter Besant, Stead goes on to imagine a reunion of sorts with the United States at the center of an Anglophone empire. This federation of English-speaking peoples would not be without its drawbacks for the British, Stead admits, and his treatise ends on a note of ambivalence as he contemplates a certain future with uncertain consequences. Drawing on the moralist writings of figures such as William Gladstone and William Wordsworth, he cautions against the enervating influence of an American consumerism that "lays waste our powers" and leaves "none for the cultivation of the higher soul."

A century later Robert Rydell and Rob Kroes subtitled their own study of US popular cultural exports with a nod to the British journalist. *Buffalo Bill in Bologna: The Americanization of the World* invokes Stead with a measure of irony given the highly varied ways the process of Americanization played out in the early twentieth century.[18] Pointing out that the concept derived initially from French cultural observers, including Baudelaire, who used it as a short hand for changes they associated with American influence, Rydell and Kroes's study differentiates among a range of cultural, social, and economic trends. This nuanced portrait shows that European uses of the term reject the "one-to-one relation between the ideological program of American culture as Americans willfully project it abroad, and the ideological reading given to it at the receiving end."[19] This volume, in turn, builds on their work while striving to keep to Rydell and Kroes's injunction to contextualize these complex historical processes in ways which demonstrate that they are neither monolithic nor static. It also expands on other key treatments in recent years that have placed the Wild West's foreign tours within its most immediate political and social contexts. Most book-length studies in this category neither devote their entire focus to the show's international history nor, if internationally focused, address subjects beyond Buffalo Bill's Wild West. In the former category, work by Joy Kasson and Louis Warren, in particular, has established a critical vocabulary foundational to subsequent studies for thinking about Buffalo Bill and the Wild West as a cultural phenomenon. Other scholarship includes linear surveys on specific topics that encompass the Wild West as a key phase. Research by Paul Reddin, Sam Maddra, and Laura Scarangella McNenly has established a foundation for studies of Wild West shows and Indian performers, just as Glenn Penney and Kate Flint have examined specific areas of European reception. Working within this tradition, this volume considers how the Wild West in Europe ritualized multiple strains of nationalist discourse that were, in turn, part of a broader shift in transatlantic culture of the late nineteenth century.

The essays that form the body of this volume extend beyond past conversations in pursuing a range of geographic and thematic priorities. The first five chapters emphasize key contexts for the international exhibition that go beyond the confines of nation-states-as-consumers with their own discrete imperatives. Among the extra-commercial ambitions for Buffalo Bill and the Wild West was the role of cultural ambassador. Essays by Robert Rydell and Jeremy Johnston consider how the concept of an exhibition operates in the contexts of peace and war. Rydell places the exhibition against the backdrop of an emerging international peace movement in the 1890s. He explores the paradox of a Wild West performance that promoted the martial values of conquest and colonial expansion while framing its broader endeavor as a form of cultural education. Johnston addresses another key pairing for Europeans in their perceptions of the American frontier—William Cody and Theodore Roosevelt. His study shows how each embodies a version of frontier masculinity that was simultaneously distinct and mutually dependent and considers the legacy of their collectively formed type on European views in the decades that followed.

The masculine ethic promulgated by Roosevelt's and Cody's cowboy figure saw its counterpoint in the Wild West's other most enduring persona: Annie Oakley. Two scholars explore the impact of Oakley's celebrity as it expanded beyond US borders. Monica Rico considers the gender politics surrounding Oakley's international debut in 1887, which took place both with and without the Wild West exhibition and helped forge the particular version of womanhood she came to embody. For the British, Oakley demonstrated a unique capacity to accommodate her gender to her place in the Wild West framework in the figure of the "New Girl." Rico traces the roots of this capacity to Oakley's own account of her early life in her memoirs. J. R. Henneman in turn situates Oakley's gender performance within the visual culture of 1887 London as it was represented in the arena and in various media, including photographs and cartoons. For a certain social set, orthodox middle-class life had, according to some social critics, produced a generation of *un*natural women. Oakley, rifle in hand, offered a return to a more organic version of womanhood, a version capable of countering the enervating effects of modern life.

Questions of gender and celebrity in an international context take on new meanings in Jamie Horrocks's essay, which identifies Cody's European tours as a vehicle for a new form of transnational celebrity. Echoing Johnston's comparative treatment of Roosevelt and Cody, and complicating the binaries that underwrite the other discussions of Cody's and Oakley's gendered self-making, Horrocks's comparative reading of Cody and Oscar Wilde shows how their lives intersected in 1887 London and how their careers paralleled each other's in remarkable ways. The comparison is in fact highly valuable to an understanding of either figure's public persona making, as together they offer a rich case study for the *new* celebrity—one that simultaneously codified and transcended particular notions of national identity at the turn of the century.

The remaining chapters follow the Wild West tour as it makes its way from France to Germany and on to Spain and Italy, with each chapter offering discrete attention to how the Wild West exhibition was translated within specific national contexts. Emily Burns considers how the visual culture—including periodical cartoons and political posters—of 1890s Paris incorporated images of the Wild West into the cultural and political narratives that preoccupied Parisians and Americans at the fin de siècle. Burns's account centers on the American expatriate community pursuing artistic refinement and finding in Paris its own form of frontier ethos, one that invited comparison with the Wild West exhibition when it made its debut in 1889. Julia Stetler follows the Wild West's 1890 German tour to explore various ways the German audiences interpreted the exhibition's representation of frontier life. In particular, she demonstrates, primarily through the newspaper coverage of the tour, the gap between the show's aims and the audiences' expectations. Ultimately, her analysis supports a broader consideration of the link between the American frontier experience and the roots of early German nationalism. The national moves regional in Chris Dixon's account of a largely ignored chapter in the Wild West's European tours: its visit to Barcelona following the Exhibition Universelle in 1889. The relatively short stay was the Wild West's one and only stop in Spain, and the weeks in Barcelona were marked by hardship as well as by the peculiar inflection of Catalan culture in how audiences received and interpreted the performances. Renee Laegreid's study examines a later Italian nationalist phase by considering the legacy of the Wild West during that country's political foment of the 1920s and '30s. Cody's popular culture afterlife—particularly in the form of mass-market fiction—provided a potent iconography for parties from across the political spectrum, eventually making its way into the hands of Mussolini's mythmaking machine. There the question of legacy becomes a contest over heritage—Cody's specifically—as fascist propaganda seeks to adopt the frontiersman both literally and ideologically.

Collectively the essays in this volume break new ground in accounting for the expansive influence of the Wild West exhibition as a transnational phenomenon while also showing how the exporting of Cody's enterprise contributed to the ongoing project of American national definition. Buffalo Bill's Wild West in Europe took place alongside other spectacles of cultural nationalism, such as Queen Victoria's 1887 Jubilee celebrations and the 1889 Exhibition Universelle. The coincidence of these mass-consumed performances of nationhood and their at-times literal convergence affords a unique opportunity for exploring how late nineteenth-century conceptions of national affiliation emerged through engagement with a transatlantic imaginary. On the one hand, the history of Buffalo Bill's Wild West is the history of how the frontier went global, as one feature of the broader phenomenon of European Americanization. On the other hand, the Wild West's foreign tours suggest that Buffalo Bill's brand of frontierism was, to some extent, actually a *product* of globalization. For many Europeans, the story they witnessed on the Wild West showground began or accelerated their own process of *naturalization,* leading eventually to their resettlement in the United States. For the Wild West's American audiences, the story of the Wild West's international exploits—by 1893 incorporated into the spectacle through the Rough Riders of the World—became integral to the drama of Americanization as it played out *domestically.* Ultimately, the worldliness of the Wild West advanced the process of national consolidation by bringing the outside in, even as it sold the story of the Wild West to the rest of the world.

Notes

1. These could range from specific historic events, such as Custer's Last Stand, to more generalized episodes making up a frontier iconography that would include Indian attacks on a stage coach and on a settler's cabin.
2. Warren, *Buffalo Bill's America*, 254.
3. Burke, *From Prairie to Palace*, 204.
4. Cody, *The Wild West in England.*
5. Ibid., 15.
6. Warren, *Buffalo Bill's America,* 302.
7. Bender, *Rethinking American History,* 11.
8. Peyser, *Utopia and Cosmopolis,* 7.
9. Ibid., 14. See the preface to the present volume and Wrobel's *The End of American Exceptionalism* and *Global West, American Frontier.*
10. Rowe, *Post-nationalist American Studies*, 23.
11. Ibid., 2.
12. Tamarkin, *Anglophilia*, xxvi.
13. Stead, *Americanization.*
14. Wiener, *The Americanization of the British Press*, 10. Wiener points to Henry Fox Bourne's history of English newspapers for its "substantive" treatment although the term had appeared in British newspapers as early as 1882.
15. Ibid., 4.
16. Ibid.
17. Stead, *Americanization*, 396.
18. Rydell and Kroes, *Buffalo Bill in Bologna*, 9.
19. Ibid., 167.

1

"It Looks like Peace in the Indian Country"

The Wild West, the Great Far East, and the Transatlantic Optics of Peace

ROBERT W. RYDELL

> Many strange things have happened. Why should not Buffalo Bill become a Quaker if he sees fit?
>
> *William F. Cody, commenting on himself (1894)*

In all of the scholarship on Buffalo Bill's Wild West, there are abundant references to guns and gunplay, violence between whites and Indians, and the myth of the American West. There is growing attention to issues of race, gender, class, and imperialism as they pertain to the Wild West. As evidenced by the other essays in this volume, the show's transatlantic travels are also on scholars' radar screens. Peace, on the other hand, is not a concept generally associated with the show or with William F. Cody, although Cody believed his show helped bring peace to the upper plains—a claim that the US military also seemed to endorse when General Nelson Miles dispatched Cody to the Pine Ridge Reservation (too late!) to ease the tensions that would explode in the 1890 massacre at Wounded Knee. Since there is little doubt, as historian Louis Warren has suggested, that Cody's show helped "Americanize the global frontier,"[1] might the Wild West, which spent nearly seven years in Europe between 1887 and 1907, be understood in transatlantic context, not only as an instrument of US foreign policy but as a spectacle of peace (at least a certain kind of peace) that helped shape the cultural context for the Hague Peace Conferences of 1899 and 1907? Did any of the roads traveled to the First and Second Hague Peace Conferences pass through the Wild West? As the world moved toward the cataclysm of the First World War, did the meaning of peace itself become part of a spectacle shaped by the optics of Buffalo Bill's show? And what about America's place at the negotiating table at both Hague Conferences as a "great power"? Did Buffalo Bill's stagecoach diplomacy have an effect abroad? And what about its effect at home, especially after Buffalo Bill's Wild West merged with Pawnee Bill's Great Far East Show in 1909? What exactly did it mean to be a great power? Did the Wild West (and its eventual combination with Pawnee Bill's Great Far East Show) position both Americans and Europeans to think of the United States as a major actor on the world stage?

As far-fetched as these suggestions may appear, I believe they do have merit, especially when we reflect on the immediate context for the First Hague Peace Conference. The prime mover behind the conference was not exactly known for his deep knowledge of international diplomacy. According to historian Robin Sharwood, Czar Nicholas II, whose diplomatic note set things in motion, "was an amiable if somewhat obtuse young man of 30, some four years in the throne, languid rather than energetic, whose passions were the army, his family and a determination to maintain the most rigid autocracy."[2] Other European and American political leaders may have had greater knowledge about foreign affairs, and they did not exactly rush to embrace the czar's proposal to hold an international conference that seemed intended mostly to give Russia some "breathing space" amidst its domestic financial and political problems.[3] So what brought these rivals together? A half-century of war on both sides of the Atlantic might seem a sufficient explanation. After all, the US government, newly reunited after a devastating civil war, had been prosecuting its relentless wars against American Indians between 1865 and 1890 and had embarked in 1898 on a "splendid little war" with Spain. Meanwhile, Europeans had been fighting one another, as had the English and Irish. And all of the so-called civilized powers, when not fighting among themselves, had been hell-bent on quashing colonial insurrections across their increasingly far-flung empires. But the experience of wars alone would not have brought these nations together. As Sharwood points out, national governments everywhere had to contend with popular peace movements and peace congresses—many of which took place at international exhibitions on both sides of the Atlantic.[4] All of these factors doubtless played important roles in advancing conversations about peace, but it is perhaps worth noting in passing that Czar Nicolas's favorite uncle, Grand Duke Alexis, had become infatuated with Buffalo Bill and had joined him on an excursion of the American West in 1879.

Like war, talk of peace was in the air—and on the ground—by the close of the nineteenth century.[5] Discussions of peace were advanced by a cadre of diplomats, including that well-known (at least in his day) and now forgotten (a lesson to us all) French diplomat Paul-Henri-Benjamin Balluet d'Estournelles, Baron de Constant de Rebecque. Born into a French aristocratic family that traced its geneaology of begats and begottens back to the Crusades, he entered the French diplomatic corps in the 1870s and rode the waves of international diplomacy until his death in 1924. He is relevant to my story for these reasons. First, he received the 1909 Nobel Peace Prize. Second, he played a crucial role in both the 1898 and 1907 Hague Peace Conferences. Third, in 1900, he was appointed to the Permanent Court of Arbitration in The Hague. And, fourth, perhaps because of his American wife, he wrote a fascinating, if not well-known, account of his travels to the United States in which he recorded a meeting he had with Buffalo Bill in person. "Nos maux," Buffalo Bill declared (although probably not in French) in reply to a question d'Estournelles put to Cody about the showman's eternal youth, "n'existent que dans notre imagination: 'it is in the mind,' disait-il. 'it is in the mind!'" That Buffalo Bill became something of an oracle for d'Estournelles is worth mentioning in passing; more noteworthy is what the French diplomat recorded Cody as having said: "it is in the mind . . . it is in the mind."[6]

Cody, most scholars would agree, was "in [and not just "on"] the mind" of many Europeans and Americans between 1887 and 1907. True, Cody's reign did not last as long as Queen Victoria's, but considered in terms of the cultural imagination, it would make an interesting study to rethink Victorian culture in terms of its Buffalo-Bill-ian qualities. After all, Cody got out more and put more miles on his frequent-traveler account than did the queen. And it is arguable that more people saw both him and his show than ever set eyes on the "Empress of India." What about his influence on matters of foreign affairs as they related to peace? In the contest between Buffalo Bill and Queen Victoria, the queen surely wins hands down. Or maybe she does not win—at least not when it comes to the cultural construction of the meaning of peace in an age of empire.

Cody's influence on discussions of peace is clear from the event that catapulted him to international fame: the Wild West's appearance at the 1887 American Exhibition, an event held at Earls Court in London and the first in a series of national exhibitions organized at this exhibition site by the English engineer and linoleum investor John R. Whitley.[7] So much has been written about what transpired during the show's appearance at the American Exhibition that only a brief summary is required. Before the show opened to the public, it became, if not the jewel, then the bauble in the crown of English royal family. The rakish Prince of Wales, the future Edward VII, and a set of his royal pub crawlers and hunting enthusiasts learned about the show and, through the prince's handlers, arranged a private, behind-the-scenes performance and tour. That they were drawn to the Wild West is hardly surprising. As Monica Rico points out in her *Nature's Noblemen,* the virtual American West was almost as good as the real thing for British and European elites concerned about issues of masculinity and retaining political power in an age of social upheaval.

The Prince of Wales and his entourage attended a rehearsal of the show on May 8. Cody arranged for his crews to construct a royal box and invited the prince to stand and signal when he would like the show to begin. According to Cody, when the prince gave the signal, "the Indians, yelling like fiends, galloped out from their ambuscade and swept round the enclosure like a whirlwind."[8] Thrilled down to the tips of his royal boots, the prince led his cohort in roaring their approval. Afterward, the future monarch greeted Annie Oakley and offered a cigarette to one of the Indian performers, the Sioux Chief Red Shirt. What happened next was even more important. The prince returned to the palace, spoke with his mother, Queen Victoria, and persuaded the queen to command a performance of the show one week later and another as part of her Jubilee Year celebrations. Cody, needless to say, obliged, and the rest is part of a contested history. In Cody's retelling of the events, when the May 11 performance began and a rider entered the arena carrying an American flag, the queen (and everyone else in the audience) stood and bowed, and the military officers in her company saluted. Historian Louis Warren has described the event differently based on newspaper reports that had the rider, with Cody at his side, lowering the flag before an "all-but impassive queen."[9] Did the queen really get out her chair? Or did she sit on her hands? Cody was not one to get hung up on the details and doubtless would have agreed with the newspaperman in the film *The Man Who Shot Liberty Valence* who told James Stewart, "When the legend becomes fact, print the legend."

FIGURE 1.1. *Distinguished Visitors to Buffalo Bill's Wild West, London, 1887.* Poster, c. 1887, Gift of The Coe Foundation.

Courtesy of the McCracken Research Library, Buffalo Bill Center of the West (accession no. 1.69.458).

Less in dispute is what happened at the Jubilee Day performance a month later. For this occasion, the queen brought with her to the show over three hundred invited guests, including "kings from Belgium, Denmark, Greece, and Saxony; crown princes from Austria, Germany, and Sweden; and a grand duke from Russia."[10] These heads and near-heads of state were in for a royal treat. With Cody literally in the driver's seat, the Deadwood Stage was packed with King Leopold of Belgium, King Christian IX of Denmark, King Albert of Saxony, King George I of Greece, and the Prince of Wales (the future Edward VII). Cody raced them around the arena with American Indian performers in hot pursuit. The breathless Prince of Wales told Cody after his ride, "Colonel, you never held four kings like these before!" Cody's reply has become part of the legend. "I've held four kings," Cody replied, "but four kings and the Prince of Wales makes a royal flush, such as no man ever held before." Other aristocrats and ministers would soon join in this vortex of sociability, and a ride in the Deadwood Stage became a rite of passage for policy makers in the summer and fall of 1887.

So did meetings of British and European leaders with the Wild West Indians. The queen recorded her impressions in her private diary (the Indians were "very alarming"). The former British prime minister William Gladstone paid the show a visit and made it a point to meet personally with several of the Indian performers, including Red Shirt.[11] For the duration of the American Exhibition (and beyond), the Deadwood Stage afforded opportunities for countless political leaders to make deals on wheels, or at least to engage in both serious and frivolous conversations about the meaning of peace.[12]

Some clues about the content of those conversations come from Whitley, the organizer of the American Exhibition. Described as having a "Samson-like physique and force of character,"[13] Whitley managed his father's engineering firm and set up exhibits at industrial, national, and international exhibitions in Paris (1867 and 1878), Moscow (1872), and Vienna (1873). Taxed by overwork, he retreated from engineering, turned to art, and acquired an interest in developing linoleum, a new product that he believed would have an extraordinary value as an industrial art applied to domestic use. He likely commissioned a study of his own physiognomy, which provided these particulars: "He possesses an enormous front head, the length from the ear to the outer corner of the eye denoting a quick intellect and marvelous powers of comprehension." As Whitley explained it, he put his intellect to work in organizing the American Exhibition (and the succeeding Italian, French, and German Exhibitions—all held in the Earls Court Exhibition complex) "to assist in causing those conglomerations of humanity we call 'Nations' to *work* together [rather] than to incite them to maim and slay each other."[14]

To make this vision work for Europe, it was crucial, Whitley believed, for England and the United States to join as allies. As he declared in remarks delivered for its opening, the American Exhibition "would deal the final death blow to the suggestion that any remnant of ill-will or jealousy could linger on between the two great nations of the English-speaking world."[15] Gazing into the future, Whitley predicted that "the English-speaking race may most confidently look for a continuance of material and moral progress on both sides of the Atlantic."[16]

Peace, however, was not just an ideal for "the English-speaking race." He believed peace was utterly within reach for all "civilized" nations and that exhibitions, like the American Exhibition and outdoor exhibitions like the Wild West, were the means to attain the end. As if to hammer this message home, Whitley brought the American Exhibition to a close with a conference that drew together prominent American and English political and business leaders at Earls Court in Trophies Hall (an exhibition building that displayed "trophies only of man's war against the lower animals, not against his fellows"). The conference concluded, as the *Illustrated London News* reported, by adopting a resolution calling for the establishment of a court of arbitration between England and the United States.[17] What animated this resolution? Whitley was blunt. Quoting and paraphrasing a story from the *London Times*, he declared that "although at first sight it might seem a far cry from the Wild West to an International Court (or as *Punch* phrased it, from Earls Court to an International Court), 'yet the connection is not really so very remote, . . . and civilisation consents to march onward in the train of Buffalo Bill.'"[18]

The American Exhibition, in short, concluded with an invitation to hop aboard Cody's peace train. But as it traveled around the United Kingdom, Europe, and the United States in the ensuing decades, the show came to resemble nothing so much as an Orientalist express intended to wed the ideal of peace among "nations" to the goal of keeping subaltern populations at bay.

This preoccupation with conflating ideas about peace with emerging Orientalist presuppositions that underwrote the cause of empire on both sides of the Atlantic became clear just before the American Exhibition closed. Ever the promoters, Whitley and Cody arranged a meeting at Earls Court between one hundred "Arabs" who had been performing at the Olympia

Theatre and one hundred of "Buffalo Bill's Braves." This meeting between the "dusky denizens of the East" and the "Wild Indians of the West" is worth quoting at length.

> All present were anxious to see the meeting between these Eastern 'children of the desert' and the Red Men from the plains of the Far West. About two o'clock the Olympia company arrived, with the Arabs in their picturesque native dress—white burnous, baggy trousers, red leather boots, &c, and proceeded at once to the Indian encampment. Here they were received by 'Buffalo Bill,' Mr. Nate Salsbury, and all the cowboys and Indians. Much shaking of hands took place between the Red Skins and the swarthy Arabs, the latter entering the wigwams of the Braves and generally making themselves at home.[19]

This scene captured Whitley's notice and, as the subsequent history of the Wild West attested, certainly stuck in Cody's mind as well. By the early 1890s, he was reinventing his show as a "Congress of Rough Riders" and incorporating performers from the Middle East, Russia, and South America.

To what end? Obviously, Cody was interested in making money. But Cody was part of a long line of ideological innovators who were constantly updating and applying ideas about race and empire in new ways. Could the Wild West show become a "soft" instrument of empire? Could it be a vehicle for cementing what many elites considered common racial interests among "civilized" nations and provide a vehicle for containing dissent among subaltern populations in the colonies? Could the Wild West help secure peace? As early as 1886, Cody had advertised his belief that the Wild West could turn into a "grand council" that would "cement a lasting peace between [Crow and Sioux Indians]."[20]

Cody got an opportunity to put these possibilities to the test in late 1890, when, after returning from Europe, he received a telegram from General Nelson Miles to travel to the Pine Ridge Reservations in South Dakota. With tensions escalating between whites and Sioux Indians, Miles ordered Cody (who had military standing in the Nebraska National Guard) to "secure the person of Sitting Bull" to prevent him from joining the Ghost Dance movement, which in the eyes of the military would have resulted in open warfare between Indians and whites. Cody headed to the Dakotas but was prevented from meeting with Sitting Bull by a corrupt Indian agent who wanted the honor of arresting Sitting Bull for himself. The result was the wanton slaughter of several hundred Indians. As historian Joy Kasson notes, Cody always insisted that, had he been allowed to meet with Sitting Bull, who had toured with the show in 1885, he could have prevented the massacre.[21]

Perhaps he could have. Exactly what Cody had in mind in advance of his aborted meeting with Sitting Bull is not clear, but his claim is certainly plausible given that other Indians who had helped lead the Ghost Dance resistance at Pine Ridge agreed to join the show after they surrendered instead of enduring long prison terms. So, it is certainly possible that Cody would have offered Sitting Bull an even more prominent role in the Wild West—a role that would have enhanced Sitting Bull's status as well as Cody's reputation as a public diplomat. What is clear is that after the massacre, Cody weighed in with his thoughts about peace in a telegram to the *New York Herald* that bore the title "It looks like Peace in Indian Country." In revealing language, Cody made clear that the events at Wounded Knee represented "a war with a most wily and savage people, yet the whites are restrained by a humane and peaceful desire to prevent bloodshed and save a people from themselves." Military action, he argued, was necessary and just, but Cody further argued that the Indians required "sympathy and immediate assistance." "Intelligent and quick legislation can now do more than the bullet," he insisted. Entertainment, he knew, had a role to play as well and Cody's artists wasted little time generating this poster depicting (falsely) Cody's arrival at Pine Ridge before the massacre and depicting (more revealingly) the Wild West show as an agent of peace.

In the years leading up to the 1899 Hague Peace Conference, the show, as it toured America and Europe, hammered home the theme that just as the Wild West had brought "peace to Indian Country," so it could be an instrument for securing peace among imperial powers and within empires themselves. Press accounts of the spectacle as it traveled around the United States sometimes heralded Cody as "a new, but peaceful Napoleon"[22] and sometimes compared him to Stanley and Livingston, who had "shown how war, well-ordered, / In peaceful triumph ends." By May 1899, a *Philadelphia Record* cartoonist seized on the opening of the Hague Peace Conference and the Wild West's appearance in Philadelphia to draw parallels between the two events. The cartoonist got this much right—since the 1880s, as Louis Warren has made clear, the Wild West had been globalizing ideas about the American frontier and promoting the idea that the United States had, through its bringing "peace to Indian country," earned a seat at the table of "great powers." In 1899, European and American diplomats were just catching up with a reality that Cody had shown them a decade before.

After the 1899 Peace Congress, Cody continued to advocate for peace from a great power's perspective. With his life in turmoil because of financial setbacks and his infamous divorce trial, Cody's Wild West made four tours of Europe and England between 1902 and 1906. In 1903, he brought his show to Oxford. Could the young T. E. Lawrence, the future "Lawrence of Arabia" and then a student at the City of Oxford High School for Boys, have missed the show or the excitement surrounding it?[23]

Described everywhere as an "imperial figure,"[24] Cody dazzled his English audiences and evoked discussions not only of war but of the importance of peace. In February 1903, for instance, this account of the show's appearance in London made its way back to the United States: "There was a great scene of enthusiasm at Buffalo Bill's show to-day when over 3,000 boys from the London schools attended the performance, carrying little American and British flags. They vociferously sang 'The Star-Spangled Banner' when Colonel Cody appeared in the arena. The colonel made a patriotic speech, and predicted that the flags would continue to wave in unison and that the peace of the world would thereby be maintained."[25] That Cody built the rhetoric of peace into his show was also clear from this 1907 account: "In dissipating the then innate hatred that for generations had been existing between the misguided red men and the antipathetic white, through making them both better acquainted—the one with the industrial habits and peaceful instincts engendered by commercial progress and the other with respect and pity for a foe defeated . . . —it accomplished in a brief time what otherwise would have taken years." Calling attention to the show's "aggregation of nations and races," the newspaper underscored the Wild West's role in securing "the great peaceful American continent."[26]

Could peace, at least as Cody understood and represented it, be extended beyond America's shores? He certainly seemed to think so. In 1908, short of capital but long on vision, Cody agreed to enter into a partnership with his former employee and rival, George Lillie, better known as Pawnee Bill, to form a "combined" show—so called because it combined Buffalo Bill's Wild West with Pawnee Bill's Greater Far East extravaganza that Lillie had organized in 1906. Surprisingly little has been written about this show, perhaps because it went bankrupt in 1913. But last acts, however depressing, are still

FIGURE 1.2. "Buffalo Bill's Peace Congress, as the members will appear in the Parade to-day." Cartoon, *Philadelphia Record*, May 29, 1889, p. 7.
Courtesy of the McCracken Research Library, Buffalo Bill Center of the West.

worthy of critical notice—especially when they raise the curtain on how entertainment could function to promote a view of the world that made imperialism and cosmopolitanism seem synonymous and necessary for achieving world peace.[27]

The 1910 show that opened in Madison Square Garden and made its way across the nation included an advertisement in advance of its stop in Butte, Montana. Billed as "AN ORIENTAL SPECTACLE" and as "A GREAT DRAMA OF COSMOPOLITAN LIFE," the show also received notice in the same broadsheet as "Holding the Mirror of Nature for Reflections of Oriental Pageantry and Splendors." Clearly, from the vantage point of the show's promoters, imperialism and cosmopolitanism, anchored to racial categories deemed natural, informed one another.[28]

To make sense of the combined show, it is important to understand that Lillie's decision to acquire an interest in Cody's Wild West had been building for a long while. From the time he first encountered Buffalo Bill as storybook hero in novels, Lillie, fourteen years younger than Cody, was enraptured with Buffalo Bill's adventures. As a young man, he met Cody, he helped secure Pawnee Indians in 1883 for Cody's earliest Wild West performances, and he performed in the show himself. But in 1888, Lillie broke with his idol and organized his own Wild West show, taking it on both US and European tours. Over the next decade and a half, Cody and Lillie engaged in a bitter competition, deploying their advance agents to paper over their rival's billboards in towns awaiting the shows. Like Cody, Lillie made money and a lot of it, but unlike Cody, Lillie invested wisely, first in Oklahoma real estate and then in oil. Like Cody, he kept looking for ways to keep his show competitive, and in the 1890s he internationalized his performers with equestrians from Mexico, South America, and the Middle East. In 1906, no doubt to distinguish his show from Cody's and to capitalize on growing interest in Asia and the Middle East, Lillie refocused and rebranded his production as the Great Far East. Then, in 1908, with Cody facing financial collapse, Lillie purchased a share of the Wild West. He merged the two shows the next year into a "Two Bills" extravaganza that was billed as "Buffalo Bill's Wild West and Pawnee Bill's Great Far East." For four years, the combined show ricocheted across the United States, entertaining audiences coast-to-coast while showing how, in America's hands, the world, if understood in racial terms, could be tamed.[29]

The racialized footings for the show's ideological scaffolding were clear in the 1909 program produced for the show on its tour of the United States. According to this publication, which ran to over thirty pages, the show would help audiences decide "whether mankind was descended from one original source—the 'Garden of Eden'—or whether the human animal has evoluted [*sic*] from different origins of a lower species." The answer seemed clear: "The classification of mankind into a number of permanent varieties of nations rests on grounds that are within limits, not only obvious, but definite. From a popular or scientific point of view, it would be admitted that a negro, a Chinese, and an Australian belong to three such permanent varieties of men, all plainly distinguishable from one another and distinctly differing from any Europeans." Each group, the program insisted, "is due to special ancestry, each race thus representing an ancient breed or stock, however these breeds or stock may have had their origin."[30] Understanding how races, organized into political and geographical categories called nations, made progress provided the central narrative structure of the show. The story unfolded in a hyperbolic spectacle of Anglo-Saxon masculinity,

> wherein the dusky-skinned Arabian vies with the American cowboy in displays of equestrian expertness; the camp life of the native American Indian is shown in contrast to the nomadic domiciles of the desert-born Bedouin; Russian Cossacks, the proudest representatives of the Czar's cavalry, display their saddle expertness in contrast to the horsemanship of Uncle Sam's soldiery; the slow but sure camel and the lumbering and bulky elephant may be compared with the eagle and bucking broncho and the prancing steed of the exhibition arena.[31]

So complete was the imperial choreography that even the animals bore ideological markings of reputed national identities.

To call the show a spectacle is probably to understate its effect. Again, Butte, Montana, was typical.[32] A local newspaper drummed up interest in the production with this description of the show's progress toward Butte: "The combined shows carry 78 60-foot cars in two sections, which, if made up into one train, would be nearly one mile in length. There are 1,100 people and 600 horses in the organization. Twenty-seven distinct nationalities are represented. Among them are Cossacks, Arabs, Nubians, Kurds, Persians, Turks, English, French and German army officers, Dahomians, Australian bushmen, Hindoos, Japanese Ceylonaise, Malays, Mexicans, South Americans, and Pategonians. There are 136 Sioux and Cheyenne Indians with the shows." Add to this fourteen bison, a physician and surgeon, two hospital stewards and three graduate nurses, a veterinarian and staff, carpenters, laundresses, seamstresses, and cooks. "All the supplies," the newspaper told eager merchants, "are purchased locally," including the "three thousand pounds of meat consumed each day."

The show, organized into eighteen acts, fully tripled the number of acts in the "Drama of Civilization" in Cody's original Wild West and lasted two hours. It opened with a "Grand Review" that harkened back to the American Exhibition and allowed visitors to see the "Red Men of two hemispheres ride side by side" and noted that "Many Nations contribute Man and Beast to a Triumphal March of the Ethnological Congress." Then came a series of acts featuring equestrian events, the fictitious story of Cody's involvement with the Pony Express, and US military drills featuring former soldiers. Other acts included sharpshooting and lassoing, a game of football (really a cross between polo and soccer played with an outsized ball) between cowboy and Indian riders, and multiple acts featuring train robberies and attacks on settlers by Indians. The most extensive act, the sixteenth, was called simply "The Far East" and resembled nothing so much as an amalgam of Wild West narratives about the contest between "civilization" and "savagery" now projected on the world stage.[33]

The Far East segment opened with a camel caravan resting in front of a massive panorama painting depicting the Egyptian deserts complete with pyramids and the Sphinx. A reputed group of "Bedouin bandits" who had kidnapped some foreign tourists were portrayed awaiting a delegation bringing a ransom payment for the release of the captives. When the delegation arrived and the ransom was paid, the "Sheik of the Bedouins" ordered the tourists released and for a festival to begin. It resembled nothing so much as a hybrid circus and midway parade. A performance by Rossi's Musical Elephants kicked things off. Next came an eclectic series of performances by "Arabs, Japanese, Singhalese, Russian Dancers, Dahomeans, Australian Boomerang Throwers, Hindu Fakirs, Illusionists and Wonder Workers."[34]

This "dream of the Orient,"[35] as it was billed, surely whetted appetites for the sideshow entertainments that Cody and Lillie erected on their show grounds, likely with some of the same performers, but this show-within-a-show was also intended to reinforce the combined show's claims of ethnological authenticity. For instance, the Australian aborigines, the program emphasized, "are the lowest type of humanity, but little removed from the dumb beast in the matter of intelligence."[36] Hardly held simply for fun, these shows, like the "anthropology live" shows along midways at world's fairs, claimed ethnological authenticity and purported to be educational as well.[37]

The Far East act did not end the show. Rather, the entire program concluded with a "Final Salute" featuring Buffalo Bill "and all of his Rough Riders, Indians, and White Men side by side, in a final and friendly salute to the audience."[38] This seemingly banal gesture, coming at the end of so many enactments of violent scenes of racial conflict, may seem like proof positive that the Wild West, even combined with the Far East, had simply run out of gas. But the show's denouement was wholly consistent with one of its key themes—peace.

The *Seattle Post-Intelligencer* captured this part of the show's dynamic with its headline: "Peace Promoted by Buffalo Bill." After recalling the role of the show at the 1887 American Exhibition in fostering better relations between England and the United States and noting that the 1910 show's performances in New York City had attracted the visit of Chinese dignitaries, the newspaper described the opening of the show's equestrian events: "the ride by the people of all nations, with the flags of all countries, side by side, saluting a central flag in pure white, with a laurel wreath embroidered in it, a white dove with extended wings perched upon the standard, typical and known as the flag of peace." Cody, the newspaper insisted, "is trying to spread the gospel of universal friendship through a picture of many people of many flags, riding side by side and led by the white emblem of amity." The show, the newspaper summed up, illustrated "that modern man wants prejudice dispelled and [that] the prevailing sentiment is for peace."[39]

From the 1887 American Exhibition forward, first the Wild West and then the combined show made the point of helping audiences on both sides of the Atlantic envision peace as the outcome of imperialism. To help persuade audiences in the United States—especially those antiimperialists like Mark Twain, who condemned America's violent occupation of the Philippines at the turn of the century—that imperialism and peace could march hand in hand, the Wild West increasingly embraced the rhetoric of cosmopolitanism. In 1910, the managers of the combined show billed it as "the great drama of cosmopolitan life." The *Seattle Post-Intelligencer* claimed the show reflected well on its audience with its "appeals to a cosmopolitan people," before adding that the show really represented a "combined kindergarten of Wild West and Maj. Lillie's Far East." Cody and Lillie had certainly merged their talents to take up the "white man's burden," extending the logic of their earlier shows to the world stage. And, as was the case with their original Wild West entertainments, this was only one aspect of their combined show. They made the burden seem light and even fun. No less important, performances helped audiences visualize world peace as contingent on imperial powers maintaining peace among themselves while subduing potentially unruly colonial subjects.

At the same time that European powers were ramping up their plans for a war that would erupt in August 1914, the Wild West's contributions to peace might well have been more substantive than anyone has thought. What Cody and Lillie understood, perhaps better than anyone else, was that peace, for Europeans and Americans alike, had become a show.

Notes

This essay is a revised version of the paper I presented at the 2014 European American Studies Association Conference. I am grateful to Rob Kroes and Jap Verheul for their comments. I am also grateful to Frank Christianson and Jeremy Johnston for their insights and to Mary Robinson and her staff at the McCracken Library for their assistance. The Montana State University Center for Western Lands and Peoples has also been generous with its support.

This chapter's main title comes from Burke, *"Buffalo Bill" from Prairie to Palace: An Authentic History of the Wild West*, 254.

Epigraph: "May Yet Be a Quaker," 1. The story is about Buffalo Bill allowing a Quaker community to settle on his land in Nebraska.

1. Warren, *Buffalo Bill's America*, 430.
2. Sharwood, "Princes and Peace Makers," 448.
3. Ibid.
4. *Encyclopedia Britannica*, 11th ed., s.v. "peace."
5. Calls for the international arbitration of disputes had a long history dating at least to Hugo de Grotius and gained momentum across the nineteenth century. My claim, of course, is not that Buffalo Bill "invented" the concept of peace,but that he shaped how "peace" was seen at the fin de siècle. On the earlier history of peace proposals linked to international arbitration, see Scott, "Peace Conference."
6. D'Estournelles de Constant, *Les Etats-Unis d'Amerique*, 362.
7. Lowe, *Four National Exhibitions.*
8. Quoted in Kasson, *Buffalo Bill's Wild West*, 179.
9. Warren, *Buffalo Bill's America*, 287.
10. Reddin, *Wild West Shows*, 91.
11. Huxley, "Buffalo Bill and William Gladstone."
12. In his autobiographical recollections, Lew Parker, one of Cody's managers, provided the names of well over one hundred monarchs, crown princes and princesses, aristocrats, ambassadors, and celebrities who packed into the Deadwood Stage and, to the cheers of crowds, thrilled to being chased by Indian performers. See Parker, *Odd People I Have Met*, 90–94. Lest anyone think that the relationship between the conduct of diplomacy and popular exhibitions is tenuous, it is worth recalling the famous "kitchen debate" that occurred at another American Exhibition, held in Moscow in 1957, between US Vice President Richard M. Nixon and Soviet Premier Nikita Khrushchev.
13. Whitley, quoted in Lowe, *Four National Exhibitions*, 15.
14. Ibid., 23.
15. Ibid., 92–93.
16. Ibid., 94. See also, *London Times*, November 1, 1887. This and all other newspaper clippings cited in this chapter can be found in the William F. "Buffalo Bill" Cody Collection, MS 6, McCracken Research Library, Buffalo Bill Center of the West.

17. *Illustrated London News*, November 5, 1887, William F. "Buffalo Bill" Cody Collection.
18. Whitley, quoted in Lowe, *Four National Exhibitions,* 119.
19. Lowe, *Four National Exhibitions,* 115
20. "Buffalo Bill's New Show," *New York Times,* November 15, 1886, William F. "Buffalo Bill" Cody Collection.
21. Kasson, *Buffalo Bill's Wild West,* 183. For a very different view of the events at Wounded Knee, see Vuillard, *Sorrow of the Earth.*
22. "The Great Buffalo Bill," *Baltimore Herald*, May 1, 1898, William F. "Buffalo Bill" Cody Collection.
23. Did the Wild West show influence how Lawrence projected his own image? At this point, one can only wonder. But it is worth nothing that Lawrence's popularizer, Lowell Thomas, came of age in Denver, Colorado, just as the show was in its last years, and that at least one writer has likened Thomas to Ned Buntline. See Florence, *Lawrence and Aaronsohn.*
24. "Buffalo Bill's Wild West Show," *Dresden Daily,* August 19, 1906, William F. "Buffalo Bill" Cody Collection.
25. "'Buffalo Bill' Declared for Peace of the World," *San Francisco Call,* February 21, 1903, William F. "Buffalo Bill" Cody Collection. I am grateful to Jeremy Johnston for this reference.
26. "Buffalo Bill's Wild West Returns," *Washington* (PA) *Daily Reporter,* August 31, 1907, William F. "Buffalo Bill" Cody Collection.
27. I have developed this argument in "When the Cosmopolitan Was Not a Drink," 67–79, and in "Buffalo Bill's 'Wild West.'"
28. Martin, "'The Grandest and Most Cosmopolitan Object Teacher.'" Note that this important analysis does not carry the analysis forward into the period of the combined show.
29. Contrasted with the overflowing cup of scholarship on Buffalo Bill's Wild West, the absence of scholarship on Pawnee Bill and his operations is notable. My information about Pawnee Bill is gleaned from Shirley, *Pawnee Bill.* I am deeply grateful to Erin Brown and the staff of the Pawnee Bill Ranch in Pawnee, Oklahoma, for sharing their archival resources with me.
30. *Buffalo Bill's Wild West Combined with Pawnee Bill's Great Far East 1909 Courier,* William F. "Buffalo Bill" Cody Collection, MS6.1970, 6.
31. Ibid., 3.
32. Claims of typicality should be treated with skepticism, but the same advertising material that appeared in the Butte papers appeared in the *Tacoma Times,* September 15, 1910, p. 3, William F. "Buffalo Bill" Cody Collection.
33. *Buffalo Bill's Wild West Combined*, William F. "Buffalo Bill" Cody Collection, box 9, fol. 2.
34. Ibid.
35. Ibid.
36. Ibid.

37. See, for instance, Blanchard et al., *Human Zoos.*
38. Ibid.
39. "Peace Promoted by Buffalo Bill," *Seattle Post-Intelligencer,* September 6, 1910, William F. "Buffalo Bill" Cody Collection.

2

"Not National Merely"

Oscar Wilde, Buffalo Bill, and the Performance of National Identity

JAMIE HORROCKS

In 1899, the American humorist and transatlantic entertainer Marshall Wilder recorded his recollections of some of the most memorable figures of the latter half of the nineteenth century, celebrities with whom his own celebrity status had brought him into contact. About one such personality (clearly a personal favorite), he effused: "He fills a full-dress suit as gracefully as he does [other types of clothing], carries himself as elegantly as any English gentleman of leisure, uses good grammar, speaks with a drawing-room tone of voice, and moves as leisurely as if he had nothing to do all his life but exist beautifully."[1] It is especially this last—his description of the cultivated affectation of beautiful indolence—that brings to mind a man who basked in the spotlight of popular acclaim in both England and America in the 1880s and '90s: Oscar Wilde. Wilder's focus on physical appearance, tone of voice, and sartorial selection replicates a pattern of description used in hundreds of press clippings generated in America by Wilde's 1882 cross-continental tour. Even Wilder's observation that this man possesses a keen sense of humor seems to indicate Wilde, who famously (and apocryphally) quipped upon disembarking in New York, "I have nothing to declare except my genius."

But the man Wilder describes is not Oscar Wilde. The omitted section of the quotation above, which reads in full, "He fills a full-dress suit as gracefully as he does the hunter's buckskins," reveals the actual subject of Wilder's praise: Buffalo Bill Cody. That Cody, who similarly embarked on a famous transatlantic tour in the 1880s, here shares the signifiers of the archetypical Victorian aesthete gives reason for pause. Readers might well wonder what, exactly, the signs of aestheticism mean when associated with America's most celebrated frontiersman or, even more compellingly, what the signifiers of the American frontier mean when a frontiersman as quintessentially American as Cody can so easily pass for Wilde.[2] The ambiguity raised by Wilder's description suggests that what Daniel Novak has called the "bizarre parallel" that exists between Cody and Wilde[3]—a parallel made explicit in the 1892 image Kate Flint reproduces from the *Evening News* in her *Transatlantic Indian* (fig. 2.1)—might more accurately be described as a complicated entanglement of cultural meanings that brings together the unlikeliest of bedfellows. After all, while "The *Wilde* West" cartoon does intimate parallels between Cody and Wilde in the parallel lines of lower limbs and walking sticks, it is the merging of the two figures—the way that Cody's hat slides neatly beneath the brim of Wilde's, the near-meeting of Cody's vest and Wilde's elbow, the impossibly slight white space between the men that eclipses the ocean that should divide them—that suggests the affinity recognized by this illustrator.

This affinity was remarked widely by writers and cultural critics in the nineteenth century and is still mentioned today (by critics like Novak, Flint, and Perry Meisel). For their contemporaries the pairing of the British and the American frontiersman was the occasion of humor; a one-liner in the Comanche, Texas, *Chief*, for example, describes skinny young cowboys who will need to give their calves some hay before they can live up to the infamous knee breeches that made the tour with Wilde.[4] But innocuous barbs like this one remind readers of the larger cultural tensions that existed in the 1880s and '90s between what Paul Giles describes as a thoroughly transatlantic aestheticism and the notions of British identity circulating within the global network of empire.[5] The "bizarre parallel" between Wilde and Cody, a pairing that Novak uses to preface his discussion of queer Westerns and that Flint uses to augment her argument about British perceptions of the American Indian, is situated squarely within these tensions. It prompts readers to consider what the Atlantic crossings of the two men meant and continue to mean in the narrative of transatlantic influence that helped define both British and American national identity at the fin de siècle.

FIGURE 2.1. "The Wilde West," *Evening News* (London), May 19, 1892.
Courtesy of the McCracken Research Library, Buffalo Bill Center of the West.

Jokes framing this influence in terms of rivalry abound, as when an 1882 squib in the New Orleans *Times Picayune* claims that Buffalo Bill will shoot Oscar Wilde on sight for unlawfully pirating his trademark curling locks.[6] And yet considering the two men merely as rivals obscures many of the interesting complications of their relationship. As the *Picayune* joke demonstrates, when Wilde arrived in America, one way that his performance of Britishness was made to signify was by locating it within a discursive space already occupied by Cody. It was Cody that American commentators often drew on to explain, to contextualize, to define Wilde. But only five years later, it was Wilde—his manipulations of the press, his deployments of body and brand, and especially his cultivation of celebrity—that Cody drew on in his own transatlantic tour. In this sense, Wilde is both antecedent and precedent to Cody, while Cody is both precedent and antecedent to Wilde.

Such intertwined and mutual reliance suggests that the narrative of Cody's transatlanticism cannot be told fully without Wilde, and vice versa, for each man provided the other with certain tools of cultural navigation. What Cody offered Wilde at the outset of Wilde's tour was a readily legible version of Americanness against which British aestheticism could be, and would be, posited. What Wilde, in return, offered Cody was a model of national identity that simultaneously acknowledged the constructedness of categories of nation, self, and other and asserted their authenticity. For Wilde in America, this model served the characteristically Wildean purpose of unsettling the notion of a stable identity, national or otherwise. For Cody in Britain, however, this model provided a means by which a performance, a spectacle of stagecraft that everybody recognized as such, might also be regarded as an authentic expression of national identity.

Identity as "What Is to Be"

The magnificent performance that was Wilde's lecture tour through America's major cities, a theatrical sensation that lasted almost the full duration of 1882, was first and foremost a trumpeting of Britishness. It was, in other words, a performance enmeshed in the politics of national identity from the outset. Arriving with a slim volume of poems and the outlines of three lectures, Wilde disembarked in New York and immediately began the work of deconstructing the transatlantic symbolism that framed the journey from old world to new. The man who struck many as awash in affectation pronounced himself surprisingly *un*affected by the Atlantic Ocean. "I am not exactly pleased with the Atlantic," he quipped. "It is not so majestic as I expected."[7] His comment sardonically reversing the conventional gesture of appreciation for America's greatness (geographical as well as ideological and commercial), Wilde represented himself and came to be represented by critics and reporters as "symptomatic of a certain kind of national identity."[8] The *Nation* acknowledged this when, reporting Wilde's arrival in the United States, it suggested that Wilde's "extravagant" otherness—the very substance of the attraction he offered—would spell the failure of his undertaking in America. The author wrote, "Mr. Wilde is an essentially foreign product, and can hardly succeed in this country."[9] However, it is this very foreignness that made Wilde's booking agent and American manager, Colonel W. F. Morse, certain of Wilde's success. As Morse told a reporter before Wilde's first lecture in New York, his speech "will be a fine thing. It will be a definition and a description of English culture as applied to social life."[10] Morse's assessment seems particularly apt, not only with regard to "The English Renaissance of Art," Wilde's lecture, but with regard to Wilde himself. Wherever he went during his sojourn in the United States, Wilde was looked on as "a definition and a description of English culture."[11]

The irony of an Irish poet being considered the very definition of Englishness was not lost on Wilde, but an equally compelling irony immediately manifested itself in Wilde's principal lecture. "The English Renaissance of Art," the repertoire piece that Wilde would polish to perfection over the course of his lecture tour, gives little scope to Englishness, Irishness, Britishness, or any other form of nationalism in relation to aesthetic values. Instead, as Benjamin Morgan points out, Wilde imagines a post-national empire of art that will bring all nations together in aesthetic fraternity.[12] Emphasizing the artistic contributions of artists from England, America, France, Germany, Italy, Greece, and countries of the Middle East, Wilde asserts, "All noble work is not national merely, but universal. The political independence of a nation must not be confused with any intellectual isolation."[13] Indeed, the kind of intellectual isolationism that Wilde associates with nationalism inevitably results in international conflict, "wars and the clash of armies and the meeting of men in battle." It is only art that transcends race, nation, and ethnicity and "makes the life of the whole race immortal." Wilde writes, "I think that art, by creating a common intellectual atmosphere between all countries, might—if it could not overshadow the world with the silver wings of peace—at least make men such brothers that they would not go out to slay one another."[14]

Coming near the end of "The English Renaissance," this cosmopolitan vision of art is a culminating thesis in Wilde's lecture and a surprising assertion, given Wilde's supposed embodiment of a strictly nationalist enterprise. And yet this key point was never remarked on by listeners, never queried by reporters who conducted an endless series of interviews with Wilde in between his lectures. Instead, the popular discourse that surrounded Wilde in America continually asserted his foreignness, "emphasiz[ing] his strangeness in the language and visual imagery of retrenched culture, national, and racial categories."[15] Ever the opportunist, Wilde used his exotic public image to his advantage. As Gregory Castle has demonstrated, Wilde maneuvered the public's recurrent "misrecognition" of him toward the creation of an inchoate persona that allowed him to become Irish, for example, when speaking in cities like Boston and San Francisco with large Irish populations, or to assert Confederate sympathies when lecturing in Georgia.[16] In such moments, nationalism is not swallowed up in the kind of aesthetic fraternity postulated in Wilde's lecture. Rather, the opposite happens, as an asserted affiliation (with the Irish, the South) serves as a rhetorical indicator of difference. Oddly, however, the effect is the same in both circumstances. Whether nationalism is effaced by the brotherhood of art or brought to the fore by repeated affiliations with various national communities, the boundaries of identity become elastic and identity itself becomes fungible. Although Wilde's Britishness was central to American perceptions of him throughout his US tour, it is instead this notion of the variability of identity that is conveyed by Wilde's performativity.

The figure of the British lecturer as public performer was by no means new to American audiences of the 1880s. Charles Dickens perhaps most famously performed the dual role of author/actor when he lit up American stages forty years before Wilde attempted to do the same. However, although Wilde felt the long shadow of Dickens throughout his transatlantic journey, Wilde exemplified a different kind of performativity, a model of public presentation that would have enormous effect on Cody. This is, in part, because both Wilde and Cody operated within a cultural milieu that witnessed the supersession of "character" by "personality," a late nineteenth-century phenomenon that Warren Susman explores at length.[17] While character was associated with moral qualities of *being,* personality was associated with *doing.* Hence, "the social role demanded of all in the new culture of personality was that of a performer."[18] A performer Wilde certainly was; in fact, performativity was central to the unique form of celebrity that he came to embody.

This modern version of celebrity premised a paradoxical blend of artificiality and authenticity, a combination of attributes that would prove just as useful for Cody as it did for Wilde. American commentators emphasized most frequently the artificiality of Wilde's performances, using terms like *posturing* or *posing* to preclude the possibility that there was anything authentic about the man or his message. Aestheticism itself was believed by many to be little more than an affectation, a pose, and thus Wilde was often accused of posing as an apostle of posturing. This is the sentiment behind the quip made in the *Milwaukee Daily Sentinel* that "Oscar Wilde is about to depart from this country with his lily, his sunflower, his knee-breeches, his twaddle, and his apish posing."[19] As this quotation makes apparent, visuality is the primary medium for posturing, the look of the poseur being paramount. Audiences flocked to see Wilde being "Wilde," even more than to hear his lectures; London's *Daily Telegraph* reported that "not a few persons may have paid their money to receive 'impressions' through the eye rather than through the ear."[20] What they saw, however, was not Wilde but Wilde performing "Wilde," a persona that replaced the lecturer and could be visually consumed by spectators as a commodity.[21]

Many critics regarded this performance of self as a sign of charlatanry, an indicator of inauthenticity, and said as much in their reports of Wilde. A writer for the *Charleston News and Courier*, for example, describes Wilde's arrival in that city after a long train ride by saying that "the door of the ladies' entrance being locked, the two hundred pounds of aestheticism posed about on the doorstep, grim and dusty, and uncomfortable, but looked all the same like a magnified photograph of Geo. Denham in the role of 'Bunthorne,'" the character in the Gilbert and Sullivan operetta *Patience* that Wilde had been hired to promote in America.[22] In this reporter's reading of Wilde's performance, Wilde quite literally becomes the commodity that he peddles: "two hundred pounds of aestheticism." His appearance, as he "poses about on the doorstep," is that of an enlarged representation of a character in a play that featured tableau caricatures of cartoon prints drawn by artist George Du Maurier—a reproduction of a reproduction of a reproduction. Little wonder that the writer later describes Wilde as "lolling" on a sofa, strategically "ornamented" after having completed a quick "costume" change.[23] He is all stagecraft here, an empty suit of art for art's sake.

At the same time, however, such stagecraft could and did convey, in the minds of nineteenth-century spectators, a powerful legitimacy. Writing of Victorian theatricality and celebrity figures of the Victorian stage, Lynn Voskuil has demonstrated how Victorians on both sides of the Atlantic "developed a sophisticated capacity to . . . act authentically and be theatrical at the same time. In this way, they theatricalized the ideas and institutions they believed to be most authentic even as they authenticated the spectacles they made of themselves."[24] This notion is the basis for what was called "natural acting" in the late nineteenth century, a style of showmanship in which "the entire apparatus of illusive theater—the state-of-the-art stagecraft, the elaborate costumes, the larger-than-life characters—was paradoxically essential to the experience of genuine intimacy."[25] For modern spectators (and some Victorian critics of Wilde), a performative self is antithetical to a genuine self.

Yet in the world of late-Victorian theater, a world inhabited wholeheartedly by Wilde and by Cody after him, this antithesis did not necessarily exist. For those who believed that "the player's own identity [was] the core theatrical element," the alignment of identity and performance carried no contradiction and conveyed no element of deception.[26] As Voskuil explains, the "image of a performative self entails not role reversal—the exchange of authenticity for theatricality, or theatricality for authenticity—but a logic of self-construction that authenticates theatricality, that sees the self as spectacular to its very core."[27]

This does, as Amanda Adams claims, "cloud the notion of a stable limited self," but it concomitantly "allows identity to be realized—as an action, not a state of being."[28] Gregory Castle describes Wilde as profoundly aware of this conception of identity as a spectacular performance in process. He quotes from a letter Wilde wrote while in New Jersey, in which Wilde states that "while one is living, one can only work for what is to be."[29] This suggests that rather than conceiving of himself as already being or embodying any fixed idea (Irishness, Britishness, or even aestheticism), Wilde "is always working towards a being-in-the-future, a possibility."[30] Identity conceived in the future progressive tense, not as "what I am" but "what I will be," complicates the idea of a single, essential self, but it restores to performance the authenticity that Voskuil finds attributed to numerous Victorian showmen and women. In the process of becoming, one may be a great number of selves, but each self, each persona, remains a genuine expression of identity.

It should be immediately apparent why this model of identity—at once performative and authentic, dynamic and evolving—would be as attractive to Cody as it was to Wilde. The celebrity of both men relied more on their theatricalization of an idea than on any particular action or accomplishment. In 1882, Wilde had published only a handful of poems, none of the essays or society dramas for which he would gain literary fame. And the pre–Wild West Cody was largely a dime-novel name, an adventurer whose early exploits would remain a lifelong subject of debate. It mattered little; what Wilde established on his transatlantic tour, and what Cody likewise adopted on his, was a performative model of identity that recognized the impossibility of embodying any single or stable category, that welcomed the persona as a legitimate expression of self, and that regarded theatricality and authenticity as symbiotic rather than antagonistic. This model defied the American perception of Wilde as the very "definition and description" of Englishness, a role he played quite happily from time to time. It suggested instead that national identity—Britishness, Americanness—was a construction, as fungible as every other category of identity. And this is the theme that Wilde's performance begins to adopt as he moved away from the East Coast and into the frontier states of America. Here Wilde seems to have found a geographical counterpart to a performative notion of identity, a space in which the boundaries of identity were elastic and the transparent juxtaposition of myth and reality presented no challenge to authenticity. Not surprisingly, it is also in the American frontier that the British aesthete encountered and began to shape his performance in accordance with the quintessentially American persona of Buffalo Bill, a merging of personalities that would align Wilde with Cody long after the former had returned to Britain.

Wilde in the "Glorious Occident"

Wilde liked the American frontier; "The West," he told a reporter in the "western" city of St. Louis in 1882, "I like best."[31] He claimed it was "the most beautiful part of America"[32] and had a special attraction for visitors from Britain. "After once dining at Delmonico's," the famous restaurant in New York, Wilde wrote, English people "start off for Colorado or California, for Montana or the Yellow Stone Park. Rocky Mountains charm them more than riotous millionaires; they have been known to prefer buffaloes to Boston. Why should they not?"[33] Like Frederick Jackson Turner, whose thesis on the frontier would appear shortly after Wilde's tour, Wilde believed there was something more real, closer to nature and therefore more authentic, in the people he met west of the Mississippi River. "The East I found a feeble reflex of Europe," he reported, but in the West, "The people are stronger, fresher, saner than the rest."[34] They lack the "foolish prejudices that have influenced East America."[35]

While these pronouncements, made by a savvy showman dependent for his success on gaining the good graces of his audience, must be taken with a grain of salt, Wilde's affection for the American frontier was an oft-repeated refrain, even years after he had returned from his tour. What intrigued Wilde about the West, however, may not have been its seeming authenticity but rather its ability to seem in and of itself—to seem unbounded, to seem original, to seem pristinely untouched, to seem whatever Wilde happened to want it to be. To a Cleveland reporter Wilde explained, "The side of your American civilization those of us in Europe . . . are most interested in is not the East but the West. We want to see what civilization you are making for yourself and by yourselves."[36] Potential as yet unrealized, place in process of becoming: this quality piques Wilde's interest in the frontier. And if the West is mythically characterized, for Wilde, by "its grizzly bears and its untamed cowboys, its free open-air life and its free open-air manners," it is also characterized by "boundless prairies and boundless *mendacity*."[37] The duplicity of the frontier, once again its ability to seem to be something whether or not it actually is, attracts Wilde. As with Wilde's own performance as Englishman, Irishman, or "Apostle of Aestheticism," the American West is where constructedness is perhaps the most cogent element of authenticity.

Wilde was correct in his perception that the frontier was (like Wilde himself) as much a construction as a reality. As Perry Meisel explains, "The West is ungraspable by definition. There is nothing after all to capture, only a horizon to be infinitely expanded and a world to be made more fluid, supple, flexible."[38] It is, writes Monica Rico, a "mythic space, in which past and present, fiction and reality could coexist."[39] For Wilde, fiction and reality not only coexisted in the American frontier but also coincided, fiction merging into reality and reality into fiction. "I have, you will be interested to hear, seen Indians," Wilde wrote to Mrs. Bernard Beere in a letter from Denver, March 20, 1882; "The squaws are poor imitations of Clara Jecks"—a British actress whom Wilde had seen play an American Indian on stage in J. B. Buckstone's *Green Bushes*.[40] Of the miners he met in Leadville, Colorado, Wilde wrote on the same day to Mrs. George Lewis to confess that "I secretly believe they read up Bret Harte privately; they were certainly almost as real as his miners, and quite as pleasant."[41] The irony of this inversion is that it is, in part, true—not that the miners perform their roles less convincingly than Harte's characters, but that Wilde's perceptions of the West are almost entirely constructed of representations held up as authentic in dime novels and melodramas. These textual representations, the fictional posturing of cowboys and miners and Indians, therefore become the standard against which Wilde measures the real and (not surprisingly) finds it lacking. He, like Louis Warren, recognized that "western reality" was "an imposture of frontier imposture," a performance carried out on a variety of stages.[42]

This must have made the American West all the more attractive to Wilde, a sign of its alignment with the model of identity Wilde espoused. Indeed, the evident affinity between Wilde and the frontier becomes a principal theme in the poetic "Apostrophe" written to "O. Wilde" by the American humorist Bill [Edgar Wilson] Nye. Nye's 1883 poem makes full use of the mythic narrative of the American frontier, inviting Wilde to "Come to the mountain fastness," to "Sit on the fuzzy cactus," and to "Ride the fierce broncho o'er the dusty plain."[43] The West is markedly different from the cultured East; the "cordial home" of the cowboy and the coyote is awash with "alcoholic inspiration" rather than with the more reputable muses of civilization and progress.[44] However, if the frontier is "raw / And uncouth," populated by men of "untutored ways and wild," it is also "free," the "home of genius," in which a "son of Albion" like Wilde might find a queer sort of welcome: "The cowboy yearns to yank thee / To his brawny breast."[45] Where else, Nye suggests, would a "soft eyed" Briton with "low neck shirt / And high neck pants" belong but beside the "pack mule" with its "soft demeanor" and equally "peculiar mien"?[46]

Both "uncouth" and inspiring, "mobbish," perhaps, but "high toned" in its mobbishness, the West's strange foreignness makes it a "glorious Occident" for Nye, but an Occident in which Wilde inherently fits.[47] Wittily positing New England and England as "Oriental" by comparison, the term *Occident* allows the otherness of the American West (and Wilde, by analogy) to effectively other the Anglophone places that assume, with great national pride, the global self-designation of "western." Here the western world is eastern, the boundaries of familiarity shifted by the (purportedly) more authentic Occidentalism of the West. Wilde's foreignness to America is emphasized recurrently by Nye: Wilde hails from "across the main," "from o'er the sea," "from far-off lands."[48] And yet this becomes a point of kinship in the West. Wilde is no more different, no less foreign, than the space through which he travels. As the western European who has come west to reach the American West, Wilde's national identity—indeed, the very idea that nationality rather than personality might constitute affiliation—becomes muddied. In the ambiguous psycho-geographical space of the frontier, Nye's identification of Wilde as ersatz "bard and champion aesthete" signifies belonging much more so than an accent, a passport, or the lack thereof.[49]

Wilde as "authentic" westerner: the image this conjures up—of an Irishman who travels to America to represent Englishness and is there welcomed by a frontier narrative that regards the Occident as Orient and Wilde as brother rather than other—is wickedly Wildean in its inversions of logic and expectation. Nevertheless, it is the image that gets repeated in the popular press as Wilde moves speedily through Kansas, Missouri, Nebraska, Texas, Colorado, Utah, and California. It is the image we find, for example, in the 1882 "big cut" in *Harper's Bazar* titled "Wilde on *Us:* Something to 'Live Up' to in America"[50] (fig. 2.2). Like Nye's poem, which sees a natural home for Wilde in the American West, the title of this engraving by Thomas Nast reverses the standard journalistic assessment of Wilde as foreigner in the spotlight of critical opinion. Here it is Americans who fall under Wilde's measuring glance rather than "*Us*" (the United States as a critical body) passing judgment on Wilde. In this way, the illustration defamiliarizes America instead of the British aesthete.

The engraving, which depicts Wilde's visit to Leadville, a mining town in central Colorado, presents a portrait of incongruity that unsettles viewers' knowledge of themselves as American and Wilde as not. Casting the rough and tumble miners of Leadville as "picturesque," the adjective stamped onto the slouch hat that Wilde holds up, Nast aims at drawing a laugh from viewers who know that mining boomtowns (not to mention the miners who populated them) are nothing of the sort. The heavily masculine connotations of manual labor associated with silver-lead mining contrast sharply with the effeminacy conveyed by Wilde's slender legs and s-curving, contrapposto stance. The masculinity also emphasized by the fistfight hieroglyphically depicted above Wilde's head (next to a whisky bottle and a cockfight, should viewers require more obvious suggestions of the dangerous male virility associated with Leadville) throws into relief the domestic ideals implied by the sunflowers and lily, the squat decorative vase, the subject of Wilde's lecture ("The House Beautiful"), and the two homes sketched below the embattled men and roosters.

The figure of Wilde himself—impeccably clean, impeccably dressed, and impeccably coiffed—embodies a number of contradictions. While he seems the very picture of leisure and the life of the mind, the "ugly $" stashed in his pockets and the dollar sign in the center of his sunflower buttonhole convey both the crassly commercial machinations of Leadville inhabitants and the crassly commercial motivations of Wilde's lecture tour (and aestheticism itself). Thus depicted, Wilde exemplifies rather than repudiates America's commercial ethos, which is magnified by the good citizens of Leadville whose pursuit of wealth will continue "rain or shine," as the hat's tag indicates. If "art for art's sake" celebrates beautiful uselessness (as the antecedent to this image, George Du Maurier's 1880 cartoon depicting aesthetes striving to "live

FIGURE 2.2. "Wilde on *Us*: Something to 'Live Up' to in America," *Harper's Bazar* (New York), June 10, 1882, p. 361.

Courtesy of the L. Tom Perry Special Collections, Harold B. Lee Library, Brigham Young University.

up to" their blue and white china, suggests), Wilde here celebrates something else as he points approvingly at work boots and hat, symbols of American productivity. It is difficult to imagine Wilde swapping out his dainty, beribboned slippers for the creased knee boots that dangle from his hand, and yet he has already claimed the boots that flank him on either side, turning them into vases that now sprout the ubiquitous symbols of aestheticism.

The illustration, which places Wilde in a position of considerable ambiguity (praised or censured? praising or censuring?), serves as a vehicle for American readers of *Harper's* to reflect not on Wilde's otherness but on the disappearance of the boundary between self and other that his tour occasioned. What viewers and readers of the text that accompanies the image are led to realize is that far from being an interloper in Leadville, Wilde's appearance there discovers Leadville's innate aestheticism. "In all his travels," claims the blurb beneath Nast's engraving, "the only well-dressed men he [Wilde] has seen have been the miners of the Rocky Mountains." Their "wide-brimmed hats" and cloaks "may well be dwelt on with admiration," as might their "high boots," remarks Wilde; the miners "only wore what was comfortable, and therefore beautiful." Wilde continues, "As I looked at them, I could not help thinking with regret of the time when these picturesque miners should have made their fortunes, and would go East to assume again all the abominations of modern fashion attire."[51] The miners cannot help themselves; without intending to, they embody the aestheticist ideals that critics identified with Wilde's alienage. By traveling eastward and acculturating themselves to the "foreign" customs of dress prevalent there, the men of Leadville will lose the quaint beauty of their native ways of life—native, that is, to an America that is not the America of the East Coast. The illustration's contrast between Wilde and "*Us*," in other words, reveals Americans' foreignness within America, the differences that separate West and East, and the similarities that posit Wilde at home in Leadville.

Wilde's circulation through the frontier did much the same thing that this image does—it deconstructs the signs by which one identifies the self and distances the other, ultimately making national identity more and more difficult to define. Benjamin Morgan notes that this was also the suggestion conveyed by E. B. Duval's popular "National Aesthetics" trade cards, which were printed in 1882 to coincide with Wilde's tour. Each card features an unflattering caricature of a national type, a stereotypical figure (German, Chinese, French, Irish, etc.) aping the tropes of aestheticism. Rather than discrediting the philosophy of "art for art's sake," however, the cards suggested to viewers that nationality itself might be little more than an affectation or pose. "As the iconology of aestheticism comes into contact with the iconology of the nation," Morgan explains, "it renders the latter startlingly fungible."[52]

"Wilde on *Us*" raises the stakes of this interaction still higher, for in it we find the iconology of aestheticism *becoming* the iconology of the American frontier, the two signifying systems merging into a single type. The more time Wilde spent in the West, the more identifiably "western" he appeared to become. Pundits and reporters in the frontier states, for example, occasionally joked about the effeminacy that had been much commented on by eastern critics of Wilde; just as often, however, their accounts contradicted this. In Leadville, a reporter claimed that Wilde "stumbled onto the stage with a stride more becoming a giant backwoodsman than an aesthete"; in California, another reporter observed that "many an ox must have yielded the broad sirloin' [*sic*] to put two hundred pounds upon so large a frame."[53] Fellow British aesthete Arthur Symons additionally noted that as Wilde traveled through the West, he gained both confidence (he "spoke without a manuscript") and authenticity (he left off "parody[ing] Pater and Swinburne"), traits Wilde himself associated with American frontiersmen.[54]

To these qualities, critics in the West began to add also the material accoutrements of an increasingly popular frontier persona. The hip boots and hat pictured in the "Wilde on *Us*" engraving are key elements of that persona. So, too, is the title Wilde was given in Texas. He writes, "It is a popular superstition that in America a visitor is invariably addressed as 'Stranger.' I was never once addressed as 'Stranger.' When I went to Texas I was called 'Captain'; when I got to the centre of the country I was addressed as 'Colonel.'"[55] For good reason: Wilde was made a colonel in the Texas Rangers in Galveston (the rank was confirmed in Houston).[56] In Dallas, the white hat that "Col. Wilde" (and thousands of other frontiersmen) wore began being advertised by at least one storeowner as an "Oscar Wilde hat," but most who saw it were reminded of someone else.[57] With the "large, wide-brimmed, white slouch hat he wore," from which fell "long light-brown hair, reaching in somewhat straggling masses to the shoulders," Wilde struck many as "something after the style of Buffalo Bill."[58] In neither figure nor face does Wilde resemble Cody, but this did not prevent the frequent referencing of the latter to describe the former. Humorous scenarios in which the one man is mistaken for the other fill dozens of odd corners of newspaper columns. In the *Los Angeles Daily Times*, for example, "a gentleman well known in commercial circles rushed madly home" to tell his wife that he had caught a glimpse of "Oscar Wilde, of course. Met him on Spring street [*sic*] all dressed up in long hair, knee-breeches, yellow cravat and everything." The man dons a clean collar and "his best sunflower" and rushes out to meet Wilde, "unconscious that the party he mistook for Oscar, the aesthete, was none other than Buffalo Bill, the Comanche scout."[59] As with Marshall Wilder's description of Cody, here again we find the physical signifiers of aestheticism (long hair, knee breeches, yellow cravat) written onto the body of Buffalo Bill.

From Wilde's West to the West End

Pundits who provide anecdotes of misrecognition like this one do so with tongue in cheek, but the convergence of Wilde and Cody is telling, nevertheless. The two men should have been—and were, in many cases—antithetical, Cody providing a classic model of virile American masculinity against which Wilde's effeminacy registered as all the more foreign. But as Wilde traveled west, calling into question the possibility of inhabiting a stable identity with his ever-evolving performances of self, the cultural relationship he shared with Cody evolved as well. On the one hand, a general transatlantic pattern of response to British aestheticism entailed the reassertion of certain codes of masculinity embodied by a frontiersman like Cody. This response emphasized the distance that lay between aestheticism and the American frontier, the essential difference separating a long-haired dandy like Wilde from a long-haired dude like Cody. On the other hand, however, Wilde's performance of aestheticism in America offered Cody a model of transatlantic celebrity, premised on the authenticating nature of performance, that would become crucial to Cody's success in England. In fact, one might argue that Cody became the Buffalo Bill of mythic status, celebrated on multiple continents, by becoming like Wilde. For Cody, like Wilde, was above all else a performer who relied on the capacity of his late-Victorian audiences to interpret a theatrical performance as an authentic expression of self. In America, this capacity allowed Wilde to unsettle the notions of otherness required by definitions of self. In England, this capacity allowed Cody to present an elaborate spectacle, the constructedness of which was always apparent, as a legitimate version of Americanness.

This gunslinging, Stetson-wearing version of Americanness was, of course, well-known to British consumers of popular culture in the fin de siècle. But before the 1887 arrival in England of Cody's Wild West show, it was often posited as antagonistic to, rather than emulative of, aestheticism. The best example of this comes from a comic melodrama written by F. C. Burnand and called, appropriately enough, *The Colonel.* Premiering in London in 1881 (it would open in America in 1884) just prior to Wilde's American tour, *The Colonel* brought the British aesthete and the American frontiersman into a shared cultural space, the same space used to comic effect by writers of the Wilde/Cody jokes that would appear in the American press the following year. In Burnand's play, however, there is no mistaking the aesthete for the frontiersman, whose role it is to contain and to counteract the pernicious influence of art for art's sake.

The colonel's success in this endeavor is made possible by what the play posits as the specifically American qualities that he brings from across the Atlantic. Burnand's colonel, Woottwweell W. Woodd of the US Cavalry, is a pure specimen of American masculinity ("genus masculine—species named on the label"),[60] a straight talker and a straight shooter who immediately ascertains the root of the problem (aestheticism) that has thrown the family of his friend Forrester into disarray. The play's Wildean aesthete, the duplicitous Lambert Strekye, suspects a fellow charlatan in Colonel Woodd, a man he characterizes as "a Yankee, with a soul of shoddy, devoted to drinks and dollars." But Colonel Wood insists that he is a simple man who finds solace in the amenities offered by the American frontier: "hunting, shooting, fishing," and for repast, "anything will do for me—a cut of old beef and no fixings, with a cup of coffee and a cigar."[61] With nothing but his good sense and his no-nonsense attitude, Colonel Woodd reveals Streyke and his aestheticist friends to be a bunch of "affected caricatures," an "effeminate invertebrate society."[62] He restores order to the British home by demanding from his friend Forrester a healthy dose of vigorous action ("Now's your time! . . . [S]trike the first blow at the enemy"), a reassertion of traditional masculinity ("Be a man!"), and an American-style "declaration of independence" from aestheticism. When, in the last line of the play, the characters realize that happiness reigns once more and that they "certainly are indebted for it all to The Colonel," Woodd is acknowledged as the preserver of the institutions—family, home, dominant masculinity and passive femininity, reputation, and aristocratic fortune—that uphold Britishness itself.[63]

Although neither the illustrations of Colonel Woodd that accompanied the published version of the play nor the actor (Charles Francis Coghlan) originally cast to play him resembles Cody, it would have been difficult for British audiences not to associate Woodd with the Buffalo Bill of dime-novel renown. Burnand's ridiculous doubling of the consonants in Woodd's name (something made apparent to theater-goers when one character asks Woodd to spell out his name) parodies the double "b" in Buffalo Bill, and the character (who is referred to as "an American giant") possesses all of the personality traits and speech patterns of the frontiersman.[64] Six years before Cody would bring the Wild West to England, then, his persona was already attached to a position antithetical to aestheticism, a fact reinforced in the play when the aesthete Streyke admits in an aside, "Somehow I shan't feel quite safe till the Colonel has disappeared."[65] Colonel Woodd's staunch and steadfast Americanness, most beneficial not to Woodd, but to his British friends, clearly offers one response to what Paul Giles describes as the threat to "coherent liberal forms of national identity posed by aestheticism"—and specifically in the 1880s, by Wilde.[66]

One might expect that when Colonel Cody arrived in England, he would play the role already scripted for him in the guise of Colonel Woodd, presenting himself as an antithesis to aestheticism and the ideologies it encompassed. Instead, Cody posed, postured, and performed, adopting a persona very similar to that which Wilde assumed on his transatlantic tour. So apparent was this similarity that in London, as in the American frontier years earlier, commentators placed the two men side by side, carrying into the 1890s an association that by then had become almost commonplace. By doing so, they acknowledged, perhaps unwittingly, the dependence of Cody's success as a public figure on Wilde and on the performative identity that Burnand's Woodd regarded as antagonistic to the very idea of the American frontiersman. Wilde's modeling in 1882 of a type of celebrity that was at once artificial and authentic thus did not provide a type against which Cody could distinguish himself as much as it prefigured a persona that Cody himself would employ. Adopting this performative persona allowed Cody to assert an identity just as constructed as Wilde's but used instead to provide both Britons and Americans with a mythic narrative of American national identity.

Cody was well aware that the version of Americanness he presented to British audiences was mythic, fabulous in every sense of the word, and rife with the potential vacuity that performativity inevitably suggests. As early as 1882, Cody expressed a concern that if he took his show to England, he "might be classed among the many impostors who have gone before [him]."[67]

The elaborate spectacle of his show—from the livestock and Indian village to the costumes worn by all players at all times—attempted to counter this anxiety, to announce to spectators that Cody was the genuine article. And yet the artificiality of the Wild West was as apparent to spectators as Cody feared it might be. As one *Punch* critic writes, "From what I saw [of the Wild West show], I gather that Life in the Wild West is a theatrical, circus-like sort of existence; that everyone dresses in a fancifully embroidered costume; . . . that there is a good deal of tan about; and that there are highly-coloured canvas mountains."[68] No amount of (mock) gunfire, it seems, sufficed to pull the wool over this visitor's eyes.

At the same time, however, those very audience members who recognized the Wild West as simulacra also insisted on the show's authenticity. This aspect, the Wild West's coincident realism and constructedness, was the show's principal selling point for both Mark Twain and Henry Irving, two men who made performativity their lifelong career. In his 1884 letter to Cody, Twain encourages Cody to take his show to England and, while recognizing that it is a reproduction of life in the West as it no longer exists, insists that the show is "wholly free from sham and insincerity," genuine "down to its smallest details."[69] It is "painfully real" (especially the "bucking horses") for Twain, who signs his letter with his pseudonym, a gesture that reiterates his affirmation of the authenticity of performance. Louis Warren contends that Twain's recognition of representation as reality in the letter "reflected his subtle appreciation of the artifice and imposture that went hand in hand with the display of real western figures."[70] Certainly Cody's show offered "an outrageous collapsing of fact into fiction," but this did not delegitimate the performance for late-Victorian audiences.[71]

Henry Irving, perhaps the most popular actor in late nineteenth-century England, agreed. Irving saw the Wild West in New York in 1886, before it moved to London's West End, and recommended it to British audiences in glowing terms. A transatlantic counterpart to Twain, Irving understood perfectly well the theatrical nature of the "entertainment," speaking of the "performance" as a "scene" that is "played" in monumental terms, the "stage extend[ing] over five acres." But he goes on to emphasize the realism of the performance: "You have real cowboys, . . . real buffaloes, . . . and real Indians," he writes. "Hordes of cows" are "lassoed and stampeded in the most realistic fashion imaginable." Yes, Irving admits, the performance is "rehearsed," "the greatest care [being] taken that it shall go properly," but "it is impossible to avoid a considerable share of the impromptu and the unforeseen. For you may rehearse with buffaloes as much as you like, but no one can say in what way they will stampede when they are suddenly turned loose in the open." It is this coexistence of the rehearsed and the impromptu, the artificial and the genuine, that leads Irving to predict that the Wild West will "take the town by storm" when it comes to London.[72]

Irving's recognition of the authenticity of Cody's performance as Buffalo Bill in the Wild West reflects both his own investment in the "natural acting" that Voskuil claims distinguished Irving's career as well as his belief that "the electric force of a strong personality" was essential for success on stage. "To act naturally for Irving," writes Voskuil, meant employing the mechanisms of performance so as to "awe spectators into believing that what they saw on stage was real." And Irving's emphasis on the necessity of personality "both tapped into and enhanced an intensifying cultural desire to minimize the line between actor and role."[73] Cody's performance was premised on the same theatrical philosophy, as was Wilde's before him. If, as Voskuil contends, late-Victorian spectators "knew themselves" individually and collectively through a "paradoxical" combination of "theatricality and authenticity," then the performative model of identity exemplified by Wilde and adopted by Cody could be both genuine and simulated at once.[74] Thus for many, Cody was the unforgettably American "Buffalo Bill," on stage and off, and while the mountains that comprised his Kensington set were constructed of canvas, what took place in their shadow was, as Twain wrote, "wholly free from sham."

The same might be said of the visual representations of Cody that flooded England before, during, and after the Wild West tour, which offered viewers a commodified version of Cody that was both an idea (of Americanness, of westernness, of triumphant white masculinity) and a living, laboring version of the man himself. In this, Cody's debt to Wilde is once again immediately visible. Wilde's success in America, as many critics have noted, relied heavily on his strategic deployment of new media and advertising techniques.[75] The man behind this deployment was Colonel W. F. Morse, Wilde's American front man and booking agent, who worked in conjunction with Richard D'Oyly Carte in London. Morse made sure that "Wilde"—as image, idea, and commodity—preceded the aesthete into every city on his lecture tour.[76] By the time Wilde himself arrived, spectators already knew him, or felt they knew him, with a level of intimacy directly related to his ownability as a commodity. Wilde was, as the *New York Herald* observed, "a perpetual and magnificent advertisement," not only for Gilbert and Sullivan's *Patience* but also for the brand "Wilde."[77] Cody's similarly styled ex-military impresario, Major John Burke, followed this pattern of commercial dissemination, saturating London (and later Manchester and Birmingham) with visual and textual advertisements for the Wild West show. These advertisements cultivated anticipation and brand recognition, and they make the dual status of Cody as person and as thing readily apparent. One *Punch* writer, commenting on the incredible proliferation of Buffalo Bill circulars before the opening of the show, jokes about this; he writes, "At present we don't know much about 'Buffalo Bill,' but one thing is certain, that the Buffalo Bill-poster is doing his work uncommonly well."[78] The ambiguous "his" in this statement (Cody's work, or the poster's work?) humorously suggests a subjectivity on the part of the Cody advertisements. The representation is hard at work, as much an authentic part of the show as the man represented therein.

The sentiment expressed by this *Punch* writer, of not knowing much about Buffalo Bill and yet knowing a great deal about the man represented as Buffalo Bill, indicates that despite the massive publicity campaign waged by Burke and others, questions lingered in the minds of Britons regarding the identity of the man at the center of the Wild West. These questions echo ones voiced by Americans about Wilde, the "magnificent advertisement" whose face and figure everyone recognized but whom few seemed to know anything about. It is not surprising, then, that Cody turned to the same technology of representation that Wilde turned to in his attempts to project a "real" version of the man capable of supplementing the handbill version: photography. Cody's enormously popular *carte-de-visite* photographs bear a compelling record of Wilde's influence in this arena as well. In the 1870s, when Cody was gaining recognition as the hero of Ned Buntline's dime novels and the manager of the Buffalo Bill Combination troupe, Cody commissioned Napoleon Sarony—the celebrity photographer who would create the images of Wilde that remain iconic today—to take a series of photos that would appear on some of the earliest Buffalo Bill *cartes-de-visite.* Sarony produced two types of photographs, one showing a sedately ponderous young Cody in white shirt collar, black suit and vest, and heavy overcoat, and the other depicting Cody in full Buffalo Bill regalia, with fringed buckskins and rifle over his knees. Shortly thereafter, Sarony took perhaps the most famous pictures of

FIGURE 2.3. "Oscar Wilde, No. 15," Napoleon Sarony (photographer), 1882.
Courtesy Private Collection, Ken Welsh/Bridgeman Images.

his career, the 1882 Wilde photos that quickly flooded the United States and were appropriated (in violation of a copyright that Sarony had to appeal to the Supreme Court to receive) into countless advertisements and posters.[79]

Among Sarony's photos of Wilde is one in which the young aesthete lounges on a divan in aestheticist costume (knee breeches, silk stockings, and beribboned slippers), his head propped up by his right hand and his finger marking his place in a book (fig. 2.3). Making plentiful use of fur and oriental rugs, this image conveys both Wilde's fondness for lavish colors, prints, and textures and his embodiment of deliberate indolence, key characteristics of British aestheticism. Because these are not, however, characteristics typically associated with Cody or the Wild West, the echoes of them in a publicity photo that Cody commissioned in London in 1887 are all the more remarkable (fig. 2.4). In this picture, it is Cody lounging full figure, his head propped up by his right hand, Wilde's book being swapped for a rawhide quirt. The artificial rocks the frontiersman leans on neatly replicate Wilde's divan, a

FIGURE 2.4. "William F. Cody Seated with Quirt and Rifle," Elliott and Fry (photographers), London, 1887.
Courtesy of the McCracken Research Library, Buffalo Bill Center of the West.

gesture, perhaps, toward Cody's association with outdoor rather than indoor life. The image of Cody, in full western get-up but reclining as though smitten with aestheticist ennui, is almost comical in the contradiction it interjects between subject and pose. Wilde's influence on Cody's self-presentation is clearly evident when one considers the difference between this languid Cody and the active, alert Cody of the earlier Sarony photo, one entirely

Figure 2.5. "William F. Cody," Albert Naegeli (photographer), New York, c. 1894.
Courtesy of the McCracken Research Library, Buffalo Bill Center of the West.

reconcilable with the Buffalo Bill persona. More interesting still, the 1887 photo is not the only instance in which Wilde's publicity photos are recalled by Cody's. Another set—taken around 1894 by Sarony's rival Albert Naegeli, whose Union Square studio sat near Sarony's—capture Cody as a respectable businessman in a dark suit and floor-length coat with wide fur collar and cuffs, hat in left hand (fig. 2.5).[80] Alone, there is nothing particularly notable about the image, but paired with another of Sarony's Wilde photos (fig. 2.6), it, too, suggests the influence that the public figure of Wilde had on Cody. In this 1882 photo, Wilde similarly appears as a businessman or traveler rather than an apostle of aestheticism. He stands in three-quarter pose with right

FIGURE 2.6. "Oscar Wilde, No. 5," Napoleon Sarony (photographer).
Library of Congress Prints and Photographs Division, Washington, D.C. (reproduction no. LC-DIG-ppmsca-40826).

hand on hip, dressed in a dark suit and long overcoat trimmed with wide fur collar and cuffs. Instead of a hat, Wilde holds in his left hand a pair of gloves.

More than simply recording a visual similarity, what these photos—along with all of the illustrations, advertisements, and newspaper reports linking the two men—suggest is that Cody and Wilde shared the same transatlantic discursive space, a space in which the authenticity of national identity was both unsettled and unexpectedly affirmed in all of its apparent constructedness. Just as Wilde could be regarded as the "definition and description" of Englishness, Cody could be regarded as a "distinctive American type," even as each man's representativeness was challenged by his own performance of it.[81] Revealingly, however, this paradoxical narrative of national identity is recurrently told for one man in the context of the other; Cody is as important for the interpretation of Wilde as a "definition" of Englishness as Wilde is for the interpretation of Cody as a "type" of Americanness. One sees this interdependence in both an 1887 article printed in the *New York Star* (reprinted in the *Abilene Reflector*) and a full-page illustration from the British comic magazine *Moonshine* published just a few weeks later. Titled "Americans in London," the *Star* piece recounts Cody's departure for England: "We send these children of nature, with all their dirt and eccentricities of dress and manner, as true samples of our national individuality."[82] The writer contends that Buffalo Bill and his men "are not mere duplicates of the swells of Pall Mall or of the animals in the 'Zoo.' They are wildly original and unique," genuine Americans that can be recognized only as such. The piece goes on to support this assertion, however, by claiming that "Sitting Bull could never be mistaken for Lord Randolph Churchill, nor Texas Jack for Oscar Wilde." The comparison here between Cody's friend Texas Jack Omohundro and Oscar Wilde is supposed to confirm the quintessential Americanness of the Wild West show, but in fact it does the opposite. By calling to mind the Wilde/Cody mistaken identity gag used frequently in 1882 and the years following, the article brings both men together even as it attempts to distance them. Wilde is necessary to this writer's demonstration of the authenticity of Cody's national identity.

A similar joining of Cody and Wilde in an attempted exposition of difference occurs in "Days with Celebrities (301.) Buffalo Bill," drawn by Alfred Bryan and published in the London journal *Moonshine* on 21 May 1887. A collage of a dozen vignettes depicting Cody's exploits in London, this illustration features Cody's face, in profile, at the center of the page. Each of the sketches that surround him emphasizes his foreignness, the distinct version of Americanness that distinguishes him from typical Londoners. His enormous white hat contrasts with the sedate black top hats worn by members of "the profession" who flank him at the top of the page. To the right and below Cody, Irish MPs, girls in Brompton, and street urchins all denote their unlikeness to him via their professions of desire "to be like Buffalo Bill," a gap they attempt to close by adopting Stetsons or mustering up games of cowboys and Indians. Buffalo Bill "at home" (bottom) lounges in a teepee instead of a respectable townhome, and from his belt horrifically dangle several long-haired scalps (top left). At the top right, Cody strikes a pose on the pinnacle of St. Paul's, proclaiming "Yours is a great country!" Shown here in silhouette, his foot propped against a cross (which has been added to the cathedral by Bryan), Cody is the very picture of a conquistador surveying the new (old) world over which he has come from across the Atlantic to reign. Only one vignette challenges this depiction of Cody as a stranger in a strange land: a sketch of Oscar Wilde. Wilde is positioned immediately to Cody's left, his 1882 locks snipped and his rotund stomach protruding as if to emphasize the impossibility, in 1887, of mistaking him for long-haired, skinny Cody. Beneath Wilde the artist has written, "Oscar Wilde is entirely forgotten now."[83] As in the *Star* article, Bryan here calls up Wilde to demonstrate Cody's difference from him, but referencing the aesthete to remind readers that he has been forgotten does precisely the opposite. By using Wilde as a lens for interpreting Cody, Bryan reminds viewers that Wilde and Cody are not strangers at all but close cultural associates. Fixed beside Cody in the center of the image, Wilde smiles, and it is toward Wilde that Cody forever faces.

Of course, one could argue just as cogently that it is toward Cody that Wilde forever faces, that Cody was always already interpolated into the version of English national identity fashioned by Wilde and performed at home and abroad. Whether one sees, in the image, Wilde facing Cody or Cody facing Wilde, the conclusion is the same. Both a reflection of each other and a refraction of the values that each represented to a transatlantic audience, Cody and Wilde form two halves of a cultural narrative that is at once familiar and legible and oddly unexpected. This narrative possessed what Warren calls a "symbolic facility," not just to represent the self (American frontiersman, British aesthete) to the other (British audiences, American audiences), but to represent the self as an other, an estranged and estranging figure whose constructedness confounds received notions of national identity even as it performs them.[84] In the American West, Wilde's difference from the Cody-esque American male posited a formulation of Britishness that concurrently questioned the stability of that formulation and other formulations of identity as well. And in London's West End, Cody reproduced a mythic version of Americanness apparent to all as both a reproduction and a myth and yet obtaining just the same. "Not national merely," the pair of men thus make paradoxically evident the insignificance of the transatlantic boundaries that divided them and the extreme importance of those boundaries in the performance of a self whose celebrity was shaped largely in the context of the other.

Notes

1. Wilder, *People I've Smiled With,* 111–12.
2. Though Cody and Wilde share a special relationship, Cody was not the only American frontiersman to be described in terms that bring the Wildean aesthetic dandy to mind. An "immaculate boiled shirt, with much collar and cuffs to match—a sleeveless Zouave jacket of startling scarlet, slashed with black velvet, . . . trousers [of] either black velvet or buck skin [and] jacket fitted with buttons quite beyond useful requirement; . . . french [*sic*] calf skin boots . . . polished as if the individual wearing them had recently vacated an Italians [*sic*] arm chair throne on a side street near Broadway" is how one associate describes "Wild Bill" Hickok. Davis quoted in Rosa, *They Called Him Wild Bill,* 108.
3. Novak, "Performing the 'Wilde West,'" 455.
4. MacInerney et al., "Oscar Wilde Lectures in Texas," 556.
5. Giles, *Atlantic Republic,* 149.
6. "Oscar Wilde, Probably Owing," *Times Picayune* (New Orleans, La.), November 24, 1882.
7. The feeling, according to one witty critic, was mutual; a letter reading "I am disappointed in Mr. Wilde" soon appeared in the London *Truth,* signed "The Atlantic Ocean." Quoted in Friedman, *Wild in America,* 60.
8. Giles, *Virtual Americas,* 2.
9. Quoted in Mendelssohn, *Henry James, Oscar Wilde,* 29.
10. Quoted in Symons, *Essays and Biographies,* 171. Writing in the 1930s, Symons comes to the same conclusion, claiming that "the chief secret of [Wilde's] success was his complete unlikeness to any American home product" (180).
11. "Marshall P. Wilder, James Russell Lowell, and Buffalo Bill," *Puck* 21 (April 20, 1887): 224.
12. Morgan, "Oscar Wilde's Un-American Tour," 669.
13. Wilde, "English Renaissance of Art," 73.
14. Ibid., 74.
15. Morgan, "Oscar Wilde's Un-American Tour," 672.
16. Castle, "Misrecognising Wilde," 106; Morgan, "Oscar Wilde's Un-American Tour," 676.
17. Susman, *Culture as History,* 273–77.
18. Ibid., 280.
19. "Oscar Wilde is about to depart," *Milwaukee Daily Sentinel,* May 18, 1882, 4.
20. Quoted in Castle, "Misrecognising Wilde," 103.
21. Adams, *Performing Authorship,* 11.
22. "Oscar Dear, Oscar Dear!" *Charleston News and Courier* (Charleston, S.C.), July 8, 1882, 4.
23. Ibid.
24. Voskuil, *Acting Naturally,* 3.
25. Ibid., 185.

26. Ibid., 190.
27. Ibid., 11.
28. Adams, *Performing Authorship,* 11.
29. Quoted in Castle, "Misrecognising Wilde," 102.
30. Ibid., 103.
31. "Speranza's Gifted Son," *St Louis Globe-Democrat,* February 26, 1882, 3.
32. Wilde, *Impressions of America,* 26.
33. Wilde, "American Invasion," 270.
34. "Speranza's Gifted Son," *St. Louis Globe Democrat,* February 26, 1882, 3.
35. "Wilde," *Cleveland Leader,* February 20, 1882, 6.
36. Ibid.
37. Wilde, "American Invasion," 270 (emphasis mine).
38. Meisel, *Cowboy and the Dandy,* 46.
39. Rico, *Nature's Noblemen,* 133.
40. Wilde, *Complete Letters,* 152–53.
41. Ibid., 154.
42. Warren, *Buffalo Bill's America,* 296.
43. Nye, "Apostrophe to Oscar Wilde," 9, 16, 18.
44. Ibid., 25, 24.
45. Ibid., 3–4, 32, 22, 13, 5–6.
46. Ibid., 10–11, 38–39.
47. Ibid., 35, 36.
48. Ibid., 30, 47, 21.
49. Ibid., 14.
50. "Wilde on *Us*: Something to 'Live Up' to in America." *Harper's Bazar* 15 (June 10, 1882): 361.
51. Ibid.
52. Morgan, "Oscar Wilde's Un-American Tour," 675.
53. Quoted in Novak, "Performing the 'Wilde West,'" 454.
54. Symons, *Essays and Biographies,* 185.
55. Wilde, *Impressions of America,* 27.
56. MacInerney et al., "Oscar Wilde Lectures in Texas," 562.
57. Alford, "Oscar Wilde in Texas," 193.
58. "Oscar Wilde: An Interview with the Apostle of Aestheticism," *San Francisco Examiner,* March 27, 1882, 2; "Oscar Dear, Oscar Dear!" *Charleston News and Courier* (Charleston, SC), July 8, 1882: 4.
59. "Too Tenderly, Utterly Too," *Los Angeles Daily Times,* April 11, 1882.
60. Burnand, *Colonel,* 8.
61. Ibid., 8, 13, 12.
62. Ibid., 71.
63. Ibid., 26, 69, 77.
64. Ibid., 20.
65. Ibid., 61.

66. Giles, *Virtual Americas*, 150.
67. Quoted in Warren, *Buffalo Bill's America*, 294.
68. "With the Indians on the Derby Day," *Punch* 92 (4 June 1882): 269, William F. "Buffalo Bill" Cody Collection.
69. "Wild West: Buffalo Bill's Great Show Booked for Next Week," *Wheeling Register* (Wheeling, W.Va.), October 1, 1884, 4.
70. Warren, *Buffalo Bill's America*, 295.
71. Meisel, *Cowboy and the Dandy*, 42.
72. "Wild West Show," *The Era* (London, England), September 18, 1886, 10.
73. Voskuil, *Acting Naturally*, 192; 190.
74. Voskuil, *Acting Naturally*, 2.
75. Gagnier, *Idylls of the Marketplace*, 52–55; Friedman, *Wilde in America*, 91–97.
76. Adams points out that the impresario or booking agent, while not an entirely new concept (the *OED* notes "impresario" first being used in the mid-eighteenth century), developed in conjunction with the celebrity lecture tour and reached a height of popularity in the late nineteenth century (Adams, *Performing Authorship*, 2).
77. Quoted in Powell, *Acting Wilde*, 15.
78. "The Wild West." *Punch* 92 (30 April 1887): 205.
79. Powell, *Acting Wilde*, 25.
80. Kasson reproduces this photograph of Cody with the date ca. 1876, which she attributes to the Buffalo Bill Center of the West in Cody, Wyoming (126, 303). Although the Center's William F. "Buffalo Bill" Cody Collection does date this image ca. 1876, this date does not accord with the other Cody photos taken by Naegeli ca. 1894 that use the same backdrop. Cody also appears much older in this photo than he does in the 1870s photos.
81. "Marshall P. Wilder, James Russell Lowell, and Buffalo Bill," *Puck* 21 (April 20, 1887): 224.
82. "Americans in London," William F. "Buffalo Bill" Cody Collection.
83. Alfred Bryan, "Days with Celebrities. (301). Buffalo Bill," Moonshine [London], May 21, 1887, p. 241, William F. "Buffalo Bill" Cody Collection.
84. Warren, *Buffalo Bill's America*, 298.

3

"The Wild West Side of American Existence"

Theodore Roosevelt, Buffalo Bill Cody, and American Military Exceptionalism

JEREMY M. JOHNSTON

In 1910, shortly after his African safari, former president of the United States Theodore Roosevelt traveled throughout Europe on a goodwill tour. In the course of his trip, he received three honorary doctoral degrees and delivered a number of significant speeches on topics ranging from the evolution of Western civilization to responsibilities of a citizen in a republic, as well as delivering lectures regarding the conduct of British imperialists in Africa, Egypt, and the Sudan and reciting a history of colonial policies of the United States. Roosevelt presented these lectures at prestigious universities throughout Europe, including the Sorbonne, University of Berlin, Cambridge University, and Oxford, in addition to addressing the Nobel Prize Committee in Christiana, Norway, and various businessmen at London's Guildhall. Crowds greeted Roosevelt as a celebrity in most of the European countries he visited, and he met a number of scholars, writers, political leaders, and monarchs.

Later recalling his European trip to fellow writer and British historian Sir George Otto Trevelyan, Roosevelt noted that various kings and queens of Europe "were always sure to wish to hear from me about some of the things that I had done while I was President."[1] In addition, Roosevelt noted, "they were at least as anxious to hear about my [Rough Rider] regiment, and especially about my life in the West, evidently regarding it as an opportunity to acquire knowledge at firsthand and at close range concerning the *Buffalo-Bill and Wild-West side of American existence.*"[2] Roosevelt the politician realized the power of Buffalo Bill's popular entertainment throughout his European trip and how it shaped Europe's perceptions of America, foregrounding its frontier character. Both men, Roosevelt as a statesman and Buffalo Bill as a cultural ambassador, elevated the image of America's martial values to both American and European audiences—a perception that would be put to the test during America's intervention in World War I.

Buffalo Bill's dramatic depiction of the American West through his three Wild West European tours set the stage for Roosevelt's 1910 European tour. Buffalo Bill's Wild West filled Europeans' heads with glamorous and violent images of the American frontier through his form of popular entertainment; these images shaped Europeans' perceptions of Roosevelt, the cowboy president, and influenced his own diplomatic mission and efforts to shape America's role on the world stage. Recognized as an expert of the American frontier experience, Roosevelt eagerly associated himself with Buffalo Bill's narrative of frontier exceptionalism throughout his tour of Europe, placing special emphasis on the rugged military attributes of American fighting men.

It was during this visit that Roosevelt also truly recognized the international popularity of Buffalo Bill and his Wild West tours throughout Europe and how deeply many Europeans associated him with the excitement and romance of the American frontier. Roosevelt discovered that Europeans viewed him not only as a statesman who served as governor of New York and as vice president and president of the United States, but also as a "cowboy" who ranched in the Badlands of Dakota, a cavalier who led the famed Rough Rider regiment, the rugged sportsman that hunted mountain lions and bears throughout the Rocky Mountains. In addition to being an international diplomat representing the United States, then emerging as a world power, Roosevelt became the political personification of the mythical American West, a rugged individualist who appeared to live the adventurous lifestyle that Buffalo Bill encapsulated in his earlier European tours of Buffalo Bill's Wild West as a cultural ambassador.[3]

Buffalo Bill assumed the role as cultural ambassador for a dramatic vision of the American frontier experience during his first European appearance in 1887. American writer and humorist Mark Twain encouraged the role of cultural ambassador for Buffalo Bill, writing that "it is often said on the other side of the water that none of the exhibitions we send to England are purely and distinctly American. If you will take the Wild West Show over there, you can remove that reproach."[4] Although Buffalo Bill's Wild West was billed as entertainment, it assumed an ambassadorial posture in its self-promotion. Buffalo Bill claimed that Queen Victoria nodded toward the American flag during the show's presentation, the first salute from a British monarch. Cody later recalled, "All present were constrained to feel that here was an outward and visible sign of the extinction of that mutual prejudice, sometimes almost amounting to race hatred, that had severed the two nations from the times of Washington and George the Third to the present day. We felt that the hatchet was buried at last and the Wild West had been at the funeral."[5]

After watching the performance, Queen Victoria praised Buffalo Bill's rugged appeal and successful military record in her diary: "Col. Cody 'Buffalo Bill' as he is called, from having killed 3,000 buffaloes, with his own hand, is a splendid man, handsome & gentlemanlike in manner. He has had many encounters & hand to hand fights with the Red Indians."[6] With the international success of his first British tour, Buffalo Bill returned to Europe in 1889, opening at the Paris Exposition. Historian Allan Gallup noted, "The French edition of the Wild West wielded the same magic on Parisians as the British version had on Londoners four years before. President Carnot and his wife, plus his entire cabinet and their families, attended the opening performances."[7] This success was repeated in Spain, Italy, Austria, Germany, Belgium, and once again in Great Britain. Following this prolonged European tour, Cody returned to the United States and debuted the Congress of Rough Riders of the World at the Columbian Exposition.

Buffalo Bill's Wild West successfully promoted itself as an educational experience, one that presented an authentic depiction of the frontier experience. It successfully blended history and histrionics by hiring real frontier figures—such as Sitting Bull, who appeared in the 1885 season—to dramatically reenact their past exploits, or at the very least to authenticate the storyline with their presence. This tradition carried over to the European tours when Cody recruited a number of Lakota Ghost Dancers to tour with the Wild West through Europe. These were not pretend Lakota but prisoners of war that he acquired from General Nelson A. Miles shortly after the Wounded Knee Massacre.

In addition to hiring Lakota performers and authentic cowboys, Cody incorporated new performance technologies and perfected his dramatic storylines to create a very realistic performance. Sitting in the grandstands watching the Wild West provided Europeans with a dramatic perspective on Americans and their frontier qualities, supplementing the stories and tales they may have read from James Fennimore Cooper's novels and journals of European travelers in the American West. Recreations of historic events, both factual and mythical, entertained European audiences: Pony Express riders, the attack of the Deadwood Stage, the attack of homesteaders in their cabin. Within these acts, Buffalo Bill and his cowboys always saved the intended victims of Lakota Indians at the last minute. Tom Cunningham noted in his history of Buffalo Bill's Wild West in Scotland that Buffalo Bill's version of Custer's Last Stand was "so real to 400 boys from St. Joseph's Industrial School that they believed the palefaces had been slaughtered by Indians in the arena before their eyes."[8]

These staged performances stressed the ideal character of the American fighting male as shaped by the frontier: independent, self-reliant, aggressive, and quick to defend any innocent person found in harm's way. Audience members witnessed cowboys and cavalrymen working as a team under the leadership of the famed scout Buffalo Bill to defend the innocent stagecoach passengers or homesteaders from savage Indian attacks. Through these European tours, the management of Buffalo Bill's Wild West envisioned an international assemblage of famed equestrian groups from Europe and Asia that were worthy of riding next to American Indians and cowboys. This vision resulted in Buffalo Bill's Congress of Rough Riders of the World. Now audiences witnessed cowboys and Indians riding alongside well-disciplined European cavalrymen representing Germany, France, and Great Britain, giving the impression that frontier experience made Americans equal to European soldiers. In addition, the placement of Boers, Arabs, and "Cossacks" (who were really Georgian trick riders) alongside Vaqueros and Lakota riders indicated Americans shared the challenge of facing worthy foes through their imperial and expansionist policies.

Back in the United States, audiences appreciated Buffalo Bill's elevation of the American fighting man's status next to European soldiers within the Congress of Rough Riders of the World. Again, Cody blurred entertainment with perceived reality. In a 1901 article written for *Collier's Magazine* entitled "Mobilizing a Mimic Army," Cody described the Congress of Rough Riders as follows:

> Have you ever watched a man at work making a mosaic floor? Stone by stone, bit by bit, each carefully selected, he adds and adds, putting each piece exactly in the right place, the job, when completed being harmonious in color, definite in form, and

> meaning something. Our Show [of Congress of Rough Riders] is a mosaic of horsemen. Each is a picked man, chosen because of his record as a soldier or plainsman, his physical perfection, and his ability to be always an integral part of a horse. . . . Here the riders of many nations break bread, and have soup, fish, roast beef, pork, coffee, together. . . . The Rough Riders' Congress can go on indefinitely as long as men ride horses with the abandon of a child on a hobby-horse. Neither bicycle nor automobile will soon supplant our great four-footed friend in the unsettled portions of the earth, and hence for years to come the rough and ready horseman may continue to give exhibitions of the strength, courage, and vigorous and virile manhood which he represents.[9]

On the surface, this article about a mimic army seems somewhat superficial; however, reports of current American military achievements appeared in the same issue. These articles included a comparison of regular and volunteer military units by General Nelson A. Miles and accounts detailing the capture of Filipino insurrection leader Emilio Aguinaldo. Clearly the editor of *Collier's* determined an article about Buffalo Bill's mimic army warranted placement alongside contemporary news of American military accomplishments in the Philippines.

During his last tour of Europe, audiences must have found Buffalo Bill's presentation of a well-organized group of rugged individualists fighting for a common cause to be an interesting phenomenon. At the time Buffalo Bill appeared in Europe, many European men were being conditioned along nationalist tendencies, where one's military service not only fulfilled one's patriotic duty but also supposedly provided heroic adventure and a gallant cause. Those serving in the European cavalry regiments figured as modern *cavaliers,* knights in shining armor, defending their respective nations. James J. Sheehan, author of *Where Have All the Soldiers Gone? The Transformation of Modern Europe,* noted that "the military was grand and distant, connected to great deeds and powerful men, but also familiar and close, part of everyday life. . . . States wanted, above all, to be identified with the heroism, self-sacrifice, and duty that had made their victories possible and their defeats endurable. . . . By 1900, two developments had transformed both war and states . . . both were democratized . . . both were profoundly affected by industrialization."[10] The well-regimented fighting men of Europe must have wondered not only about the military accomplishments of Rough Riders in the American West and through the course of the Spanish American War but also about how closely Buffalo Bill's Rough Riders reflected Theodore Roosevelt's Rough Rider Regiment. From the perspective of twentieth-century combat, what role could these rugged individualists, who clearly possessed wonderful fighting abilities, if properly commanded, serve on the battlefields of Europe?

Throughout the course of his visit through Europe, Roosevelt reviewed many European troops demonstrating their prowess. While in France, Roosevelt hoped to forgo a review of French military maneuvers for visits to galleries and museums; however, upon hearing that the kaiser planned a military review in Roosevelt's honor, French ambassador Jean J. Jusserand insisted the former president must review the French troops. "Yet I did not take [France's] military power seriously, nor deem her soldiers worth seeing; for, said Jusserand, the French pride themselves upon being a military nation, and admit no military inferiority to any people," wrote Roosevelt. "Of course I hastily withdrew my declination, saying with entire sincerity that I was a very great admirer of the French soldiers; and so off I went and saw a sham battle."[11] Following a French colonel's request that he ride with the troops, Roosevelt borrowed some leggings and rode with the soldiers, although wearing a frock coat and top hat. The French regiment later wrote Roosevelt to note they would honor the horse he rode; in turn, he promised to send them a photo of himself in his Rough Rider uniform.

When Theodore Roosevelt arrived in Europe in 1910, following three successful tours of Buffalo Bill's Wild West, statesmen and royalty indeed welcomed a diplomatic representative from the United States who embodied the American West, one with a firsthand perspective on the American frontier experience. "Accordingly, after the usual formal and perfunctory conversation with the new king or crown prince, or whoever it was, he would, with a little preliminary maneuvering, ask me if I would mind repeating the story I had told some preceding king about this, that, or the other frontier hero [Ben Daniels] who had afterwards become a public servant holding my commission," Roosevelt noted. Many of these stories reflected the violent side of the American frontier experience, similar to the scenes presented in Buffalo Bill's Wild West. Roosevelt noted the following:

> [Various royalty] wishing to know just how and why it was that Benjamin Franklin Daniels, afterwards Marshall of Arizona,

> had his ear 'bit off' in the course of the exercises of his duties as peace officer, or why Hon. Seth Bullock, who was Marshal in South Dakota . . . had regarded homicide as a regrettable but inevitable incident of a political career in territorial days; or he might (and in two cases actually did) say 'I beg your pardon, but I do not quite understand what is a two-gun man,' which would necessitate a brief review of the exercise of the right of private war in the Far West, and the advantages accruing to the cause of virtue if its special champion was able to use a revolver in either hand.[12]

Ironically, when Roosevelt recommended Ben Daniels's appointment as a US marshall in Arizona to Senator Clarence Clark, he equated his rough background to that of a Viking: "[Daniels] was born and brought up in the West when it was a very wild West indeed, and his early life was passed in conditions which have now as completely vanished from this country as the age of the Vikings has vanished from Europe."[13]

This interest in the American frontier inspired Roosevelt to stage his own version of the Wild West by inviting his friend Seth Bullock, the former sheriff of Deadwood, South Dakota, to join him in Europe to fortify his frontier connections and to impress upon the British the appearance and character of a true westerner. Estelline Bennett, a Deadwood resident, described Roosevelt's living personification of an ideal American: "Seth Bullock, tall, lean, with drooping mustache, keen gray eyes, a whimsical humor, a soft voice that spoke English like the educated gentlemen he was, and always, even when he went to Washington as the guest of the President, wearing a soft white Stetson. His friendships could run the gamut from Roosevelt to Calamity Jane and back again without stumbling."[14] Roosevelt used these relations with the rougher elements of the American West to burnish his authentic connections to the American frontier and the violent men who brought law and order to the West.

During his tenure in Great Britain, Bullock enjoyed playing the backwoodsman, gently poking fun at their proper manners and formality with his colloquial sense of humor. Bullock speculated how the elaborately dressed "Major-domos" who announced the names of guests at banquets would fare on horseback during a roundup. "He certainly would have been the envy of every Sioux brave in an Indian dog dance," recalled Bullock.[15] Roosevelt chuckled when Bullock, while crossing a bridge, asked an Englishman the name of the "creek" beneath them. "That my good fellow is our River Thames," replied the incredulous Englishman.[16] Bullock's remarks, seemingly flippant, emphasized the westerner's tendency to ignore the trappings of aristocratic European society and establish a bond with whomever, regardless of their social status. Roosevelt also exhibited these egalitarian values and associated them with the frontier.

Things were quite different in the United States, where in the realm of national politics Roosevelt curtailed his rhetoric about his western and military experiences. In a letter to historian James Ford Rhodes shortly after the 1904 presidential election, Roosevelt detailed his efforts to downplay both. "It would have been an absurdity for my supporters to say anything about my having been a military man, or having been a ranchman; for one appeal would have looked ridiculous in view of my having served only four months in a very small war, and the other would have looked demagogic," noted Roosevelt. Yet Roosevelt realized that the popular image of his cowboy and Rough Rider days proved to be powerful in drawing popular support. Instead of resorting to braggadocio, Roosevelt let his political opponents draw attention to his adventuresome life. Roosevelt noted that "opposing papers, and especially the opposing caricaturists, invariably represented me in the rough rider uniform, or else riding a bucking broncho [*sic*] and roping a steer, or carrying a big stick and threatening foreign nations, and thereby made me to the younger among their own readers the very kind of *ad captandum* appeal on my behalf which it would have been undignified for my supporters to have made."[17]

In European affairs, Roosevelt felt no qualms in promoting his self-image as a rugged western rancher and Rough Rider. As president of the United States, Roosevelt was not above defending his international policies using western rhetoric. In explaining his reluctance to join a European coalition and intervene on behalf of Jews suffering from the Czarist policies in Russia, he noted, "I thoroughly believe that in national affairs we should act in accordance with the plains adage when I was in the ranch business: 'Never to draw unless you mean to shoot.'"[18] While in Europe, Roosevelt continued to play up his Rough Rider image; however, there was a downside. Many now focused on the Buffalo-Bill side of American life, which overshadowed Roosevelt's scholarly interests and a more nuanced diplomacy. In the same letter in which he detailed European's fascination with the American West to Trevelyan, he also complained, "I know nothing that the average scholar does not know, yet that I know a good deal as to which the average politician or man of affairs is abysmally ignorant; and as naturally my life has been chiefly led among politicians and men of affairs, when it was not led among frontiersmen, there are a great many things I have studied about which I have rarely or never had a chance to speak."[19] Roosevelt's frontier persona obscured his intellectual gifts and his diplomatic skills, conveying to key political figures and royalty the image of the rough American bumpkin and recalling Frances Trollope's popular account of American culture from the mid-nineteenth century.

Although Roosevelt noted the German people did not warmly welcome him, the kaiser greatly appreciated his record as a soldier and his western experiences. "It was evident that, next to England, America was very unpopular in Germany,"[20] recalled Roosevelt. Despite the cold shoulder from the citizens of Germany, the military establishment and the kaiser welcomed Roosevelt warmly as a fellow soldier. Tirpitz, Germany's secretary of war, noted Roosevelt and the kaiser "were alike, that he now saw the resemblance, but of course I had had to take responsibilities and win my own way and do things for myself, which naturally made much difference between us!"[21] Prince von Bülow recalled in his memoirs that Theodore Roosevelt, the president of the United States, exercised a quite particular fascination of the kaiser: "'That's my man!' [the kaiser] used to say, as soon as the name of Roosevelt was mentioned. He read in dispatches from our ambassador that Roosevelt performed feats of riding equal to those of a cowboy, that, like Buffalo Bill, he could just hit the bull's eye with deadly marksmanship at a prodigious distance, that his spirit was unquenchable, fearless, and ready for anything."[22] Clearly, Roosevelt's aggressive demeanor and military background resonated for the kaiser with the memory of Buffalo Bill, whose performances he had attended during the German tours.

At a dinner served the night before King Edward VII's funeral, the official purpose of Roosevelt's European trip, he again attempted to mingle with European royalty, only to be thwarted by the kaiser, who either wanted to test this cowboy president or perhaps provoke an "incident." The kaiser found great humor in introducing Roosevelt, the famed Rough Rider who stormed San Juan Hill, to the king of Spain. Finding himself face-to-face with Roosevelt, his country's former enemy, King Alfonso reportedly said, "I am glad to meet you, Mr. Roosevelt, I have admired your public career, and I have also admired your military career, though I am sorry that your honors should have been won at the expense of my countrymen."[23] Roosevelt bowed and diplomatically replied, "Your Majesty, I have always borne testimony, and I always shall bear testimony, to the gallantry and courage your countrymen showed in battle; although frankly I cannot speak as highly of their leadership."[24] The king replied, "I should think not! I should think not! But I am glad to have you speak thus of the courage of the soldiers."[25] If the kaiser hoped to provoke a western-style brawl between Roosevelt and the king of Spain, Roosevelt's diplomatic handling of the incident disappointed him. Roosevelt's diplomatic replies distinguished him from the blunt frontier rhetoric associated with Seth Bullock.

The morning of King Edward's funeral, Roosevelt again found himself caught in the complexities of European diplomatic decorum. Stephen Pinchon, the French minister of foreign affairs, expressed a number of complaints to Roosevelt about various slights to the representatives of France and the United States. Roosevelt and Pinchon were placed behind the prince of Persia in the funeral procession, and the Chinese representatives were placed in front of them both. Roosevelt defused the Frenchman's anger by threatening to play cowboy. According to Keith Eubank, author of *Paul Cambon—Master Diplomat*, "Teddy Roosevelt aided the confusion by announcing [to Pinchon] that he would ride on horseback dressed in 'khaki, in boots, with a Buffalo Bill hat, a saber, and pistols.'"[26] Once again, Roosevelt's frontier rhetoric poked holes in the royal trappings of European society. Roosevelt recalled, "I think my advice had a sedative effect; it certainly prevented any public explosion."[27]

The Roosevelt family sailed home aboard the SS *Kaiserin Auguste Victoria* and arrived to a tremendous public welcome in New York City on April 18, 1910, concluding a prolonged overseas trip that began with his departure on March 23, 1909. The cowboy president was now home. In 1912, he ran under the banner of the Progressive Party against the Democratic presidential candidate Woodrow Wilson and President William Howard Taft, defeating Taft but losing to Wilson. In the years 1913–1914, Roosevelt, seeking another dangerous adventure, went to explore an unchartered river in the Brazilian rainforest, where he nearly lost his life. As before, Roosevelt remained an international representative of an adventurous life, one that began in the Dakota Badlands and took him to the wilds of Africa and South America. Like Buffalo Bill, Roosevelt continued to develop his persona as a cosmopolitan frontiersman exploring an unknown territory with countless natural and human dangers.

On June 28, 1914, the assassination of Archduke Franz Ferdinand of Austria and his wife brought Europe into the conflict that European nationalism and imperialism would spread across the globe. At first, both Cody and Roosevelt recommended American neutrality yet argued that America must prepare its military forces, just in case military intervention in Europe became a reality. Despite propaganda depicting the German occupation of Belgium, Roosevelt defended early German tactics in western terms. Focusing on the occupation of Brussels, Roosevelt detailed the potential consequences of German withdrawal: some of the Belgian "'Apache' type, in spite of everything that good citizens may do, will from some building fire upon the retiring soldiers."[28] In this situation, Roosevelt argued that the German Army possessed the right to punish the offending "Apache," yet if the German forces destroyed Brussels, as they had done with Louvain, then a collective, international power should hold Germany accountable for their misuse of military force.

During the early stages of the Great War, Roosevelt also represented the military conflict in Europe using analogies of the early lawlessness of the Old West. Roosevelt argued Europe needed an international police force, one with teeth, to end the conflict. Passing resolutions and arbitration treaties, according to Roosevelt, did not deter the spread of war and could not bring about its end. Harkening back to his past experiences in the Badlands, Roosevelt noted that

> most Americans who are past middle age remember young, rapidly growing, and turbulent communities in which there was at first complete anarchy. During the time there was no central police power to which to appeal every man worth his salt . . . had to be prepared to defend himself . . . under these conditions each man had to keep himself armed and both able and willing to respond to the call of the peace-officer; and furthermore, if he had a shred of wisdom he kept himself ready in an emergency to act on his own behalf if the peace-officer did not or could not do his duty.[29]

In Roosevelt's mind, the world must form an international *Posse Comitatus* to take the law into its own hands and to restore world order through the collective action of concerned citizens. This organization was not to be another Hague but an organized collection of military might that could enforce the peace. If it did not have military backing, it would be similar to western communities that attempted to disarm themselves and "passed self-denying ordinances, saying nobody was to carry arms; but they failed to provide methods for carrying such ordinances into effect . . . [and] the result was the same. Good citizens for the moment abandoned their weapons. The bad men continued to carry them."[30] Many of Roosevelt's readers likely recalled the lawlessness of the cattle towns like Abilene and Dodge City, or the chaotic mining communities of Virginia City, Montana, or Deadwood, South Dakota. In these towns, community members turned to strong lawmen like Wild Bill Hickok and Seth Bullock, or they took the law into their own hands through groups such as the Montana Vigilantes, Granville Stuart's Stranglers, or the Johnson County Invaders. Hinting at this history, Roosevelt argued that when "things grew worse instead of better . . . the good men came to their senses and clothed some representative of the police with power to employ force, potential or existing, against the wrong-doers."[31] Clearly, then, what Europe needed was a strong force to restore peace, enforced by a western posse monitoring law and order on a world stage.

Roosevelt's *America and the World War*, a collection of articles written before the sinking of the *Lusitania* and before confirmation of German sabotage against the war industries in the United States, is ambivalent about taking sides among the European warring nations. Using the war as an educational opportunity for the American people, Roosevelt argued for the necessity of enforcing the "peace of righteousness" through a position of military strength. Roosevelt did not choose sides in the conflict; he was just as critical of Great Britain seizing American ships during the emerging conflict as he was of Germany's occupation of Belgium. Yet if the United States ignored the conflict and refused to prepare its defenses, "What befell Antwerp and Brussels will surely some day befall New York or San Francisco, and may happen to many an inland city also, if we do not shake off our supine folly, if we trust for safety to peace treaties unbacked by force."[32]

After the sinking of the *Lusitania* on May 7, 1915, an event that killed 1,198 people, including 128 Americans, Roosevelt's writings became more militant, calling for a more direct response against Germany, harkening back to the days of the Spanish-American War when he donned his Rough Rider outfit. Roosevelt took great umbrage at Wilson's proclamation that America "was too proud to fight." Roosevelt's next collection of essays, published under the title *Fear God and Take Your Own Part*, clearly expressed his frustration with Woodrow Wilson's administration: "During the last three years we have been technically at peace. But during those three years more of our citizens have been killed by Mexicans, Germans, Austrians, and Haytians than were killed during the entire Spanish War."[33] Roosevelt also expressed his growing frustration with Germany, arguing that "for many months Germany has waged war against us, the war being conducted by openly authorized agents of Germany on the high seas and within our land against our munition plants by men who have been shown to be the direct or indirect agents of Germany."[34]

Using his frontier rhetoric, Roosevelt again argued for military preparedness to prevent German aggression or aggression from other foreign countries. In describing his role as a sheriff in the Badlands, Roosevelt noted he "carried what was then the best type of revolver, a .45 self-cocker," and he "was instructed never to use it unless it was absolutely necessary to do so."[35] Roosevelt made it clear his success as sheriff depended on strength through weaponry, "if in the interest of 'peace' it had been proposed to arm me only with a .22 revolver, I would promptly have resigned my job."[36] Roosevelt's preparedness campaign was now couched in western terms. America needed to be a well-armed Seth Bullock patrolling the dusty streets of a lawless frontier town—in this case, the battlefields of Europe—to face down the villains led by the savage kaiser.

Roosevelt's writings reached an international audience. His first collection of essays was published in English and Spanish in 1915 and then in Italian in 1916. His second collection, *Fear God and Take Your Own Part*, appeared in English in 1916 and then French and Spanish in 1917. Roosevelt's essay entitled "Utopia or Hell?" first appeared in the magazine *Independent* and was later reprinted not only in *America and the World War* but also in Great Britain under the title "Why America Should Join the Allies." Clearly the allies received the impression from Roosevelt's writings that the Americans would likely side with them against Germany and her allies. Many readers may have envisioned some form of "Rough Riders" from America arriving in Europe to save the day and drive the Germans from France and Belgium.

Cody also argued for military preparedness at the outbreak of World War I, and sources indicate he even offered his military service to Great Britain. In *Under the Big Top*, Courtney Ryley Cooper offers one version of this:

> The King of England may remember the fact that he received a cablegram in the early days of the war with Germany. I know it was an enthusiastic thing, because I wrote it myself. It offered the services of Buffalo Bill and his Congress of Rough Riders of the World to go through the German lines like rain water through a gutter. If I am not mistaken, His Majesty replied. I guess my apologies are due the King. Buffalo Bill didn't O.K. that cablegram

> until after it was sent. But let this be known: the 'Old Man" . . . was just enough of a fighter, just enough of a youth in spite of his white hairs and three-score-and-more years, to have gone![37]

As European tensions escalated into a global conflict, Cody's career was on the wane. After the loss of Buffalo Bill's Wild West in 1913, Cody appeared with Sells Floto Circus for the seasons of 1914 and 1915. After breaking with Sells Floto, Cody collaborated with the Miller Brothers and Arlington 101 Ranch Show. The Miller Brothers show was struggling after a disastrous European tour when, upon the outbreak of the Great War, the British government seized the Miller Brother's horses and some of their equipment. Returning to the states, the Miller Brothers hoped a partnership with Cody would rejuvenate their enterprise, as Cody hoped it would improve his financial situation as well. The combined enterprise toured the United States in 1916 and promoted its connections in its billing: the "Miller and Arlington Wild West Show Co., presents the Military Pageant Preparedness, Buffalo Bill (himself) Combined with the 101 Ranch Show." The new presentation included a few "Wild West" acts, such as a Pony Express demonstration, along with a modern cavalry charge, a field battery demonstration, and a number of equestrian events.

Cody and his partners, despite the sinking of the *Lusitania* and the preparedness theme, remained very cautious not to offend their German-American audiences. Owing to large German immigrant populations in Chicago, Cody and his partners changed the name of the show to the Chicago "Shan-Kive" and Round-up, hoping to avoid alienating potential German audience members. The program for the Chicago venue explained that *Shan-Kive* was an American Indian phrase for "good time." Dropping the military preparedness theme, the Chicago performance became a rodeo, which the program explained was another term for roundup, and Buffalo Bill and various Chicago dignitaries served as judges of the equestrian events.

One must wonder how Roosevelt would have viewed Cody's willingness to drop the military preparedness theme and thereby accommodating German-Americans' views of America's role in the war. In his essay "Hyphenated Americanism," which appeared in *Metropolitan* magazine in October 1915 and was later reprinted in *Fear God and Take Your Own Part,* Roosevelt decried any American immigrant who advocated strict neutrality. In the essay, Roosevelt wrote, "As for the hyphenated Americans . . . the effort to combine fealty to the flag of an immigrant's natal land with fealty to the flag of his adopted land, in practice means not merely disregard of, but hostility to, the flag of the United States."[38] Roosevelt made his opinion clear that the alliance of any citizen of the United States should not be "in accordance with the interests of the European nation from which some or all of his ancestors have come. If he does not act along these lines, he is derelict in his duty to his fellow citizens and he is guilty of betraying the interests of his country."[39] Quite probably Roosevelt would have expressed vehement displeasure with Cody and the Miller Brothers for suppressing their preparedness message and acquiescing to German-American audiences' national ties to their former homeland to increase ticket sales.

After the Chicago "Shan-Kive" and Round-up performances, Cody and the Miller Brothers continued the Wild West portion of the show. Upon the end of the tour in November, Cody returned to the TE Ranch and contracted a serious cold. He traveled to Glenwood Springs in the hopes that its therapeutic waters would restore his health. After collapsing from exhaustion, Cody traveled to his sister May's home in Denver, where he passed away on January 10, 1917. Upon his death, President Woodrow Wilson sent a telegram expressing his condolences, as did General Hugh Scott and retired General Nelson A. Miles; however, in the archived list of dignitaries expressing their sympathy, Theodore Roosevelt's name is absent. Also in the extensive Library of Congress collection of Roosevelt correspondence, letters and telegrams from Roosevelt to Cody's family are nonexistent, implying any relationship between the two Rough Riders was not as close as many assumed.

Shortly after Cody's death, the United States entered the Great War. With America's entry into the war, Roosevelt hoped to create another Rough Rider regiment; this time they would storm the trenches of the western European front and drive back the German Army. Before America declared war, Roosevelt wrote French president Jean Jules Jusserand on February 16, 1917, that he would "raise a division of 20,000 men, even if the [American] government declined to hold out the promise of an expeditionary force . . . to go at the earliest moment."[40] After America entered the war, Roosevelt requested permission from Secretary of War Newton D. Baker and President Wilson to form such a "Roosevelt Division" to fight overseas. Both houses of Congress agreed and voted a clause to allow for the raising of volunteer regiments within the conscription bill, and Roosevelt claimed he received over 2,000 requests a day from men wanting to join his division, allowing him to raise an army of 250,000 men in a short time.

When Secretary Baker inquired with General Hugh L. Scott about Roosevelt's request, the general dismissed it, saying that the political nature of Roosevelt's effort ran up against the government's efforts to build a true national army. He concluded by pointing out the possibilities of such a crazy idea: "Consider what a ridiculous figure you would cut, attempting to punish Mr. Roosevelt by a court-martial. No, it will never do, Mr. Secretary; France and England would feel that you are not serious in this war and your promise of help would be disbelieved. This proposition goes directly athwart our plans for raising a real army."[41] President Wilson also refused to support Roosevelt's volunteer regiment: "It would be agreeable to me to pay Mr. Roosevelt this compliment and the Allies the compliment of sending to their aid one of our most distinguished public men . . . but this is not the time or the occasion for compliment or for any action not calculated to contribute to the immediate success of the war. The business now in hand is undramatic, practical, and of scientific definiteness and precision."[42]

After learning that Roosevelt's request to form a regiment was turned down by Wilson, French premier Georges Clemenceau, "the Tiger," wrote a public letter to Wilson, noting "in all candor, that at the present moment there is in France one name which sums up the beauty of American intervention. It is the name of Roosevelt, your predecessor, even your rival." Clemenceau continued,

> I claim for Roosevelt only what he claims for himself—the right to appear on the battlefield surrounded by his comrades. We have just heard of the arrival of the first American unit on the front. All our hearts beat. With what joy our soldiers greeted the starry banner! Yet you must know, Mr. President, more than one of our *poilus* asked his comrade: 'But where is Roosevelt? I don't see him.' . . . the cause of humanity, which is also your cause will owe [to the soldiers of France] something approaching a miracle. Since it is in your power to give them before the supreme decision the promise of reward, believe me—send them Roosevelt. I tell you because I know it will gladden their hearts.[43]

As Wilson noted, combat in the early twentieth century was now a science, not the romantic call to arms and dashing heroic charges that Roosevelt advocated for and conducted in the Spanish-American War. Even without the creation of a Rough Rider regiment, frontier rhetoric abounded throughout the US Army as it expanded its strength through conscription as opposed to volunteer units. Some soldiers trained at Camp Cody, a military base in New Mexico named in honor of Cody. The Ninety-First Infantry Division nicknamed itself "the Wild West Division." Units from the Wyoming National Guard serving in the war proudly displayed an emblem of a cowboy riding a bucking bronco; the state of Wyoming continues to use this emblem. Aviators, the cavaliers of the sky, also selected western themes for their emblems. The American volunteers of the famed *Lafayette Escadrille* selected the profile of an American Indian chief to symbolize their unit. The Eighty-Eighth Aero Squadron of the American Expeditionary Force's emblem depicted a cowboy riding a plunging bronco while pointing his pistol in the air. Although there were no Rough Rider regiments serving in the United States Army, a number of American Doughboys certainly touted the romantic imagery of the Wild West.

The "Wild West Division" hosted a "Wild West" show before they disembarked for Europe. Daniel Moor, a former cowboy and performer for Buffalo Bill's Wild West and Pawnee Bill's Far East, described the event.

> Two months later we got our traveling orders. The division was to jump the Pond to join the fracas in France. Permission was granted for several units to put on a big division show for the town folk, who had already grown rich off the soldiers of the 91st. The cowboys in the outfit gathered every old outlaw horse in the country and put on a rodeo, and the best-drilled infantry company came up with a real snappy Butts Manuel drill team that was something to behold. The engineers built bridges in jig time, the wagon trains and transport outfits wheeled across them just before they were blown to smithereens, and the hospital corpsmen rescued soldiers wounded in the big sham battle and toted them off on stretchers, bleeding profusely (with ketchup). The bronc riders entered the arena on an old stagecoach, dressed in top hats and tails over their boots and spurs. When the stage reached the chutes, out fell the riders, and each climbed on a ready-saddled bronc and turned him out, spurring high and handsome and yelling "Powder River!" This was the war cry that later chilled many a Kraut's blood when we met them on the battlefields of France. It looked like everyone from the whole country had come to watch our going away show, and they gave us a big hand all right.[44]

Dreams of riding with Roosevelt in a Rough Riders regiment held by these cowboy soldiers would never come to fruition. Tim McCoy, who as a boy met Buffalo Bill in Saginaw, Michigan, desperately tried to raise a Rough Rider regiment in Wyoming on Roosevelt's behalf. Upon President Wilson's declination of Roosevelt's Regiment, McCoy noted, "Thus did politics and technology doom my chance to ride in an old-time cavalry charge with Teddy Roosevelt. It would certainly have been, as he was so fond of putting it, 'Bully!'"[45] Still imbued with the fighting spirit, McCoy joined the United States Cavalry to fight in World War I only to be informed that most of the cavalry forces were to be converted into artillery units. "We were stunned. Gone were the days of the glorious, thundering, saber-wielding cavalry charges," recalled McCoy.[46] He later led a funeral march on behalf of the United States Cavalry at West Point, Kentucky. "Hundreds of troops participated. Wearing black arm bands, with our heads bowed, we moved slowly through the post to the tune of a dirge. In the center of this procession was a caisson with a casket draped in black, and on a black-bordered white streamer which lay across the coffin were the words: 'United States Cavalry. Died 1918. RIP.'"[47]

When American troops finally marched down the streets of Paris, it is reported some of the crowds shouted, "Teddy! Teddy! Long live the Teddies!" Clearly, the Europeans viewed the American Doughboys as "Rough Riders" marching in to assist the war effort. In May 1917, Captain Rochambeau wrote Roosevelt that he wished to be the first soldier "to salute [Roosevelt] with the title of 'My General' on the battlefields of France."[48] Yet Roosevelt did not arrive to fight, and he later sent the regiment a photograph of himself wearing his Rough Rider uniform, which they promptly hung in their barracks without permission from their commanding officers. Even Lawrence of Arabia depicted his escapades in frontier terms. After attacking a train with his Arab allies, Lawrence wrote his colleague Major W. F. Stirling on September 25, 1917, "I hope this sounds the fun it is. The only pity is the sweat to work them up, and the wild scramble while it lasts. It's the most amateurish, Buffalo Bill sort of performance, and the only people who do it well are the Bedouin. Only you will think it heaven, because there aren't any returns, or order, or superiors, or inferior; no doctors, no accounts, no meals, and no drinks."[49]

Although the English and the French were ecstatic upon the arrival of fresh American troops, their hopes soon gave way to the Americans' stubborn reluctance to assimilate with their allies, insisting they could fight only as an American army. The only one who correctly read the American character was the kaiser. He believed America would intervene too late because of their individual nature, which would lead to an unwillingness to fight under any other nation's banner and thus give the Americans a late start. Despite this late start, American intervention did provide a psychological boost and tremendous economic resources to English and French troops. American entry disheartened many German troops raised on Karl May's stories of the fictional Apache warrior *Winnetou*—the American Indian soldiers fighting on the front lines may scalp them in their sleep! After the war, Tim McCoy's Arapaho friend Goes In Lodge, when asked what should become of the defeated kaiser, associated the consequences of westward expansion with the Great War. "This is what we should do if we really want to punish that man: send him to an Indian reservation to make him live like us."[50]

America's entry into World War I is often portrayed as the loss of innocence, where the fighting spirit of the American solider drowned in the mud of the trenches in France. Some assert the British and French troops quickly became disheartened when the American troops began their training in Europe and then entered the fight, indicating they were frustrated that the Americans appeared more like Boy Scouts than rough-riding cowboys. Pershing biographer Donald Smythe wrote, "The French . . . called the Americans boy scouts. 'We expected to see two million cowboys throw themselves upon the Boches and we see only a few thousand workers building warehouses,' they said. When an American accidently ran over a Parisian with his automobile, the French jeered that the Americans were killing Frenchmen sooner than they were Germans."[51] In his work examining the American troops who served in British units during the last major German offensive, Mitchell Yokelson noted one British officer who "was typical of those troops who believed the cowboy stereotype" and was surprised the Americans did not resemble the iconic image of a westerner.[52]

German general Erich Ludendorff noted, "The World War did not serve to furnish any proof as to what performance may be expected of the American soldier in mobile warfare as distinguished from trench warfare."[53] The image of an American mobile fighting force on horseback, the image embodied and promulgated by both Buffalo Bill and Theodore Roosevelt, did not come to fruition during the Great War. Instead new technology began to elevate new fighting types, men such as tank commander George Patton and aviators like Eddie Rickenbacker. In a way, Roosevelt and Buffalo Bill's heroic "Rough Riders" were gradually transforming into American "Rough Drivers" and

"Rough Pilots." Although the cowboy myth would continue to shape American ideology and culture through the remainder of the twentieth century, the practicality of the Rough Rider on horseback died in the trenches of France during the Great War.

World War I killed millions of soldiers, including Theodore Roosevelt's son Quentin. Upon the death of his youngest son, Roosevelt noted to his daughter-in-law Belle Roosevelt, Edith's "heart will ache for Quentin until she dies."[54] To Clemenceau, Roosevelt wrote, "It is a very sad thing to see the young die when the old who are doing nothing, as I am doing nothing, are left alive. Therefore it is very bitter to me that I was not allowed to face the danger with my sons."[55] On January 6, 1919, the former Rough Rider Theodore Roosevelt died peacefully in his sleep.

Both Roosevelt and Cody promoted a powerful vision of the American frontier and firmly established it within the European perspective on the United States. This process began with Buffalo Bill's Wild West and was furthered by Theodore Roosevelt blurring the lines between the popular vision of the American West and the realities of United States diplomacy and military might. Roosevelt and Cody's collective effort in showcasing America's fighting ability took hold in both the United States and Europe, informing how Europeans viewed American soldiers and how the United States viewed the war effort.

After Cody's death in 1917, the Buffalo Bill Memorial Association abandoned its plans for a memorial to the great scout and advocated the creation of a military school in Cody, Wyoming, the town named in his honor. An article in the *Northern Wyoming Herald* entitled "Military Academy: Cody's Unfulfilled legacy" outlined the proposal.

> A cavalry academy, in this unique spot, where both the men and horses needed, are of a very high quality; not to mention the climate and topography of the country, which is exceptionally advantageous and conducive to success . . . which had it been consummated, would no doubt now, at this critical time, form a most powerful unit in the American army on the battle-fields of Europe. . . . How fitting then it would be to open a military academy, the chief feature of which would be the training of cavalry in a country where equestrianism has reached the highest pinnacle of perfection. Without doubt, all cowboys throughout the

> western states, who have a desire to serve their country will have the additional incentive of becoming members of this institution. [*sic*] where they will meet those of their own ilk, instead of being scattered, as they are, throughout the numerous regiments of the United States army, losing much of that unique efficiency. [*sic*] their life's training has inculcated in them.
>
> It is easily conceivable, that to launch a cavalry regiment, made up of true western cowboys, into a battle at a critical time, when the contending forces were locked in a deadly struggle for supremacy, all official supervisions temporarily broken down and every man his own initiative, would be such an inspiration to disorganized troops as would lead them on to victory, in fact it takes no great power of vision to realize that the "Buffalo Bills" as they would be called, could become the terror of the enemy, as well as the chief support of the American forces, and possibly the deciding factor in many a pitched battle, in fact it is not inconceivable, that in the event of a deadlock all along the line, a few such regiments might be credited by the future historian, as the deciding factor of the great world war.[56]

Eventually two million Americans soldiers made it overseas. Their overall contribution to the allied victory of World War I is still debated. Although the United States may not have contributed to a smashing victory against Germany, and the Great War was a precursor to the even greater global struggle of World War II, the cowboy-soldier image created by Roosevelt and Cody remained a transnational phenomenon.

Notes

1. Roosevelt, *Cowboys and Kings*, 51–52. Elting Morison also included these letters in his eight-volume edited collection of Theodore Roosevelt's correspondence.
2. Ibid., (emphasis added).
3. Roosevelt's experiences and speeches delivered in Europe are documented in various biographical resources. For the text of his speeches, see Roosevelt, *African and European Addresses.*
4. Gallup, *Buffalo Bill's British Wild West*, 38.
5. Cody, *Wild West in England*, 77. John M. Burke also wrote the same lines in his Cody biography, *Buffalo Bill from Prairie to Palace*, 235.

6. Queen Victoria's Journal, quoted from Gallup, *Buffalo Bill's British Wild West*, 101.
7. Gallup, *Buffalo Bill's British Wild West*, 155.
8. Cunningham, *Your Fathers the Ghosts*, 145.
9. Cody, "Mobilizing a Mimic Army."
10. Sheehan, *Where Have All the Soldiers Gone?* 6–7.
11. Roosevelt, *Cowboys and Kings*, 70.
12. Ibid., 52.
13. Roosevelt to Clarence Don Clark, December 8, 1905, *Letters and Speeches*, 429.
14. Bennet, *Old Deadwood Days*, 54.
15. Kellar, *Seth Bullock Frontier Marshall*, 165.
16. Ibid., 163.
17. Roosevelt to James Ford Rhodes, November 29, 1904, *Letters and Speeches*, 376–77.
18. Roosevelt to Jacob Henry Schiff, December 14, 1905, *Letters and Speeches*, p. 439.
19. Roosevelt, *Cowboys and Kings*, 57–58.
20. Ibid., 83.
21. Ibid., 86.
22. Bülow, *Memoirs of Prince von Bülow*, 337.
23. Roosevelt, *Cowboys and Kings*, 112.
24. Ibid.
25. Ibid.
26. Eubank, *Paul Cambon*, 133.
27. Roosevelt, *Cowboys and Kings*, 115.
28. Roosevelt, *Works of Theodore Roosevelt*, 18:38.
29. Ibid., 18:71.
30. Ibid., 18:71–72.
31. Ibid., 18:72.
32. Ibid., 18:68.
33. Ibid., 18:210.
34. Ibid., 18:216.
35. Ibid., 18:245.
36. Ibid.
37. Cooper, *Under the Big Top*, 47.
38. Roosevelt, *Works of Theodore Roosevelt*, 8:278.
39. Ibid., 8:283.
40. Roosevelt to Jean Jules Jusserand, February 16, 1917, *Letters of Theodore Roosevelt* 8:1152.
41. Scott, *Some Memories of a Soldier*, 562.
42. Bishop, *Theodore Roosevelt and His Time*, 425.
43. Roosevelt to Georges Clemenceau, June 6, 1917, *Letters of Theodore Roosevelt* 8:1201.
44. Moor, *Log of a Twentieth Century Cowboy*, 27.
45. McCoy, *Tim McCoy Remembers the West*, 124.

46. Ibid., 138.
47. Ibid., 138–39.
48. Bishop, *Theodore Roosevelt and His Time*, 429.
49. Lawrence, *Lawrence of Arabia*, 132–33.
50. McCoy, *Tim McCoy Remembers the West*, 139.
51. Smythe, *Pershing*, 69.
52. Yockelson, *Borrowed Soldiers*, 67.
53. Viereck, *As They Saw Us*, 51.
54. Roosevelt to Belle Willard Roosevelt, August 11, 1918, *Letters of Theodore Roosevelt* 8:1360.
55. Roosevelt to Georges Clemenceau, July 28, 1918, Ibid., 8:1355.
56. "Military Academy: Cody's Unfulfilled Legacy," *Northern Wyoming Herald*, 19 December 1917. This newspaper clipping can be found in the William F. "Buffalo Bill" Cody Collection, MS 6, McCracken Research Library, Buffalo Bill Center of the West.

4

"Don't Forget This"

Annie Oakley and the "New Girl" in Anglo-American Culture

MONICA RICO

The April 2, 1887, issue of the *New York Clipper,* whose masthead billed it as "the oldest American Sporting and Theatrical Journal," contained an advertisement that stated in bold capital letters:

DON'T FORGET THIS.
THERE IS ONLY ONE ANNIE OAKLEY, THE LITTLE SURE SHOT,
And She Leaves for Europe with the WILD WEST.

Probably placed by Annie Oakley's husband and manager, the advertisement emphasized two points. For would-be spectators of other female trick riders and sharpshooters, it warned that they were settling for an inferior copy. By calling attention to Oakley's imitators, it emphasized that she was successful enough to *have* imitators while simultaneously dismissing them as ersatz. The advertisement also underscored the link between Oakley's claim to uniqueness and her tour of Europe with Buffalo Bill Cody's Wild West. She was not just another vaudeville shooting act or circus rider. Her very absence from New York evoked her uniqueness. She was in Europe with America's great frontier hero, a quasi-ambassador representing the American West to audiences in the Old World. There was "only one Annie Oakley" *because* she was in Europe with the Wild West.

FIGURE 4.1. Advertisement from the *New York Clipper*, April 2, 1887.
Courtesy of the McCracken Research Library, Buffalo Bill Center of the West.

Oakley made money and became a frequently seen figure in London's high society during the London run of 1887. Oakley made significant amounts of money from performing at private events, which her contract with Cody allowed as long as no admission was charged. On one occasion, she provided part of the day's entertainment at a party given by the Prince of Wales by shooting in a friendly match with the Russian Grand Duke Michael. She won this match, 47–36, gaining "the most amazing and unexpected publicity," as she recalled in a 1917 newspaper interview. Reporters described her act, her costume, and her overall demeanor in glowing terms. She also found herself in demand as an informal shooting instructor for fashionable women. The Wild West was a huge hit in London, and Oakley contributed hugely to that success.[1]

The Wild West had other female riders and sharpshooters at various times in its different incarnations, including a fairly well-known competitor of Oakley's, Lillian Smith, during the 1887 tour of Britain.[2] Yet Smith has been forgotten, whereas Oakley even today is a name that instantly evokes recognition.

Born Phoebe Ann Moses, the woman who called herself Annie Oakley presented herself to reporters as a person of homespun simplicity and candor, but she and her husband created "Annie Oakley" with unremitting attention to every detail of her image. Oakley adroitly combined elements of conventional gender presentation with acts and utterances that offered a new kind of modern femininity to audiences at the turn of the twentieth century. Enclosed within the oval of the Wild West arena and the quasi-domestic backstage of the Wild West camp, she avoided being associated with the sexually suggestive spaces of the London streets and the circus ring. Instead, her image connoted innocence, health, and athleticism. She embodied a gender category just emerging in late Victorian transatlantic culture—the "New Girl."

Being neither helpless children nor sexually mature women, adolescent girls preoccupied increasing numbers of educators, ministers, physicians, and commentators from around the 1880s onward. Unlike the "New Woman" agitating for suffrage, the "New Girl" existed in a world of girls' school hockey teams and comradely camping trips with other young women, never openly challenging male authority yet exhibiting conventionally male-gendered traits such as physical courage, competitiveness, ambition, and independence. Although destined for marriage and motherhood, the girls featured in the new books, periodicals, and educational materials of the 1880s were innocent of interest in boys as anything other than friendly companions for mixed doubles.[3]

Scholars who have analyzed Oakley's public image have emphasized how she conformed to her era's dominant vision of female gender. Even during the most challenging riding stunts, she always rode sidesaddle, and she did needlework in her tent between shows. She publicly disavowed support for women's suffrage, and although she was a self-made woman whose husband's occupation essentially consisted of supporting her career throughout their lives, she never spoke publicly about economic independence or professional opportunities for women. Oakley's Wild West act and persona, however, did present an alternative to the image of the middle-class woman enclosed in her parlor, consumed by family concerns. Nineteenth-century Anglo-American culture linked manhood and firearms in a powerful bond; the skilled marksman symbolized "masculine energy, individual success, and national power." Oakley "earned a livelihood by drawing a gun on her husband, shooting a dime from between his thumbs, the ember off a cigarette between his lips, a playing card in his hand held edgewise toward her, so that the bullet sliced the card in two"—all among her most famous and astonishing tricks.[4]

Oakley biographer Shirl Kasper has noted the way in which she performed "schoolgirl-next-door" youthfulness. Kasper's apparently offhanded use of this phrase lacks an accompanying analysis of Oakley's self-fashioning as a perpetual girl. Oakley presented herself as a lively, pretty, wholesome girl at the very moment when the whole notion of female adolescence was being constructed by teachers, physicians, ministers, novelists, and girls themselves.

It was in her performance of girlishness, and not womanliness, that Oakley presented a cultural model of female gender to the audiences of her day, and her fans loved her for it.

Oakley was born in 1860 in Darke County, Ohio. She was one of seven children, of whom five survived. Always struggling, her family faced destitution after the death of her father in 1866. Oakley learned to shoot as a child, providing meat for the family table and, eventually, a source of income when she started to sell game to local hotel proprietors. She became known locally as a crack shot. When Frank Butler, a vaudeville performer with a shooting act, challenged the town to put up its best shot against him in a match, Oakley was selected. She defeated Butler, and the two began a correspondence that resulted in their marriage a few months later.

Butler was older than Oakley and an experienced stage performer and competition sharpshooter. He too had faced poverty, emigrating from Ireland as a youth and supporting himself from an early age. Their joint project, the creation of "Annie Oakley," bonded them together in a journey toward the security and respectability that they both seem to have craved. Many of Oakley's most amazing stunts involved her husband, as noted above, although she was always unquestionably the star of the act. At the beginning of her career, Oakley performed mostly in the inexpensive theaters of the vaudeville circuit, but she was more suited to larger venues where her speed and athleticism could be better seen. Moreover, Oakley strongly disliked the raffish atmosphere of vaudeville in the early 1880s, where sexual innuendo and jokes about drinking and gambling satisfied a largely working-class male audience.[5] After briefly touring with the Sells Brothers circus, Oakley signed with Cody's Wild West in 1885. Their long partnership would provide Oakley with the ideal setting for her talents.

It is impossible to know what every audience member who saw the Wild West over its long history felt on viewing the show, but we can analyze the text that Oakley's performance offers us. And by further analyzing the context in which that performance occurred, we can also gain some additional understanding of how the local circumstances surrounding each performance of the Wild West may have shaped its reception. Cody's international success was a critical part of his mythic status as an American showman, and Oakley partook of and contributed to that success. To understand how this was so, we need to move out of the Wild West arena and onto the streets of what one popular song satirizing Cody's success called "The Wild Wild West of London."

Cody had anticipated going overseas since early in the 1870s. He and his partner, Nate Salsbury, were aware of the cachet that success abroad conferred on an American entertainment. However, the 1887 London season was more than a mere bid to increase the show's prestige. Publicity materials and the 1888 version of Cody's autobiography, *Story of the Wild West and Campfire Chats,* interpreted the Wild West in England as the culminating moment in civilization's conquest of savagery. Paradoxically, the final act in the *westward* movement of Anglo-Saxons toward the frontier occurred when the frontiersman—Cody—moved east, back across the Atlantic, to link "American and European histories together by redirecting the grand narrative of American expansion" into the heart of the British metropole.[6]

In her autobiography, Oakley described the London season as a magical time when "tons of beautiful flowers poured in upon me. Books, dainty handkerchiefs, pretty lace, ties, gloves, fans and silk for a dress were sent to me." As this list of feminine gifts indicates, a major part of Oakley's success with London audiences was her "modest" demeanor, her "decidedly pretty and winsome face," her "sweet and gentle manners," and "the quiet and ladylike manner with which she" played "the part of hostess" when welcoming visitors to her tent. Her fan mail contained several marriage proposals, attesting to her appeal and also to the ways in which her stage persona avoided recognition of her married state. In Oakley's account, one of these proposals came from a young man whose mother, "a woman of breeding," came to see her and declared, "'I knew that my boy would never love any girl who was not of the highest type.'" Even though Butler assisted during some of Oakley's tricks, the show's announcer did not identify him as Oakley's husband. While occasionally a reporter would note that "in private life" Oakley was "Mrs. Frank Butler," more often she was described in terms such as "a modest little girl."[7]

Oakley thus balanced youthful femininity and stunning skill with a dangerous weapon. This combination of traits resonated with audiences because it contributed to the emerging cultural phenomenon of the "New Girl." The "New Girl" image unfolded within the gradual development of educational opportunities for middle-class girls on both sides of the Atlantic. In the United States, more and more girls were receiving some form of high school education. In Britain, feminist reformers began the first academically serious secondary schools for girls. By the turn of the century, day and boarding schools for middle-class girls, modeled on the institutions their brothers attended, flourished throughout the United Kingdom. In many ways, these schools challenged earlier assumptions about gender.

For instance, the schools emphasized athletics and outdoor recreations along with academics. Tennis, badminton, cycling, swimming, shooting, archery, skating, golf, hiking, field hockey, and gymnastics, as well as more sedate games such as croquet, all formed part of a new ideal of femininity, one of strength, vigor, and health. As the author of *Girls and Their Ways,* an 1881 "book for and about girls," declared, the most advanced parents and teachers no longer tried to keep girls supine on the sofa or laced into tight corsets: "Happily for our Girls, these ultra 'fine-lady' notions are becoming more and more things of the past, and a free, more active life is being advocated, which bids fair to win the day." Girls would develop "health of the mind" as well of the body from "regular and prolonged exercise." In response to anticipated criticism of athletic girls, the author acerbically stated, "I cannot think that our Girls will be less modest or maidenly from being permitted to indulge in healthy and exhilarating exercise, or that they will grow up unfeminine because the free use of their limbs is granted them in girlhood." However, more traditionally minded adults might have been somewhat troubled by this author's assurance that exercise would promote "self-reliance" and a competitive spirit in young women.[8]

"What means this modern craze for mannish sports and mannish ways, which has of late seized upon a certain section of young women in polite society; and what are the reasonable limits that should be set to the pastimes of womankind?" asked the author of "Modern Mannish Maidens" in *Blackwoods Edinburgh Magazine* in 1890. The author emphasized that women were not men and should not try to become them; that too much participation in competitive sports may lead to them becoming overly assertive; and that young women needed to pay particular attention to their clothing when participating in sports, lest they appear immodest or unattractive. Yet this commentator concluded that far from avoiding exercise, girls should go riding, walking, rowing, skating, and cycling. They could pursue tennis, badminton, and golf. Indeed, they could participate in nearly any activity as long as it didn't involve "violent running," a stipulation that allowed quite a lot of movement and would certainly have included shooting.[9]

Even less-privileged girls became the object of concerns about lack of health and exercise, as suggested by the decision of the London school board to appoint a gymnastics teacher. The woman chosen for the position, Martina

Bergman Österberg, eventually founded a teachers' college for physical education instructors and advocated that gymnastics be taught to both sexes as part of a national curriculum. Advocates for the new model of girlhood often envisioned cross-class alliances between working-class young women and those above them on the social ladder. Such sisterly concern could even be constructed as a kind of imperial service, uplifting the British nation as a whole and strengthening its potential points of fracture along class lines.[10]

Novelists writing for adolescent girls often imagined their heroines as actively taking part in adventurous pursuits. Rescuing someone in danger, surviving shipwreck—these protagonists avoided actual violence while still demonstrating courage and hardihood. Particularly in colonized spaces, they contributed to the maintenance of social order and, often, racial hierarchies. Such narratives suggested that quintessentially "British" qualities usually gendered as male, such as daring, determination, and self-discipline, could be exercised by women as well. Adventure stories for girls even depicted them as capable of using firearms when in extreme necessity. The heroine of *In the Toils of the Tribesmen: A Story of the Indian Frontier* (1900), by the top-selling Bessie Marchant, is adept enough with guns to handle being attacked by "tribesmen" on the "Indian frontier" of the British empire. Marchant's heroines also use guns in castaway situations to defend themselves and find food.[11]

Skill with firearms was among the useful traits promoted by the Girl Scout movement. The vision of stalwart and helpful girls strengthened through daily exercise in order to be of use to their country reached its apotheosis in Girl Scouting, both in the United States and Great Britain. The founder of the Boy Scouts, British soldier Robert Baden-Powell, was initially reluctant to expand the Scouting program to girls, but the thousands of girls who formed Scout troops without waiting for approval from his headquarters pushed him into forming a new organization that would be specifically directed at girls and differentiated in key ways from the Boy Scouts. The girls' program, dubbed Girl Guiding, told girls to imagine themselves primarily in supportive roles, and the Guides' handbook provided an example of such support in the guise of a brave girl who alerted the police when a "rowdy man" was in the street.[12] However, such anecdotes coexisted in the handbook with examples of girls acting heroically during sieges in South Africa, shooting dangerous tigers in India, and warding off "Red Indians" in colonial America.[13]

Similarly, in the United States, Scouting manuals assured "girls that they could inherit a male tradition of chivalry and frontier scouting by strengthening their minds and bodies practicing rescue skills, and adhering to the Scout law." As in Britain, the development of girls' health and character through "outdoor activity, self-improvement, and homemaking" occupied many American educators, physicians, parents, ministers, and reformers who hoped to establish a nonsectarian American ideal of healthful adolescence around the turn of the century.[14]

The founder of the Girl Scouts of America, Juliette Gordon Lowe, was a friend of the Baden-Powell siblings. She modeled her organization on the British one, with only slight changes of wording in the Scout law and manuals in the early years. In fact, the first editions of the Girl Guide and Girl Scout handbooks retained much of Robert Baden-Powell's original prose and illustrations from the boys' handbooks, and they thus addressed their girl readers as competent "people of infinite resource" who could handle danger and contribute to the welfare of the nation in multiple ways beyond domestic accomplishments.[15] While sections on cooking, cleaning, and childcare were added to the handbooks, they retained their emphases on camping, orienteering, and first-aid skills, promoted vigorous exercise, and assured girls that they had an important role in their country's future. The Guiding handbook declared that

> to be a Guide . . . means you are one who can be relied upon for pluck, for being able to endure difficulty and danger, for being able cheerfully to take up any job that may be required, and for readiness to sacrifice yourself to others. Girls can be just as good as men in these points if they like. The Guides are the frontier force, and have to do a deal of "roughing it," living far away from towns, and so having to be able to turn their hands to anything.

By linking Guiding to empire, *The Handbook for Girl Guides* recast potentially masculine qualities as furthering a cause that encompassed both boys and girls, namely, the advancement of British rule on the "frontier." Similarly, the American Girl Scouting program exhorted troop members to envision themselves as a kind of service corps: "The Union of Scouts is to be a strong union for the good of our country in the future and an ever-increasing bond for success to ourselves and aid to others." While the books told girls that they would primarily help America by exerting domestic influence on the men in their lives, much as conventional rhetoric about domesticity had been declaring for decades, Scout leaders were also supposed to encourage girls to envision themselves within a long line of patriotic Americans. The books instructed girls to think actively of ways in which they might be of use to the nation in times of war or crisis.[16]

Annie Oakley, both in her arena act and her outstanding performance in shooting matches and exhibitions sponsored by London's sporting elite, exhibited many of the traits of the "New Girl." Athletic and playful, she was also modest and pure. She presented a contrast to the stereotypical woman in the entertainment industry. In both Britain and America, representations of women in show business often rhetorically aligned them with prostitution. Actresses, dancers, singers, and acrobats displayed themselves to anyone who paid. They earned a living instead of staying modestly at home in a male-headed household, and they traveled constantly; their mobility was a threat to middle-class domestic life.

Because of their revealing costumes, dancers and acrobats in particular contended with assumptions about their sexual availability. The fact that such bodies were almost always clad in tights, and hence not technically bare, only called attention to the ways in which concealment and display intertwined to heighten the eroticism of women performers. When Oakley was touring the vaudeville circuit, troupes such as Lydia Thompson and the British Blondes had been selling out houses with their "ample, tights-clad figures" for over ten years.[17] The dangerous nature of circus performers' work heightened the intensity of the spectacles in which they were featured and necessitated physical positions that suggested sexual contact: legs open, crotches lifted, entangled with other bodies. Moreover, their bodies, like those of actresses, were featured in the vibrant world of the Victorian graphic newspaper and the street poster.[18] In the same way, Oakley's face and body were plastered on countless blank surfaces in cities around America and, eventually, Europe. Her likeness appeared over and over again in the Wild West's own publicity printings as well as in newspapers and magazines. She was a spectacle, and in her visibility, potentially disruptive to the ideal of a woman secluded with her home and family.

Oakley demonstrated remarkable inventiveness in fashioning a costume for herself that met her needs as a performer with a physically demanding act while maintaining a feminine and modest appearance. Her costumes, which she designed and made herself, modestly covered her arms, chest, and back with a loose-fitting tunic. She wore a shortened skirt and gaiters underneath so that her legs were covered loosely, rather than in a way that emphasized their shape and suggested nudity.[19]

Modest, yes, and similar to the outfits that girls in physical education classes were just starting to wear, but not boring: Oakley wore a wide-brimmed hat suggestive of those worn by cowboys, with a large star pinned to the brim. Some of her parade costumes featured elaborately stitched designs on her skirt and saddle blanket. In publicity photographs, she often wore one of the many medals awarded her by shooting clubs, though she preferred not to wear these in the arena, probably to avoid the distraction they would pose as she rapidly changed positions to make her shots. In the arena, she wore her long, curling hair loose and hanging down her back, a coiffure that became so identified with her youthful, attractive image that she had to wear a wig in her later performances as her hair began to go white. As Tracy Davis points out, Oakley's "ersatz western costuming had an exoticism of its own," but it categorized her as competent to meet the challenges of frontier life while retaining her femininity.[20]

Oakley's performance of femininity went well beyond her clothing. For instance, Oakley kept her voice as "soft and silvery as the rustling of a summer's breeze among the trees," to quote a rather smitten London journalist who also praised the "quiet, expressive eyes" and "refined English delicacy of speech of this little Diana." Oakley was just under five feet tall, and she developed a repertoire of girlish gestures that emphasized her petite stature: skipping, blowing kisses to the audience, tosses of her head, and a playful little kick as she exited the arena. In the arena, she was "a dutiful daughter with a spunky side," whose movements were "full of life and vigor."[21]

Oakley spoke often to the press about her belief that shooting was compatible with respectable womanhood, and she encouraged women to interest themselves in shooting so that they could accompany their husbands on hunting trips. Audience members responded; one man wrote in 1900 to tell her, "For several years I have been trying to get my wife interested in guns and shooting, but until she witnessed your work with Buffalo Bill last season I had poor luck with it." Oakley argued that learning to shoot conferred "grace" and attention to detail on women, making them even more feminine than before. "You cannot imagine how shooting demands perfect balance," she told a reporter, "and how shooting vanishes carelessness and slovenly ways." The goal was not that "women should sacrifice home and family duties merely for outside pleasure"; rather, through sports like shooting, women would improve their physical and emotional health and thereby be able to create happier, healthier homes.[22]

Oakley's ability to embody gender expectations reinforced her claim to uniqueness, a claim that she had to defend even within the Wild West show. Another young woman, Lillian Smith, joined the company in 1886, and by the 1887 London tour she had star billing equal to Oakley's, as a page from the American Exhibition commemorative book shows. Oakley's picture and Smith's occupy two of the slots in a row of four featured performers' pictures. Like Oakley, Smith had a solo act on the program, and a detailed biography accompanied her photograph in the show's souvenir booklet. Journalists celebrated Smith's life as romantic and colorful, although they also confused her with Oakley on at least one occasion, identifying a "Miss Lilian Oakley" seated backstage in camp.[23]

Smith was, moreover, an excellent shot who worked quickly and accurately with her rifle and had been performing publicly since she was ten. Like Oakley, Smith was presented to the Prince of Wales and Queen Victoria on their respective visits to the Wild West. On the other hand, Oakley had an asset that Smith apparently lacked. Photographs of Smith depict a dark-skinned, dark-haired woman, and later in her career she embraced an Indian identity, using the name "Wenona" and dressing in Indian clothing. Whether Smith was actually Native American or not, she was not as unambiguously white as Oakley. In the context of the Wild West, where narratives of racial superiority underpinned the nightly reenactments of battles, Oakley's ability to portray white womanhood contrasted favorably with Smith's suspect racial origins. This was particularly the case as Smith may have lacked Oakley's self-restraint in language and gesture; some sources suggest that her voice was louder, her diction less refined, and her demeanor less dainty.[24]

In her autobiography, Oakley depicted her command performance before the Prince and Princess of Wales as the climax of her London run. Oakley made a point of breaking royal etiquette by first greeting Princess Alexandra instead of her husband Edward, the Prince of Wales, who should have taken precedence. Both Alexandra and Edward were apparently charmed. Alexandra described her as "a wonderful little girl," and Edward commented, "What a pity there are not more women in the world like that little one!"[25] Daintiness and innocence—these were the qualities that Oakley tried to present to the public during these closely watched encounters with royalty. At the time, the press reported that Oakley didn't know any better, greeting Alexandra first on the "republican principle" of "ladies first."

In her own account of the incident, however, she presented herself as displaying a kind of republican pluckiness in response to the prince's reputation for male sexual misbehavior and lack of respect for domestic ideals. It's impossible to know exactly what Oakley said or what she intended at that moment, but it is telling that years later, she represented it as a small but significant triumph, saying that "all I had heard of women trying to flirt with the prince while the gentle princess held her peace, ran before me. An English born lady would not have dared to have done as I did—they must speak to royalty according to the status of the royal personages. The prince's hand came over the low front of the box as they had all arose. I quickly proffered my hand to the princess."[26]

Annie Oakley's subtle rebuke of a royal libertine textually evokes another signature moment associated with the Wild West's first London run—Queen Victoria's recognition of the American flag at her command performance as described in Cody's autobiographical *The Wild West in England.* Not content with merely being a hit, Cody portrayed the event as a coming-of-age for the American nation, a patriotic triumph of western masculinity and republican greatness that evoked a bow even from the monarch whose reign extended around the globe. "We felt that the hatchet was buried at last," exulted Cody, "and the Wild West had been at the funeral." With the past behind them, Great Britain and the United States could salute one another across the shifting frontier of the Wild West in London.[27]

The two texts parallel each other: Overcome by the national spectacle of American greatness, the queen salutes the frontier hero; while undaunted by ceremony or title, the "little one" puts a prince in his place. Cody's moment locates him in the unfolding of radicalized history, the linking of Britain and the United States as bearers of civilization westward. Oakley's face-to-face encounter with royalty, on the other hand, scales down the meeting of nations into a handshake. As the Girl Scout manual put it, "Girls need not wait for war to show what heroines they can be. . . . Moral courage is one thing that all Scouts keep a stock of."[28]

Active, cheerful, "plucky," and patriotic, the transatlantic gender ideal of the "New Girl" emerged in response to a number of cultural shifts and anxieties: the desire to expand women's education, racial fears related to perceived declines in (white) women's health, an imperialistic preoccupation with the part that women could play to support and extend conquest, and—not insignificantly—the reading and consumption choices of girls themselves, newly marked as a group of people with their own concerns and interests.

I'm not arguing that Oakley deliberately crafted her performance to appeal to girls in particular or that she explicitly claimed to be in her teens, though she did shave about five years off her actual age to make it seem as if she was in her early twenties in 1887 when she was, in fact, nearly thirty. Her performance of gender made sense culturally because it combined the "masculine" traits of athleticism and courage with "feminine" ones, such as long hair, small dainty gestures, and a soft voice. Moreover, it did this in a way that neatly avoided the troubling sexuality of adult women onstage while also expressing a new ideal of girlishness that shaped important cultural developments, such as the promotion of athletics for girls and the Girl Scout–Girl Guide movement.

Notes

1. Oakley, *Autobiography*, 29–31; *Pinehurst* (NC) *Outlook*, February 3, 1917, as quoted in Kasper, *Annie Oakley*, 85. I wish to acknowledge the help of Mary Robinson and the staff at the Buffalo Bill Center of the West McCracken Research Library and the participants in Bozeman State University's 2014 Michael Malone Conference on Buffalo Bill's West in transatlantic context, particularly the convener, Robert Rydell. Thanks are also due to Rex Myers and Susan Richards, who gave me a place to stay in Cody, and to my colleagues Brigid Vance and Regan Bardeen, who read the manuscript. I am deeply grateful to Frank Christianson and Jeremy Johnston for their guidance, support, patience, and comments on multiple versions of this project.
2. Native American women participated in the daily openings of the company's camp to visitors, although they did not work in the arena show.
3. Mitchell, *New Girl*.
4. Warren, *Buffalo Bill's America*, 242–43, 246–47.
5. Warren, *Buffalo Bill's America*, 240–41.
6. Christianson, "Introduction," xii, xv, xxvii–xxviii.
7. Oakley, *Autobiography*, 28, 32; undated clippings in Annie Oakley Scrapbooks, William F. "Buffalo Bill" Cody Collection, MS 6, McCracken Research Library, Buffalo Bill Center of the West; undated clipping from *The Courier of London*, in Annie Oakley Scrapbooks; "Miss Annie Oakley," undated clipping in Annie Oakley Scrapbooks. On the ambiguity regarding Oakley's birthdate, see Riley, *Life and Legacy of Annie Oakley*, 18–19, and Kasper, *Annie Oakley*, 61, 247n2.
8. Anonymous, *Girls and Their Ways*, 37, 46.
9. "Modern Mannish Maidens," 253–58, 260.
10. Smith, *Empire in British Girls' Literature*, 47.
11. Ibid., 96–97, 169–70.

12. Ibid., 135, 153.
13. Baden-Powell, *Handbook for Girl Guides,* 20–21, 23, 285–86, 288–89.
14. Tedesco, "Making a Girl into a Scout," 20–21.
15. Ibid., 27–35.
16. Hoxie, *How Girls Can Help Their Country,* 103–4, 12, 14, 17.
17. Riley, *Life and Legacy of Annie Oakley,* 22; Davis, *Actresses as Working Women,* 69, 138–39, 131–35.
18. Assael, *Circus and Victorian Society,* 115–24.
19. Offstage, Oakley wore fashionable but simple designs in demure colors that perhaps reflected her family's Quaker background. Riley, *Life and Legacy of Annie Oakley,* 112, 87, 114.
20. Davis, "Shotgun Wedlock."
21. "Chit-Chat and the Drama," *The Sportsman,* Wednesday, May 4, 1887, Annie Oakley Scrapbooks; Browder, *Her Best Shot,* 89; Kasper, *Annie Oakley,* 61, 45–47.
22. "Women with Guns," *Sandusky Daily Register,* June 19, 1894; Riley, *Life and Legacy of Annie Oakley,* 54, 140; Oakley, *Autobiography,* 49.
23. Cody, *Wild West in England,* 174 (illustration 54); Browder, *Her Best Shot,* 90–91; *The Topical Times,* May 2, 1887, Annie Oakley Scrapbooks.
24. Browder, *Her Best Shot,* 91–93.
25. Riley, *Life and Legacy of Annie Oakley,* 40–41; Oakley, *Autobiography,* 29; Kasper, *Annie Oakley,* 72–73.
26. Oakley, *Autobiography,* 30.
27. Cody, *Wild West in England,* 77. See also Christianson's comments in his introduction, xxxi–xxxiii.
28. Hoxie, *How Girls Can Help Their Country,* 12, 109.

5

Annie Oakley and the Rise of Natural Womanhood in England

JENNIFER R. HENNEMAN

The 1887 American Exhibition in London showcased the technological and cultural products of a growing American capitalist empire that, according to the exhibition catalogue, had been constructed largely according to the example of Great Britain. Organizers strove to highlight the similarities between British and American imperialism, both of which relied on the conviction that their people were specially chosen and were the most evolutionarily capable of conquering and ruling.[1] Buffalo Bill's Wild West, undoubtedly the most popular component of the American Exhibition, reinforced the imperial purposes of military aggression and justified the extraction of natural resources and the control of foreign lands. Products from such expansion could be toured at leisure in the exhibition's Machine Hall, cultivated North American gardens, fine arts galleries, and the Hall of American (taxidermic) Trophies. The 1887 American Exhibition took place the same year as the Golden Jubilee of Victoria, Queen of Great Britain and Ireland and Empress of India, and these events punctuated a decade of increased imperial fervor. For Britons, Buffalo Bill's Wild West presented performances of successful American westward expansion that reaffirmed an Anglo-Saxon racial preeminence increasingly called into question by colonial mutinies and widespread anxieties regarding a decadent industrialized culture.[2] It is therefore not surprising that British viewers "saw reflections of themselves"[3] in the American Exhibition and, in particular, in the Wild West spectacle, which reasserted a shared belief in Anglo-Saxon superiority and in the imperial purposes of military force. This reflection was not simply serendipitous, but rather strategically emphasized by its organizers. The imperialism on display within the American Exhibition—evident in the different "stages" of progression from Wild West spectacle to the Machine Hall and fine art galleries—presented America and Britain as "cousins" with comparable racial and cultural affinities.[4] Organizers were careful, however, to position Britain as the "mother" country and wise Old World parent to the New World power. The catalogue emphasized that the exhibition was not an aggressive display of market competition but rather a representation of the commercial foundations on which both countries could unite as cousins in a global economic empire. "The achievements in the arts, sciences, manufactures and industrial pursuits . . . exemplified in this American Exhibition," wrote the authors, did honor to the "mother country" England,[5] and exhibition president Henry S. Russell intoned that the event would "prove another strong link in that chain, sometimes strained but never to be broken, which binds the United States to Old England, the child to its mother."[6]

Beneath this display of progress, however, ran an undercurrent of ambivalence regarding the meaning and effects of industrial expansion. By the end of the nineteenth century, America and Britain had experienced crises of conscience regarding their nonurban spaces. In the United States, the closing of the frontier corresponded with a push to preserve "pristine" wild lands—and especially those considered most crucial to American identity as places of geographical wonder and diversity[7]—via various conservation movements and the creation of national parks. In Britain, a noticeable rural decline caused in large part by mass migration to the cities "prompted a sudden rush of nostalgia for rural life."[8] Nature's cultural cachet rose in direct correlation to its perceived demise at the hands of an urban, industrialized modernity. In this context, railroads came to symbolize one of the most lauded *and* distrusted industrial technologies of the time. The completion of the first transcontinental railroad in the United States in 1869 created a powerful network of trade but also, ultimately, signaled the end of the frontier. In Britain, while the railroad supposedly allowed increased tourist access to the country's most inspirational wild spaces, some critics worried that promoting such railway tourism was actually a cover for easier exploitation of natural resources. For example, in an 1876 *Punch* illustration entitled "Lady of the Lake Loquitur," the influential art critic, educator, and author John Ruskin—his recognizable head atop a paint-tube body—protects the Lady of the Lake, a personification of nature who speaks in an accompanying poem on behalf of Britain's remote insular landscapes.[9] With paint palette and palette knife wielded, Ruskin defends nature from the snake-like train twisting along the left side of the composition, which alludes to the serpent Satan in the biblical garden of Eden as well as to the contemporary rape of virginal lands by corrupt capitalists.

While a conflation of nature and woman, such as that in the *Punch* cartoon, was hardly a new representational trope, the combination of female—and particularly adolescent female—bodies within a metaphorically virginal nature provided a powerful, if largely imagined, antidote for combatting the ills of modernity. The effects of mechanization, mass production, and materialism were considered primary culprits for the fatigue, anxiety, and other nervous ailments—grouped under the label "neurasthenia"—that negatively impacted the health of British and American men and women.[10] As one way of grappling with this "overcivilized" modern existence, T. J. Jackson Lears has argued that Americans turned to "antimodern" cultures for the benefit of their "more intense forms of physical or spiritual experience,"[11] and Kimberly Wahl has extended this argument to consider the trajectory of aesthetic dress in Britain, which was originally predicated on a return to the simpler and supposedly healthier modes of classicism, orientalism, and medievalism. She writes that "at the heart of this historically based idealism was the assumption that cultures of the past—and by association rural cultures whose inhabitants are perceived as leading lives similar to those of the past—had a more direct relationship with themselves and others."[12] By the 1880s, however, aestheticism had assumed connotations of decadence and lax morals,[13] and the presence of "unnatural" New Women agitating for female emancipation and suffrage resulted in a call by some conservative critics to return women's bodies not only to a maternal and domestic sphere but also to a more natural nonurban environment.

In retrospect, sharpshooting and trick-riding Wild West performers such as headliner Annie Oakley appear to represent new models of femininity and female labor that could have potentially aggravated already contentious debates about women's work and behavior in the late nineteenth century. And yet, the narrative arc of Oakley's performances—including "live" shows,

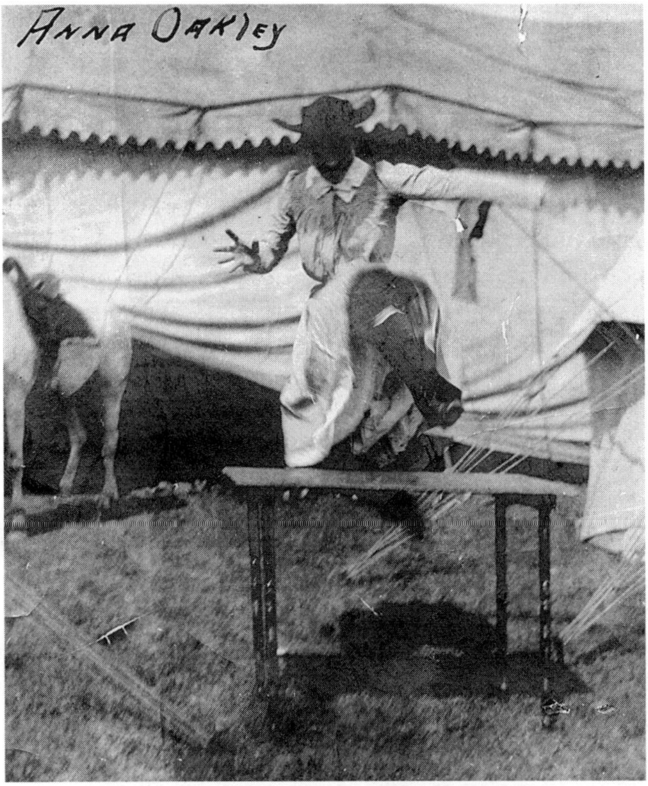

FIGURE 5.1. Annie Oakley jumps table in front of Wild West show tent. Photograph, c. 1890.
Courtesy of the McCracken Research Library, Buffalo Bill Center of the West

interviews, and printed portraits—presented a wholesome "western girl" turned modest housewife that confirmed expectations of the merits of a vigorous girlhood spent in sublime nature. Raising a girl closer to Mother Nature and without the distractions of city life, so the idea went, would render her a healthier, purer vessel. A comparison between Oakley's British reception and the writing of British social critic Eliza Lynn Linton reveals that Oakley's performances—under an entertaining guise of sensational western Americana and supposedly the result of her vigorous upbringing in the sublime landscapes of the American West—reinforced very conservative ideas regarding the appropriate maturation of Anglo-Saxon women.

Although twenty-six years old when she arrived in England in 1887, Oakley consistently reported a younger birthdate that reduced her age to twenty.[14] She performed as a highly skilled though humorously charming "Girl Shot." Reviewers noted her dexterity with a rifle, "which few only of the male sex can equal,"[15] and the "pluck and skill" of her excellent shooting, which was tempered by her "becoming modesty."[16] While in the ring, she would bow to the audience and blow them kisses, make a jaunty kick when entering and when successfully hitting a mark, pout at the audience when she did not, and then kick again when exiting. She performed cartwheels—guaranteed to show a bit of petticoat—and remarkably fast sprints. A surprisingly spontaneous photograph depicts Oakley leaping over a folding table outside the main arena. This image demonstrates not only her athletic ability but also the extent to which her skirts flew when undertaking some of her stunts. The performances of this "prepossessing young lady"[17] were precise as well as playful. Oakley's warm embrace by the British public, especially during a time when the appearance of women's bodies functioned as an important barometer for asserting racial preeminence, reveals the extent to which exhibition organizers convinced visitors of the close relationship between America and Britain, thereby allowing British viewers to claim Oakley as one of their own.

Portraits often emphasized her youth. An engraved portrait from a London newspaper clipping shows gloved hands and booted feet that have been daintily reduced by the artist. Oakley wears garters, a pleated skirt (the length of which would have been appropriate for a young teenage girl), and an uncorseted collared blouse. Under her signature wide-brimmed hat and flowing hair—also appropriate for a girl who had not yet reached the age of "coming out" to society[18]—her features have been modified: almond eyes enlarged, mouth reduced, and face rendered a pleasingly full oval.

Contemporary descriptions of Oakley as a girl or little lady reveal the extent to which the youthful ruse convinced viewers, who were already predisposed to support her entertaining role as a young western heroine because of their exposure to sensational dime-novel fiction. Portraits that circulated in London reveal Oakley's visual connections to a dime novel legacy and attest to the international influence of western Americana. For example, Oakley's long hair, wide-brimmed hat, collared shirt, short skirt, and gaiters are comparable to those worn by the western dime-novel heroine Calamity Jane from the widely popular Beadle & Adam's *Deadwood Dick* franchise.[19]

FIGURE 5.2. Engraved portrait from clipping in the Annie Oakley Scrapbook, 1887.
Courtesy of the William F. "Buffalo Bill" Cody Collection, MS 6, McCracken Research Library, Buffalo Bill Center of the West.

The bust-length portrait on the 1878 cover illustration of *Deadwood Dick on Deck; or, Calamity Jane, the Heroine of Whoop-Up* features Calamity's flowing hair, idealized feminine features,[20] long sculptural neck, and "breast of alabaster purity,"[21] all of which are shown to advantage owing to the turn of her head to three-quarter profile against her frontally posed body and open-collared shirt. The rifle slung across her back directs the viewer's eye from her left shoulder and down across her ample bosom and tight bolero jacket to the pistol at her nipped-in waist. A feather adds a musketeer-like touch to her wide-brimmed hat, tilted atop her bangs in order to frame her face in the halo of the American West. The full-length portrait on the cover of *Deadwood Dick in Leadville; or, A Strange Stroke for Liberty* shows Calamity wearing a dashing buckskin skirt-and-legging combination. Her widespread legs and thrown-back shoulders emphasize her small belted waist and vigorous action. Her pose cleverly combines the desired female hourglass silhouette with a scandalous reveal of leg under the guise of "practical" yet fashionable western attire.[22] When one commentator noted that Oakley's attire reminded him "very forcibly of the wild West,"[23] he was not referring to women's actual attire on the American frontier, but rather to the dime-novel attire of "Girl Pard" characters such as Calamity Jane.[24]

While Oakley's portraits underscored her youthful appearance and western heroine's attire, they also captured the gravity of existence on the western frontier. As stated in the 1887 American Exhibition catalogue, the "daughters of pioneers and frontiersmen" performing with the Wild West had "become accomplished rifle shots, and bold and daring horsewomen" owing to the "circumstances and stern necessities of their early life."[25] The full-length portrait used to illustrate the cover of Oakley's biography *Rifle Queen, Annie Oakley*, published in London and sold during the 1887 season, depicts her standing at attention in performance attire with a rifle. She again wears a shortened skirt, this one with embroidered panels and fringe, a loose long-sleeved blouse buttoned to the neck, gloves, a wide-brimmed hat, and gaiters buttoned over boots. Long wavy hair cascades down the front of her shoulders, while curled bangs and a wide hat brim frame her calm gaze toward a distant target. Static posed portraits such as this stem from photographic limitations and commercial studio traditions adopted from formal portraiture.[26] Portraits such as this present a serious "little lady" with correct posture and attractive, regular features: a female model of white dominance on the frontier. The combination of her legible appearance, accounts of her correct behavior, and her stunning demonstrations of physical prowess and mental focus reinforced expectations of American and British imperialism. In their mission to help bring civilization to aboriginal lands, white women would not be corrupted into something "other," but rather would maintain strength of purpose and purity of race while developing necessary skills for self-defense and self-sufficiency.

The positive reception of Oakley's persona tapped into discussions on both sides of the Atlantic regarding the maturation of female bodies. After the crisis of the Civil War, "Americans witnessed the benefits of creating physically strong, intellectually capable and emotionally resilient young women."[27] This corresponded to the increased popularity of tomboy literature and to a more vigorous model of female development that advocated "intelligence, physical fitness and health, self-sufficiency, economic self-reliance, and careful marriage."[28] However, while the boisterous activities of tomboys in American cities too often overstepped thresholds of propriety,[29] vigorous female adolescents safely distanced into the supposedly "pristine" natural environments of the West maintained steady currency as a romanticized symbol of racial health and unlimited possibility on the American frontier.

During the second half of the nineteenth century in Britain, some critics fretted about an insidious cultural corrosion resulting from an overcivilized

Beadle's Half Dime Library

Vol. III. Single Number. BEADLE AND ADAMS, PUBLISHERS, No. 98 WILLIAM STREET, NEW YORK. Price, 5 Cents. No. 73.

Deadwood Dick on Deck; or, CALAMITY JANE, THE HEROINE OF WHOOP-UP. A STORY OF DAKOTA.

CHAPTER I.

CALAMITY JANE.

FIGURE 5.3. Cover of Edward L. Wheeler, *Deadwood Dick on Deck; or, Calamity Jane, the Heroine of Whoop-Up*, December 17, 1878.
Courtesy of the Johannsen Collection, Rare Books and Special Collections, Northern Illinois University Libraries.

decadence that was discernible in the behavior and appearance of its urban women. In her most famous essay, social critic Eliza Lynn Linton[30] targeted "The Girl of the Period," the overly decorated, self-centered, thoughtless young urban women of the late 1860s.[31] These English girls, no longer "content to be what God and nature had made them,"[32] instead spent their time in frivolous and vain pursuits. Their inherently female "fine edges of feeling" had been so blunted in their desire for the fashions of the demimonde that they could

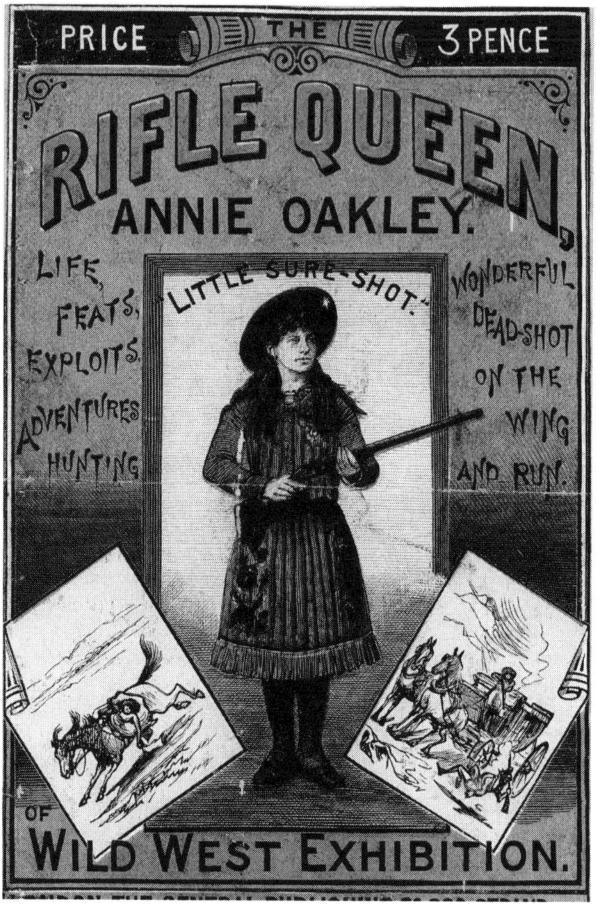

FIGURE 5.4. Cover of *Rifle Queen, Annie Oakley*, 1887.
Courtesy of the McCracken Research Library, Buffalo Bill Center of the West.

not be made to see "that modesty of appearance and virtue in deed ought to be inseparable; and that no good girl can afford to appear bad, under pain of receiving the contempt awarded to the bad."[33] Linton presented the materialistic desires of narcissistic young women as a pervasive evil threatening women's imperatives to become healthy and morally upright wives and mothers. How could England maintain its proud race, she wondered, if girls did not care to learn from their mothers but rather sought to imitate the morally degraded fancies of fashionable, and often "loose," women?

Linton focused in particular on the urban environment as one of dangerous temptation, a position reinforced starkly in her essay "Nymphs."[34] In describing the rural female adolescent type of the title—"an out-of-door, breezy, healthy girl" who frolics "among the mountains, in the secluded midland villages, or out on the thinly-populated moorland tracts"[35]—she states that the nymph cannot exist in the city but, by definition, must remain a rural type. "In the town she degenerates into fastness, according to the law which makes evil merely the misdirection of force, as dirt is only matter in the wrong place."[36] This underscores Linton's fundamental argument: in the city, a girl's energy is too often "misdirected" to frivolous concerns, whereas in the country the nymph "directs" her energies to communing with and learning from Mother Nature. Linton insists that if the nymph be allowed to mature "in the fresh pure air of her native place, she retains her youth and strength long after the age when ordinary women lose theirs, and her children are celebrated as magnificent specimens of the future generation."[37]

The backdrops for Linton's nymph—England's mountains, moors, and ruins—situate this idealized figure within a British landscape tradition that had matured alongside the visible effects of industrialization evident since the late eighteenth century.[38] These natural environments distance her subject as far as possible from the unhealthy temptations of urban modernity.[39] Like Ruskin, she decries modernity's insidious reach via transportation technology: "railroads and the penny-post, cheap trains, fashion and fine-ladyism have penetrated even into the heart of the wild mountains, and now the nymph there is only a transitional development—not, as formerly, a fixed type."[40] She directly correlates the corruption of nature with the degeneration of women's bodies and, by extension, of the British race and its culture. This vision of healthy rural women devoid of materialist and sexual desires amid a romanticized British pastoral landscape provided one powerful, if largely imagined, antidote to the perceived ills of modernity.

Twenty years after the original publication of Linton's "Girl of the Period," Oakley arrived in London and assured audiences that a vigorous rural upbringing did not compromise a girl's ability to grow into a tamable woman. While Oakley's arena performances established her fame as an accomplished sharpshooter and athlete, her performances outside of the ring were equally crucial to the construction of her persona. These included her widely reproduced portraits, which fit her into the appropriately clad and determined figure of the western heroine, and the interviews she granted to reporters and visitors during the exhibition's public hours from 10:30 A.M. to 10:30 P.M., daily. Reporters often noted her pretty features, charming banter, and soft voice. The *London Evening News* described the "decidedly pretty and winsome face . . . sweet and gentle manners, and . . . soft, girlish voice" of the young Amazon, and a rather poetic interviewer from *The Sportsman* noted her "expressive eyes" and "voice as soft and silvery as the rustle of a summer's breeze amongst the trees."[41] Descriptions such as these anticipated concerns that this western tomboy would develop into a brashly shrill woman, a criticism often leveled against American female tourists in London and increasingly applied to suffragists and outspoken New Women.[42] For added charm, reporters sometimes recorded a grammatically incorrect frontier dialect that underscored the sharpshooter's (assumed) western origins and tied her to a popular western type. For example, one journalist recorded Oakley saying "I reckon" and playfully responding to some friendly banter by saying, "Well, I'm real sorry if I've hurt your feelings."[43] Such language (whether real or invented) linked Oakley to the often humorous and colloquial language of western dime-novel heroines. However, to balance any perceived lack of femininity due to such language, reviewers also highlighted how "the refined English delicacy of speech of this little Diana" contrasted with "the hoarse gutterals of the ochre-smeared Redskins who are her neighbours."[44]

In her discussion of the nymph, Linton (not coincidentally an acerbic critic of the vocal feminists often called the "shrieking sisterhood") also invoked descriptions of voice to emphasize the girl's innocence and close relationship with nature. The nymph, she wrote, "can imitate the sounds of animals for the most part with wonderful accuracy; though she can also sing simple ballads without music, with sweetness and correctness."[45] Further, Linton emphasized the girl's inherent physical and psychological proximity to nature: "that wonderful grace of unconsciousness which belongs to savages and animals belongs to [the nymph] also, and she moves with a supple freedom which affection or shyness would equally destroy."[46] In addition to noting Oakley's vocal tone and expression, commentators reveled in the grace and ease of her athletic abilities,[47] demonstrations of which mirrored the sprinting, jumping, and riding of Linton's nymph, who enjoyed "a sharp run down a steep hill, with the chance of a tumble midway . . . clambering over gates, stiles, and even crabbed stone-walls"—even if at risk of an "undignified display of ankle"—"leaping a ditch" during a marshland walk, and riding a half-broken or bareback horse.[48]

In order for the nymph to mature into a healthy mother with an Englishwoman's "distinctive natural character,"[49] she could not be transplanted outside her natural environment. If she were, her vigorous health would give way, and in a few years she would become "nervous, emaciated, consumptive, and with a pitiful yearning for 'home' more pathetic than all the rest."[50] According to medical discourse of the time, these neurasthenic symptoms could be alleviated by various rest cures and even electrotherapy, but those who could afford it left the city to convalesce in quieter, remoter environs. These included the American West, as British traveler Isabella Bird noted during her travels through Colorado.[51] Oakley's strength, charm, and pretty features represented the healthy antidote of the American West and seemed to prove Linton's point that a nymph-turned-woman, if kept away from permanent residence in a city, would preserve the appearance of girlhood "both in looks and bearing, both in mental innocence and physical power."[52]

Although she was not often directly asked about Frank Butler, who was her husband and manager, Oakley did not purposefully disguise her wifely status. She said to one interviewer that "of course all my acquaintances know that I am Mrs. Butler in private life, although always Annie Oakley on the bills."[53] Further, she maintained a "neat and cheery" tent on Arapeah Avenue within the Wild West encampment and was admired for "the quiet and lady-like manner in which she acts the part of hostess" and "accomplished house wife."[54] She was often observed "busily engaged arranging a heap of cut flowers, and sorting them into various combinations of light and shade"[55] and serving her guests tea or juice. Witnessing Oakley sitting "composedly at the entrance of her canvas dwelling-house," one London reporter mused that she was probably thinking "of her Western home and the folks she left behind her to cross the billowy Atlantic for the purpose of giving us exhibitions of her prowess with the rifle."[56] Within the heart of London's seething metropolis, this reporter envisioned Oakley as Linton's homesick nymph, and indeed, Oakley herself admitted, "I guess I could never settle down to city life and feel comfortable or happy."[57]

Oakley's modesty, in particular, was considered an extraordinary attribute, and one reporter proclaimed that "this champion shot is as amiable as she is clever, and I don't think I can pay her a higher compliment than that. Her shooting record is quite phenomenal, and her countrymen are justly proud of her; but all their petting and enthusiasm *have failed to spoil her.*"[58] Any other woman, it is implied, would have been easily corrupted by the amount of international praise Oakley enjoyed. However, her "pluck and skill"[59] and admirable shooting, which she executed "with both eyes open, quickly and decisively,"[60] was appropriately tempered by a reluctance to focus attention on herself. She was, one commentator wrote, "the very embodiment of unassuming geniality," with "a strong vein of quiet, refined humour, and . . . a rare diffidence in one who is such a public favourite."[61] While Oakley's sharpshooting prowess created the foundation of her fame, it was her lack of vanity, apparently so prevalent in young British women of the day, that rendered her most extraordinary.

Organizers of the American Exhibition strove to demonstrate that the reasons and means for Anglo-Saxon westward expansion in America were not dissimilar from those of Britain's global expansion—that, indeed, these Atlantic "cousins" were united in a shared capitalist empire that depended on the subjugation of indigenous peoples in order to profit from the raw materials of their lands. In this context, and situated within a legacy of internationally disseminated western Americana, British audiences could interpret Oakley as a familiar, and even familial, figure developed from a "Girl Pard" type whose activities and behavior reflected the needs of the American frontier and its imperial expansion. [62] Oakley's warm British reception correlated with conservative ideas that returning women's bodies to pastoral environs would result in healthier and less narcissistic women. Just as the American Exhibition presented a country undergoing a maturation process of settling and civilizing, the narrative arc of Oakley's performances—both within and outside of the ring—reinforced a popular idea that a tomboy upbringing in "natural" spaces would not compromise an expected trajectory into tamed wives and mothers.[63]

Notes

1. In his discussion of British imperialism and literature, Patrick Brantlinger writes that, as an ideology, imperialism "bundles together different elements that more or less cohere, though these elements may also appear separately or in varying combinations, and with varying degrees of intensity." The main elements he identifies are "advocacy of territorial expansion by military force . . . a chauvinism based on loyalty to the existing Empire," and "advocacy of the use of military force to settle issues of foreign policy." Imperial ideology is predicated on a belief in "the racial superiority of white Europeans" and "a responsibility to import the light of civilization." Brantlinger points out that various political attitudes adopted the components of this "adaptable, shifting" ideology. A conviction of Anglo-Saxon racial superiority and a justification of military force to seize

indigenous lands served as underlying tenets of American westward expansion, just as they did for British imperialism. See Brantlinger, *Rule of Darkness*, 7–8.

2. The 1880s heralded what scholars have called New Imperialism and its increased jingoism. In Britain, this was in part a response to earlier colonial mutinies—particularly the Indian Mutiny of 1857 and the Jamaica Rebellion of 1865—that shook British confidence in its ability to rule abroad. Sarah Bilston writes that "white nations . . . had to find new ways of justifying their inalienable right to rule." In this context, the American Exhibition and Buffalo Bill's Wild West demonstrated the continued relevance of an aggressive imperial model. Bilston, *Awkward Age*, 5. See Brantlinger, *Rule of Darkness*, and Warren, *Buffalo Bill's America*, 282–339.
3. Reddin points out that William Gladstone, who was Britain's prime minister multiple times in the nineteenth century, stated after his visit to the American Exhibition that "God Almighty made Englishmen and Americans kinsmen, and they ought to have affections for one another." Further, according to Reddin, on April 16, 1887, the *London Illustrated News* wrote of the language, literature, social sympathies, ancestral traditions, history, manners, institutions, laws, and morals shared by Americans and Britons alike. Reddin, *Wild West Shows*, 91–94.
4. See Rydell, "London's American Exhibition of 1887," 67.
5. *American Exhibition, London, 1887*, 5.
6. Henry S. Russell, opening remarks from an undated, untitled document, microfilm roll 4564, Sartain Family Papers, Archives of American Art, Smithsonian Institution.
7. Warren writes that, in part to alleviate an inferiority complex regarding the sense that they were imitators of European culture, Americans pointed "to the uniqueness of their natural assets, particularly in the West, where natural wonders balanced Europe's cultural treasures." See Warren, *Buffalo Bill's America*, 293.
8. Marsh, *Back to the Land*, 4.
9. Translated, the title means "the Lady of the Lake *speaks*." This illustration is discussed in Marsh, *Back to the Land*, and can be viewed online at http://www.victorianweb.org/periodicals/punch/14.html.
10. *Neurasthenia* referred to the symptoms manifested by the physiological and emotional effects of modernity's influence on the nerves, some of which included fatigue, anxiety, heart palpitations, high blood pressure, reliance on stimulants and narcotics, and depression. American neurologist George M. Beard popularized the term *neurasthenia* in 1869 and published regularly on the topic through the rest of the nineteenth century. His works—such as *Neurasthenia (nerve exhaustion): With remarks on treatment* (1879) and *American Nervousness, Its Causes and Consequences* (1881)—were widely read on both sides of the Atlantic. Warren considers the relationship between neurasthenia, late nineteenth-century masculinity, and the Wild West in his *Buffalo Bill's America*, and in particular pp. 212–42. See also Wahl, *Dressed as in a Painting*.
11. Lears, *No Place of Grace*, xiii.
12. Wahl, *Dressed as in a Painting*, 30.

13. Wahl traces the changing perception of aesthetic attire from the 1860s, when it was considered a healthier and more beautiful mode of dressing than the overdecorated and tight-laced styles popular at the time, into the 1880s, when aesthetic clothing "was increasingly viewed as indicative of spiritual and physical illness as well as questionable morals." Wahl, *Dressed as in a Painting,* 145.
14. Born Phoebe Ann Mosey in Ohio on August 13, 1860, Oakley regularly cited a birthdate of August 13, 1866. She was able to maintain the ruse of younger age thanks to her pretty features and small stature: "Only 110 pounds!" was regularly crowed by astonished reporters, and the official Wild West program ended her biography by noting that "what makes Miss Oakley's feats more surprising is the fact that she is small in stature and weighs only 110 pounds." From the 1887 Annie Oakley Scrapbook, William F. "Buffalo Bill" Cody Collection, MS 6, McCracken Research Library, Buffalo Bill Center of the West, see for example various untitled and undated news clippings as well as "'Little Sure Shot.' An Interview with Miss Annie Oakley," which originally appeared as a dramatic review in *The Evening News,* Friday, June 10, 1887. See also Cody and Salsbury, *Buffalo Bill's Wild West,* 47.
15. "Miss Annie Oakley. (Little Sure Shot)," *The Rifle* (Boston), roll 1, Annie Oakley Scrapbooks.
16. Ibid.
17. Our Roving Correspondent, "The American Exhibition and the Wild West," Annie Oakley Scrapbooks.
18. Skirt length (short to long), hair style (down to up), and the wearing of corsets marked levels of maturity in girls from roughly the age of ten until their coming out between the ages of sixteen to eighteen.
19. Written by Edward L. Wheeler, *The Deadwood Dick Half-Dime Library* series encompassed thirty-three stories, the first of which began on October 15, 1877, and the last of which ended on October 20, 1885, with the hero's demise. Between 1885 and 1897, Beadle & Adams released ninety-seven stories in the *Deadwood Dick, Jr.* series, which was supposedly written by Wheeler. Johannsen argues that Wheeler died in 1885, and that ghostwriters maintained the adventures of Deadwood Dick, Jr. See Johannsen, *House of Beadle.* While Wheeler was most likely inspired to create this female character from news reports and travel accounts of the real Calamity Jane—Martha Canary living in Deadwood, South Dakota—Oakley's physical features much more closely resembled the dime-novel heroine than did that heroine's namesake. See McLaird, *Calamity Jane.*
20. These ideals were based largely on physiognomic and phrenological types, popular throughout the nineteenth century, which hypothesized that internal qualities of character manifested themselves directly through the shape, arrangement, and size of facial features and the skull. Of utmost importance were the supposed visual correlations between the features of animals and those of a particular human: the closer one looked to an animal, the more it was thought that person shared the animal's assumed behavioral characteristics. In the late nineteenth century, this

became a direct way of elevating idealized white human features—supposed to represent the upper echelon of an evolutionary hierarchy—above those of people of color. White ideals of beauty often referenced physical qualities associated with classical sculpture, thereby reinforcing assumed cultural and aesthetic superiority.

21. From the same dime novel (number 73), quoted in McLaird, *Calamity Jane,* 96.
22. The visual indicators of sexual attractiveness—namely, a small waist, dainty feet, idealized facial features, and abundant hair—come as no surprise considering that the Half-Dime Library, in particular, was marketed to boys.
23. Riley, *Life and Legacy of Annie Oakley,* 57.
24. "Girl Pard" refers to a heroine type utilized by dime-novel authors, including Wheeler. Often coarse in speech and behavior, these Girl Pards (short for "partner") nonetheless retained highly feminine, and often eroticized, physical features. Their roles were almost exclusively to aid and abet the mission of the male protagonist, to provide levity, and on occasion to provide romantic interest for the sake of the plot line, as was the case with Deadwood Dick and Calamity Jane. See Burr, "American Cowgirl" and Armitage, "Rawhide Heroines."
25. *American Exhibition, London, 1887,* 19.
26. The earliest photographs of Oakley are studio shots. Many of these would have been sold at performances of Buffalo Bill's Wild West and used as references for engraved portraits. It was not until the 1880s and 1890s that smaller cameras, improved photographic chemistry, and gelatin film allowed for more spontaneous photographs.
27. Abate, *Tomboys,* 25.
28. Cogan, *All-American Girl,* 4. For a consideration of tomboy literature, see Abate, *Tomboys,* who writes on page xv that the widespread popularity of Josephine "Jo" March in Louisa May Alcott's *Little Women,* published in two volumes in 1868 and 1869, signaled the beginning of the tomboy literature heyday in the late 1860s that lasted until the Great Depression.
29. In the first chapter of her dissertation, Gretchen R. Sinnett discusses urban adolescent mischief makers as subjects of the *National Police Gazette,* a weekly tabloid known as the "Barber Shop Bible" because of its large male readership. See Sinnett, "Envisioning Female Adolescence," 15–80.
30. Linton began her tenure with the prestigious conservative journal *Saturday Review* in 1866. This journal's essays were often so scathing in their criticism that the authors, Linton included, were referred to as "Saturday Revilers." See Anderson, *Woman against Women,* 119–25.
31. "The Girl of the Period" first appeared in Britain on March 14, 1868. While the phrase had been used prior to 1868, Linton established its currency through the rest of the century as a particularly negative identifier. The essay was published in the United States in an 1868 collection called *Modern Women and What Is Said of Them.* In 1883, seventy-four of Linton's best-known essays were collected into *The Girl of the Period and Other Social Essays* and republished in London. See Anderson, *Woman against Women.*

32. Linton, *Girl of the Period,* 2.
33. Ibid., 4.
34. "Nymphs" was republished in the 1883 collection *Girl of the Period and Other Social Essays,* but to date I have not found reference to its original date of release. Most likely it was written for the *Saturday Review* and published in the late 1860s or 1870s. See Anderson, *Woman against Women,* 119–25.
35. Linton, *Girl of the Period,* 138. Linton states that her nymph cannot be called a tomboy, since for "stricter women" the word has associations of misbehavior that cannot be associated with the innocent nymph. See Linton, *Girl of the Period,* 140. However, the similarities between her description of the nymph and a romanticized notion of American tomboyhood are quite clear. The nymph exists only in the short window "between the time of the raw school-girl and that of the finished young lady . . . when the physical enjoyment of life is perhaps at its keenest, and a girl is not afraid to use her limbs as nature meant her to use them, nor ashamed to take pleasure in her youth and strength" (ibid., 137). The age she specifies—between "raw" school girl and finished lady—would be between ten or twelve years and sixteen or eighteen years of age.
36. Ibid., 137–38.
37. Ibid., 145.
38. According to Tim Barringer, landscape painting registered "the momentous historical developments of the era—sometimes through direct transcription, sometimes by offering a commentary or an alternative vision." It also reflected the tension between the opulence and anxiety of an expanding industrial nation. Barringer, *Opulence and Anxiety,* 9.
39. Evoking such "authentically" British landscapes situates the figure in what Lynda Nead has called "the heart of the imagined indigenous community, of British civilization that is whiter than white and purer than pure." See Nead, "The Secret of England's Greatness." 173.
40. Linton, *Girl of the Period,* 144.
41. "Chit-Chat and the Drama," *The Sportsman,* Wednesday, May 4, 1887, Annie Oakley Scrapbooks.
42. For example, see Tickner's *Spectacle of Women* for a thorough discussion of representations of suffragists, both negative and positive.
43. "Camp Sketches.—No. VII. Miss Annie Oakley," August 13, 1887, Annie Oakley Scrapbooks.
44. "Chit-Chat and the Drama," Annie Oakley Scrapbooks.
45. Linton, *Girl of the Period,* 142.
46. Ibid., 139.
47. One reporter wrote that she was "small in stature, but quick and sure in her movement, [rode] with unsurpassed grace, and [shot] with unerring accuracy." See "Miss Annie Oakley. (Little Sure Shot)," Annie Oakley Scrapbooks. Oakley is reported to have said in an interview that "one of my few accomplishments is that I can

run like a deer." See "The Woman Rifle Expert. Return of Buffalo Bill's Wonderful Feminine Attraction," *The World*, January 8, 1888, Annie Oakley Scrapbooks.

48. Linton, *Girl of the Period,* 137. Not only did Oakley's athletic antics harken to such activities, but she was "passionately fond" of "horse exercise" and in 1884 (at the fictional age of eighteen and the real age of twenty-six) supposedly had tamed a horse with a vicious reputation in only three days. See "'Little Sure Shot.' An Interview with Miss Annie Oakley," Annie Oakley Scrapbooks.
49. Linton, *Girl of the Period,* 6. Linton described the characteristics of the ideal Englishwoman thus: "a creature generous, capable, modest; something franker than a Frenchwoman, more to be trusted than an Italian, as brave as an American but more refined, as domestic as a German and more graceful. It meant a girl who could be trusted alone if need be, because of the innate purity and dignity of her nature, but who was neither bold in bearing nor masculine in mind; a girl who, when she married, would be her husband's friend and companion, but never his rival; one who would consider his interests as identical with her own, and not hold him as just so much fair game for spoil; who would make his house his true home and place of rest, not a mere passage-place for vanity and ostentation to pass through; a tender mother, an industrious housekeeper, a judicious mistress." Linton, *Girl of the Period,* 1–2.
50. Ibid., 145.
51. Bird, *Lady's Life in the Rocky Mountains,* 47.
52. Indeed, Linton posits such an upbringing as a kind of anti-aging mechanism when writing that nymphs-turned-women have "the shy and innocent look of girls; they blush like girls; they know less evil than almost any town-bred girl of eighteen, mothers of stalwart youths though they may be; they can walk and laugh and take pleasure in their lives like girls; and their daughters find them as much sisters as mothers." Linton, *Girl of the Period,* 145.
53. "The Woman Rifle Expert," Annie Oakley Scrapbooks. Further, when an inquirer wrote to an unknown publication for information on Oakley, the publication's response included her married name (Butler).
54. *Daily Press,* 1887, Annie Oakley Scrapbooks.
55. "Camp Sketches.—No. VII. Miss Annie Oakley," Annie Oakley Scrapbooks.
56. *The Topical Times,* May 21, 1887, Annie Oakley Scrapbooks.
57. "'Little Sure Shot.' An Interview with Miss Annie Oakley," Annie Oakley Scrapbooks.
58. Emphasis mine. A Sightseer, "At the Yankeeries," *The Evening News and Telephone,* Tuesday May 10, 1887, Annie Oakley Scrapbooks.
59. "Miss Annie Oakley. (Little Sure Shot)," Annie Oakley Scrapbooks.
60. "Shooting at the Wild West Show," unknown publication, undated [1887], Annie Oakley Scrapbooks.
61. "'Little Sure Shot.' An Interview with Miss Annie Oakley," Annie Oakley Scrapbooks.

62. The American West was often conceived as an adolescent space undergoing a maturation process of settling and civilizing, and Armitage discusses how the western heroine came to represent this metaphor. See "Rawhide Heroines," 178.
63. While tomboyishness seemed to present an alternative model for female maturation, Abate points out that upon reaching maturity, women were expected to discard their youthful behavior and assume appropriately demure and submissive feminine behavior: "Although the nation may value strength, independence and assertiveness in young girls, it does not esteem such qualities in adult women." See Abate, *Tomboys,* xix.

6

Taming a "Savage" Paris

The Masculine Visual Culture of Buffalo Bill's Wild West and France as a New American Frontier

EMILY C. BURNS

Buffalo Bill's Wild West traveled to fin-de-siècle France twice.[1] In 1889, the show performed for seven months at Neuilly, outside Paris, to take advantage of the crowds at the Universal Exposition; it then traveled to Marseilles. In 1905–6, William F. Cody (1846–1917), by then known to the French as "*Guillaume* Bill," returned to France and toured 115 destinations across the country. A route map (fig. 6.1) published as a souvenir with dates charted the show's course across the nation. The program, presented in front of a panoramic Rocky Mountain backdrop, reenacted the mythic taming of the American West in a series of staged scenes by costumed American Indians, cowboys, and sharpshooters.[2] Though carefully constructed, its rhetoric insisted on its historical veracity.[3] French audiences celebrated the "simplicity of the performance" of the equestrian figures running around the arena, a display that matched the plain appearance of Cody and his cowboys.[4] But, in its cultural associations, the show was anything but "simple."

In addition to presenting mythologized history, Buffalo Bill's Wild West participated in wider cultural discourses in France at the turn of the century. The show invited observers to make surprising links between contemporaneous trends in Franco-American exchange. For example, while the current penchant for American art students to train in Paris might seem unrelated to

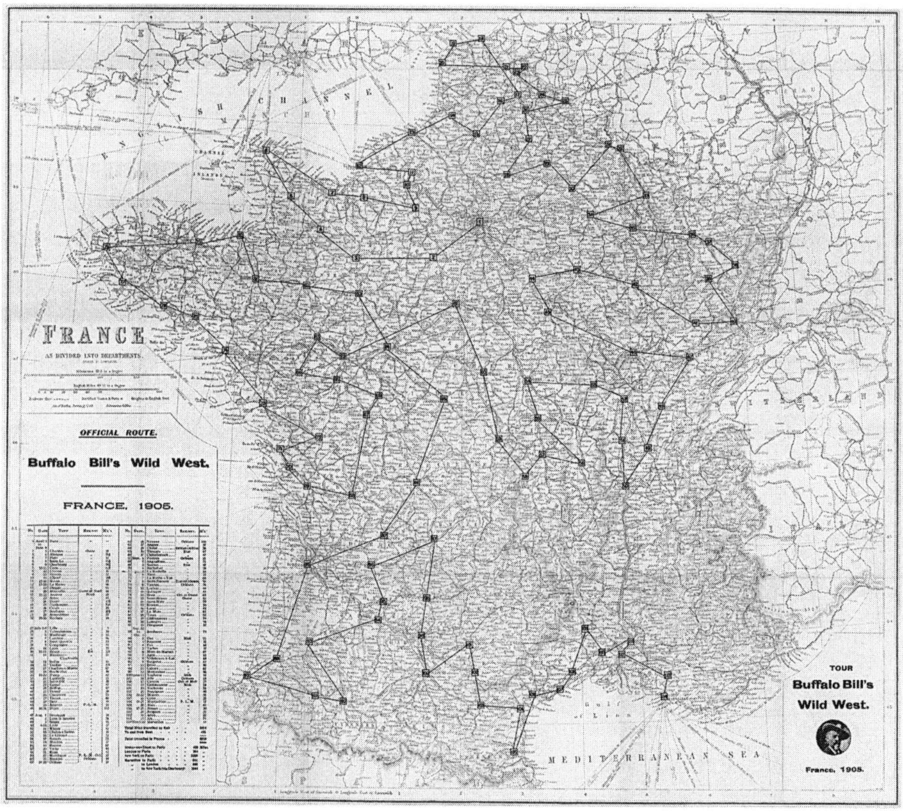

FIGURE 6.1. *Route map of Buffalo Bill's Wild West Tour of France*, 1905–1906.
Courtesy of the Center of the West.

the myths of the American West, debates about an extending international frontier as a symbol for US identity in the age of imperialism were simultaneously raised by the artists' community and by the international performances of Buffalo Bill's Wild West. To many French observers, and in the context of fears about French cultural degeneration, the "colonization" of Paris by art students and by Cody signaled a wider incursion of a US mass culture that was gendered as masculine. The spectacle came to the center of a transnational negotiation that transformed Paris into a metaphorical extension of the American frontier. In the late nineteenth century, American travelers, artists, and writers redefined Paris as an urban wilderness in need of taming. Buffalo

Bill's Wild West allegorized such taming with its putative American cultural colonization. Furthermore, Cody and his cowboys performed a version of US masculinity that centered on virility.[5] French observers took up these notions of masculinity as possible models in a troubled France, though some satirized and contested these stereotypes through caricature. Visual representations of Buffalo Bill's Wild West in posters, illustrations, paintings, and sculptures by American and French artists played a role in transforming France into a metaphorical US frontier before conquering it rhetorically. These images register cultural imperialism but also express ambivalent reactions to the spread of American mass culture and its masculine ethos in France between 1889 and 1910.

Paris as a Frontier in the American Cultural Imagination

During the late nineteenth and early twentieth centuries, Paris became an important stage for various forms of US culture. When thousands of American artists traveled to Paris to study in the foreign capital as part of a larger influx of US tourists and other students, they brought American cultural tropes with them.[6] The flood of Americans to fin-de-siècle Paris was so pronounced that in 1891, British critic Gilbert Parker (1862–1932) declared, "One cannot understand America until one has seen it in Paris."[7] Parker's irony suggests that Paris became an important staging ground for the expression of American national identity.

In 1888, British writer Lord James Bryce (1838–1922) foreshadowed Parker's observation when he mused, "Where will the American imagination of the future seek its materials when it desires to escape from the dramas of domestic life? Where will bold new spirits find a field in which to relieve their energies when the Western world of adventure is no more?"[8] On the eve of American historian Frederick Jackson Turner's (1861–1932) frontier speech at the Chicago World's Columbian Exposition in 1893, Bryce was among many contemporaries who saw the American West as a metonym for US national identity. Furthermore, Bryce implied that this frontier mythology might extend beyond the geographical borders of the so-called West. He suggested that American "energies" driving to the West would need to find new direction once that landscape was, at least metaphorically, settled.[9] Both Turner and Bryce imagined new American frontiers would be international. Indeed, ten years following Bryce's comment, the Spanish-American War produced the United States' first overseas colony in the Philippines.[10] During this same period, however, Europe became the site for a subtler cultural colonization through the rise of art study abroad and through the spread of American mass culture.[11] As the geographical boundaries of the US western frontier closed, American tourists and expatriates abroad invoked tropes of the American West in Paris.

If, for many nineteenth-century observers, the American West served as the site of American personal and national formation, late nineteenth-century Paris became a location to negotiate those displaced energies. While European civilization might seem far afield from the rugged American West and US colonies, references to US frontier culture appeared in the cultural discourse around Paris in surprising ways. Some American artists described the landscape of the Atlantic Ocean traversed en route to France as akin to the open prairie, thus making an analogy between migrating to the American West and traveling to France.[12] Some of the terms used by American writers and travelers to discuss Paris in the fin de siècle resonated uncannily with the popular idioms of the American West. For example, US critics increasingly represented European decadence as savagery.[13] These constructions challenged the notion of Europe as a site of civilization and a model for artistic development.

Labels that announced its decline marked France as a rigorous site for the negotiation of personal identity. Turner's frontier speech had pinpointed the trope of the rugged frontier of the American West as a fulcrum in establishing American selfhood; critics recycled versions of this thesis in fin-de-siècle Paris. American accounts about travel to and within Paris mimicked the idea of working through a rough landscape to define oneself. Artists discovered their identities in the imaginary frontiers of Paris just as Americans had defined themselves in the western landscapes. As applied to a civilized city, this rhetoric of taming functions as a parody of US western expansion. Furthermore, the discourse of the American West in France also defined Paris as a wilderness that warranted taming through the influx of American culture.

As the practice of American art study in Paris became an increasingly common rite of passage after the American Civil War, American artists began to draw from a cultural typology of the American West to describe French bohemian culture. These commentaries offered an antithetical understanding of European civilization as threatening, loud, unfocused, chaotic, and ill-suited for careful study.[14] American observers identified two main sources of Parisian savagery: the overwhelming traits of an unknown city and the wildness of the bohemian lifestyle.[15] These writers merged geography and national character. As early as the 1840s, George Catlin (1796–1872) described the city's "wilderness throngs of boulevards" with an "endless throng of human beings sweeping by me." He used the metaphors of wilderness to describe a wandering pack of crowds and juxtaposed this urban wilderness with the quietude of the "desert wilderness" of the American West.[16] Many American writers extended the idea of the physical wilderness of an overwhelming foreign city to descriptions of Paris as a moral wasteland. In 1885, American critic Horace Scudder (1838–1902) likened Paris to a "jungle" and "pestiferous swamp."[17] An anonymous writer echoed Scudder in 1895, insisting that Paris was filled "with devils to drag [visitors] down, and that the all-absorbing question for weak and strong alike is how to keep themselves pure in an atmosphere reeking with immorality."[18]

Expatriate writers employed the figure of the American Indian to embody the "reeking" moral climate of the French atelier. In his recollections of Parisian art study, American art student Ion Perdicaris (1840–1925) described French artists hazing the *nouveaux*, or new art students, in an atelier full of "raging chimpanzees and hideous orang-outangs": "they roar—they howl—they mew—they chatter—they grin! While the unfortunate newcomer, like the prisoner around whom the Indian braves, with brandished tomahawks, perform their savage-war dance, appeals to his tormenters in vain." In this description, the French art students are "Indian braves, with brandished tomahawks" involved in a "savage-war dance" inflicted on the American art students.[19] Such comments in American artists' letters, memoirs, and journals oscillate between describing and mythologizing their experiences of Parisian art study with the concepts of wilderness and savagery. American artist Earl Shinn (1838–86) designated such atelier behavior in Paris as "the rough, threatening coquetry of Arcadia."[20] His comment suggests a paradox—the Arcadia of Paris is not an idyllic pastoral, but a coarse wilderness. Most often found in the American mass-market newspapers and magazines such as *Harper's* and *Frank Leslie's*, these descriptions gave their readership a vision of Paris as a savage wilderness in a state of decay.

In describing French politics, American observers extended their treatments of Paris as savage beyond the physical and moral aspects of the city. For example, when American sculptor Alexander Phimister Proctor (1860–1950) moved back to Paris in 1897, his apartment overlooked the Place de la Madeleine, where riots ensued in the midst of the ongoing Dreyfus affair, in which a French Jewish military officer was charged with treason on spurious evidence, thus polarizing French observers.[21] To characterize the violence of the rioters, Proctor's recollections invoked parallels with the American Indian. In his autobiographical draft, he writes, "The Dreyfus trial for treason had just begun. Our square that night, was suddenly filled with a mob, of excited Frenchmen, yelling 'abas Dreyfus.' Frantic people swarmed from all sides carrying wood, a huge fire was built not far from the hotel. Our windows looked right out on the scene: an effigie of Dreyfus was brought up, and with fanatical pandemonium and apache yells, was cast into the raging inferno."[22] Proctor persisted with this metaphor, equating the sounds of the violent mob to "apache yells." He elaborated, "No one knew at what moment the hoodlums and apache might turn into a killing burning rampage. Panic seized the neighborhoods."[23] Proctor's commentary draws on stereotypes of American Indian character to comprehend the political turmoil witnessed in Paris. The use of the term *apache* to describe Parisian behavior was not limited to American observers, however; as historian Dominique Kalifa has noted, many French commentators on urban decline also used this term in the nineteenth century.[24] American visitors' adoption of the same language created a parallel discourse that challenged the convention of a civilized Paris.

Some writers proposed serious advice and suggestions for Americans to negotiate the Parisian wilderness. Shinn suggested that the American art student needed to maintain composure, focus, and a "Buddhistical tranquillity [*sic*]" in the face of the savagery.[25] Advice columns implied that the traversing of the urban environment was an important means of training the self. As a locus for American self-discovery, Paris exhibited parallels with descriptions of the West in the rhetorical training of American citizens. The discourse of art study in Paris repeated the myths of the American West; for example, American painter Will Hicok Low (1853–1933) explained that the artist in Paris "was not coddled in any way but left free to learn for himself the uncharted laws which governed this apparently irresponsible land."[26] The cultivation of a particular skill set suggests that the artists' negotiation of this wilderness was necessary to their self-discovery.

The practice of working through a rough landscape to define oneself recycled conventions of self-definition on the rugged frontier of the American West, in particular the ideas Turner presented in his frontier speech of 1893.[27] Turner argued that in the West, a European confronted savagery through the "primitive conditions on a continually advancing frontier line," but then conquered it, emerging an American.[28] This process of "Americanization" takes "a European in dress, industries, tools, modes of travel, and thought." For Turner, the figure of the American Indian occupied the central phase in this transition. The frontier "strips off the garments of civilization and arrays [the frontiersman] in the hunting shirt and the moccasin," and "he fits himself into the Indian clearings and follows the Indian trails." Turner concludes that by adopting strategies of the American Indian and then taming the wilderness, "the outcome is not the old Europe. . . . The fact is, that here is a new product that is American."[29] Turner coalesces individual and national character in this passage, as the transformation of the self indicates a larger, national character.

The construction of Paris as a frontier invited the same transformation of the European to the American, retaining the figure of the American Indian as the pivot. By applying the motif of the savage wilderness to Paris, it became a site that, in parallel with Turner's narrative, first turns its visitor "savage" and then Americanizes him. The negotiation of this new urban wilderness, as suggested by Low's comment, shapes the new American. The link between the frontiers of the American West and Paris extended beyond self-discovery and actualization. This cultural dialogue metaphorically redefined the Parisian landscape as a wilderness in need of taming, just as the American West had been tamed. If France was metaphorically akin to the American frontier, it unwittingly placed the French in the position of the American Indian tribes that were suppressed by US expansion.

Buffalo Bill's Wild West Tames a Foreign Wilderness

The rhetoric of taming appeared alongside language that figured the American as educator of the "savage" American Indian and the "barbaric" Parisian. Some critics insinuated that Americans abroad should culturally master and civilize French society. Other writers linked the idea of French decline with the ascension of the United States on the world stage. For example, American historian Brooks Adams (1848–1927) noted about Europe in 1899, "the energy with which those nations palpitated when I was a boy is ebbing, and with the national vitality ebbs the national art." In contrast, according to Adams, American society "is gathering momentum, and, as it surges onward, our art gains dignity and scope."[30] Adams was part of a growing chorus that linked the decline of Europe and rise of America on the world stage with burgeoning cultural forms in the United States.

American journalist Richard Harding Davis (1864–1916) implied in 1895 that the expatriate members of the American colony in Paris were like frontiersmen, embarking into the wilderness. He expressed concern that Americans could be weakened and broken down if their principles were not steadfast in Paris. He wrote, "There is something fine in the idea of a colony, of a body of men and women who strike out for themselves in a new country, who cut out their homes in primeval forests, and who make their peace with the native barbarians."[31] Davis sent a series of articles on Paris to *Harper's Weekly* and became an avid commentator and critic of Franco-American interaction.[32] He sardonically likened the American community in Paris to a society negotiating with "native barbarians," here the Parisians. For Davis, Americans who move to Paris occupy a liminal space, neither in the United States nor in France. In this frontier zone, identities are called into question.

In this context, the term *American colony* functions on an additional register, implying that the American presence in Paris marks an attempt to tame the land by colonizing it and averting its so-called savage immorality.[33] This concept was implicitly linked with late nineteenth-century imperialist rhetoric that charged American forces to seek "new frontiers."[34] In addition, as literary scholar Roxana Oltean has argued, such "othering" of Paris can be read as an inverted Orientalizing process in a colonial context.[35] American critics' claims that Paris was a barbaric wilderness justified its cultural colonization. The links between these commentaries and American imperial expansion in the Philippines, Hawaii, and Guam in the 1890s have been noted, especially as these links appeared in the exoticized displays of Cuba and Hawaii in the Trocadero in the Universal Exposition of 1900.[36] A metaphorical "colonizing" of Paris enacted this same discourse, though it did so more subtly than the overt American colonial ambition in the Pacific. As Buffalo Bill historian Louis Warren has pointed out, the Wild West abroad "reversed the course of conquest."[37]

The visual culture of Buffalo Bill's Wild West in France in 1889 allegorized the construction of Paris as a site for cultural invasion and taming. The advertising around the show signaled the spread of mass culture in France. Paris was plastered with advertisements during the performance run of seven months, which was timed to take advantage of the large numbers of tourists who visited for the Universal Exposition at the Champ de Mars.

French critics complained about brash American commercialism littering the city.[38] Although Buffalo Bill's Wild West was not an official part of the Universal Exposition, its advertisements crept into official fair publications.[39] In 1889, *Brooklyn Daily Eagle*'s Paris correspondent Emma Bullet noted, "The immense painted posters over all the city to advertise Buffalo Bill—his portraits pasted all in a row, many times larger than natural; the cowboys on their wild horses; the Indians, looking very savage—amuse the Parisians immensely." According to Bullet, however, Parisians also perceived these advertisements as a "foreign invasion."[40]

Buffalo Bill's transformative, if not imperial, presence in the city assumed a political dimension with the attempted coup d'état by General Boulanger (1837–91) early in 1889.[41] In order to gain mass support for his candidacy in the election, which enthusiasts hoped would enable him to declare a dictatorship, Boulanger's supporters covered major monuments in the city with electoral materials. One cover of *L'Illustration* shows one of the Paris lion sculptures plastered with posters on the pedestal, and even on the body of the lion itself.[42] When Buffalo Bill's Wild West's advertising materials had a similar visible presence in the city with their "giant and multicolored posters . . . [that] already have set fire to the curiosities of the gullible," French contemporaries could not help but link Boulanger with Cody.[43] Militaristic propaganda transformed into the showmanship of a so-called military hero.

American commercial projects, especially those associated with spectacular mass culture, were implicated in Cody's own cultural coup of Paris. A caricature in *L'Illustration* from 1889 linked the arrival of Buffalo Bill's Wild West in Paris with Boulanger's attempted coup, because it employed a similar overload of posters on Parisian monuments.[44] In the cartoon, two men contemplate a poster that reads "Buffalo Bill Great Exhib!" Two American Indian figures are visible on horseback in the poster image, and the figure of Cody charges out of the frame wielding a gun. Cody's placement in the composition follows the line of the figure in top hat at left who depicts none other than General Boulanger. The caption imagines Boulanger demanding that his designer "give my electoral posters the artistic character of these here, representing me in the process of toppling the government."[45] The image suggests anxiety about the guilelessness of some observers who would be swept away by such propaganda. This amusing representation also compositionally elevates the figure of Cody over Boulanger and implies the effectiveness of Cody's advertising scheme.

FIGURE 6.2. Uzés, Du haut de la Tour Eiffel, cartoon, 1889, *Le Courrier Français* (August 25, 1889), 1889 Scrapbook (Paris, France).
Courtesy of the McCracken Research Library, Buffalo Bill Center of the West.

Indeed, if there was competition for public attention between Boulanger and Cody, the press suggested that Cody won the day. *The New York Sunday News* reported that "the once popular Boulanger-cum-Paulus 'En Revenant de la Revue' is now eclipsed, and all Paris is singing the latest success." The chorus read: "Farewell, brave general / your prestige is no longer / We take for our delight / the hero of the 'Wild West' / All is in decline / Military and Civil / Sing, live France / and live Buffalo Bill!"[46] This song celebrated Cody's absorption of Boulanger's power in the public imagination. This reassignment of cultural power was signaled in a full-page illustration from *Le Courrier Français* in August of 1889 (fig. 6.2). In this image, General Boulanger's arms are tied to a post behind his back. He growls up at characters seated on the platform of the Eiffel Tower depicted in huge scale as a stage set. The figures include Naser al-Din Shah Qajar (1831–96), the Shah of Persia who visited the exposition, a bull to signal Spanish toreador bullfights in Paris, and, at right, Buffalo Bill Cody wielding puppets of an American Indian and a cowboy.[47] All three rebuke Boulanger and "force him to take second place" to the "three newsworthy events of the year."[48] Cody's placement on the tower's platform as one of the objects of Boulanger's gaze suggests a transfer of power.

Another caricature (fig. 6.3) in the satirical newspaper *Le Grelot* depicts Buffalo Bill riding a crowned centaur who thumbs her nose at General Boulanger at the right of the scene. Entitled "One Ham Actor Chasing Another" to refer to the metaphorical center of attention, Cody rides in a large circus ring labeled "La Buffalo Bill's," while Boulanger sits astride an underfed horse with its head lowered in front of a sign of "La Boulange Bill's" failed show. While Cody's crowned centaur is propped up as almost a phallic extension of the performer's body, Boulanger's horse's head reads as an impotent phallus. A bouquet thrown by the Paris region, Le Faubourg St. Germain, lays at his feet. These subtle cues emphasize Cody's virility at the expense of the French general's prowess. As in the cartoon printed in *Le Courrier Français,* Cody replaces Boulanger and his politics, which the poster at right within the cartoon lists as "Royalists, Bonapartists, Camelots, and Wild Muffles."[49] The use of the term *sauvages* on the background poster is a thinly veiled reference to the "savage" tribes of so-called primitive people who were displayed regularly in Paris during this period at the expositions as well as in the Jardin de l'Acclimatation and even found in Buffalo Bill's Wild West encampment.[50] These images highlighted the transnational framing of French political power struggles through Buffalo

FIGURE 6.3. Pépin, "Un Cabotin chasse l'autre," *Le Grelot* (June 9, 1889), 1889 Scrapbook.
Courtesy of the McCracken Research Library, Buffalo Bill Center of the West.

Bill and, by proxy, American cultural imperialism. They also suggest that Cody could tame the French people, succeeding where Boulanger had failed.

By the second tour of Buffalo Bill's Wild West in France in 1905, the images that circulated placed even greater emphasis on Cody's conquest of the city, and even the country. The visual culture of the show became militaristic to signal a cultural conquering of France. A poster (fig. 6.4)—with the vague but ominous statement "Je Viens" [I Am Coming]—was plastered all over Paris, and Cody's face in a medallion is superimposed onto the body of a charging bison.[51] The bison's head is turned so that the animal appears to be simultaneously charging

FIGURE 6.4. "*Je Viens*," chromolithographic poster, 1905.
Courtesy of the McCracken Research Library, Buffalo Bill Center of the West.

to the left and also forward from the image into the viewer's space. This more direct presentation highlighted the forceful advertising strategy and ubiquitous presence the spectacle took in the French capital.[52] In 1905, Buffalo Bill's Wild West was not on the periphery of Paris in Neuilly, as it was in 1889. Rather, it was placed in the center of the city on the Champ de Mars in the shadow of the Eiffel Tower. This placement informed the myth of Buffalo Bill's Wild West; a later poster of "Scenes of the Life of Col. W. F. Cody, 'Buffalo Bill'" imagined the performers charging "under the Tower Eiffel" in 1889.[53] By 1905, Cody's mythology exceeded the actual history of his presence in France and signaled his metaphorical conquering of the foreign nation.

In its second France tour, Buffalo Bill's Wild West enhanced tropes of colonization through its technology and methods of transit around France. Contemporaries marveled at the speed with which the show could travel, build, and take down its arena, so it became a symbol of technological modernity as well. In the 1905 tour, the ship carrying the infrastructure for the show brought about fifty Pullman railcars to transport the troupe across the nation.[54] With its self-sustained systems of transport, Buffalo Bill's Wild West captivated foreign audiences.

The mass-market phenomenon of transportation also associated the spectacle with the military. Indeed, the train system that Cody used to traverse France transformed how the country thought about its transportation. The negative association adhering to France's inefficient single-track rail lines, held to be largely responsible for the country's defeat in the Franco-Prussian War, yielded to the image of a modern success of efficient mobility.[55] Even thirty-four years after the Franco-Prussian War and the Commune, the resulting anxiety and uncertain stability of the Third Republic continued well into the twentieth century.[56] Cody's tour redirected these national fears, but also raised the idea of imperialism. The design of the 1905 Wild West route map (fig. 6.1)—with its red line moving across its 115 destinations in France as a "ZigZag tour"—is more akin to a military map than the mere mapping of popular entertainment.[57] This representation subtly implied the cultural colonization that resulted from exporting the American frontier to France through Buffalo Bill's Wild West. In the wake of the Franco-Prussian War, the map signifies the transformation of the railroad system. In the process, the image invites the viewer to consider alternatives to societal enervation through the traveling performance.

Inverting Parisian Refinement: Cody and Transnational Masculinities

The rhetorical conquering of Paris invited the replacement of the aristocratic dandy with the masculine persona of the American cowboy. A chromolithographic poster (fig. 6.5) of Buffalo Bill's Wild West and Congress of Rough Riders of the World, originally printed in the mid-1890s, opposes the military hero of the French past with the more common American man of the present. The image pairs the mythic civilizer of the American West with the imperial Napoleon Bonaparte (1769–1821), who experienced a resurgence in French public attention in the wake of Boulanger's attempted coup.[58] The poster includes French painter Rosa Bonheur (1822–99) in the center of the composition. She is seated before her easel, as she was depicted in a contemporary photograph of her visit to the Wild West Show at Neuilly in 1889 when she painted a widely reproduced portrait of Cody on horseback.[59] While both Napoleon and Cody are seated on horses, Cody is more active and in control, and Napoleon's shoulders are slumped and his belly protrudes.

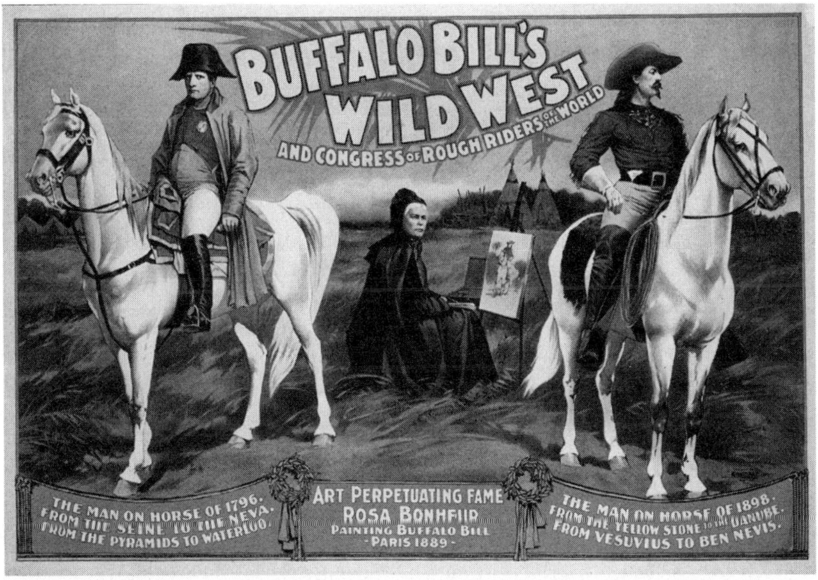

FIGURE 6.5. *Art Perpetuating Fame, Rosa Bonheur Painting Buffalo Bill*, chromolithographic poster for Buffalo Bill's Wild West and Congress of Rough Riders of the World, 1898 version of c. 1894 poster.
Library of Congress Prints and Photographs Division, Washington, D.C. (reproduction no. LC-USZC4-2350).

The advertiser's pairing of Napoleon and Bonheur with Cody furnished the newcomer greater cultural currency in France. The direction of her gaze and the subject of her portrait also bestow triumph on Cody. Compared to Buffalo Bill, Napoleon seems defeated, and his slouching posture offers a subtly ironic comment on the label describing him as the hero of 1796. The upright Cody receives the same status for 1898. The date kept changing when the poster was reprinted, so Cody's role as a victor over Napoleon was constantly updated, and the printer always kept one hundred years between them. In both cases, the text emphasized military prowess. For Napoleon, the label marked the distance he once controlled from the river "Seine to the Neva" in Russia, and "from the pyramids to Waterloo." Meanwhile for Cody, the label highlights his metaphorical cultural power, held "from the Yellow Stone [*sic*] to the Danube," and from Vesuvius in Pompeii to Ben Nevis, Scotland, marking the extent at the time of the Buffalo Bill's Wild West tour in Europe. The reference to the American victory in the

Spanish-American War implied a growing imperialism, and the parallel with Napoleon enhanced that link. A critic from *L'Illustration* referred to Cody as the "Napoleon of the Prairie," though the same author's statement, "They are all colonels," cast doubt on Cody's claim to military prowess.[60] French writers also referred to Buffalo Bill as a "musketeer, a western d'Artagnan," and "King of the Far West."[61] These posters, and the discussions they incited, elevated this exceptional American cowboy as a successor for the downtrodden Napoleon at left.

As an iconic figure, Buffalo Bill became the harbinger of a new revitalized cultural norm based on the rugged American model. He symbolized the stereotype for American masculinity: virile and strong, but also rough and uncouth.[62] Cody developed the term *Rough Riders* to describe the equestrian skills performed in the show in the 1890s, and the American military adopted the moniker to refer to the American equestrian forces in the Spanish-American War. This evolution of the term offered more credence to Cody as a military hero in the early twentieth century. The masculinized cowboy character also spread through the rise of Theodore Roosevelt (1858–1919) in American politics and his emphasis on "the strenuous life."[63] As French historian Jacques Portes has shown, early twentieth-century French writers reported that Roosevelt exported a particularly masculine American character.[64]

One of the souvenir publications produced for the traveling spectacle was entitled *Rough Riders*. The 1906 *Rough Riders* souvenir magazine depicted Cody in military garb, merging him with the contemporary history of the Spanish-American War by including a photograph of "Roosevelt's Rough Riders Héros de la Guerre de Cuba" in the text.[65] In the 1905–1906 tour, French newspapers focused on the figure of the cowboy—those "audacious cavaliers of the American prairie"—and the wild American horses that "could not be dominated."[66] Some articles emphasized the "great difficulty" of the labor to mount these wild horses, which "must be done in the most dangerous conditions."[67] French critics' emphasis on the dogged vigor of the cowboys highlighted their masculine prowess. Indeed, the cowboy figured much more prominently in the 1905–1906 tour of Buffalo Bill's Wild West than it did in 1889, when the press focused on the Oglala performers. This shift was due in part to the presence of the Rough Riders, drawn from equestrian masters from many parts of the world, but the discourse of masculinity also influenced the conversation in the press. The language of taming in France foregrounded the relationship between colonization and masculinity.

In the context of anxieties about the decadence and decline of French culture during the fin de siècle, the cowboy offered an important intervention. As Christopher Forth, Robert Nye, and other historians have considered, concerns about the feminization of French culture rose in the 1890s, incited by the character of the dandy and the elegant graceful styles of art nouveau.[68] The defeat in the Franco-Prussian War also spurred fears about cultural degeneration and enervation.[69] Aesthetes such as Robert de Montesquieu (1855–1921) prompted some French critics to claim a crisis of masculinity. Buffalo Bill's Wild West seemed to offer an alternative to the feminized grace of art nouveau; even the bold fonts of the American posters implied a sturdy and hard-edged character (figs. 6.4 and 6.5). The prototypical American presented in Buffalo Bill's Wild West became a model for a new French generation; one contemporary argued that French men would need to "prepare themselves" alongside this example for a "new generation of vigorous men."[70] The manly cowboy and rustic frontiersman became masculinized alternatives to the French dandy and the urban cosmopolite. This metaphor was extended to replace the outworn models of monarchical and aristocratic power structures in France with the rugged American common man as a republican ideal.

American critics argued that the Wild West provided to French audiences an allegory of the potential of the civilized to conquer savagery. Buffalo Bill's Wild West dramatizes and embodies the story of Western civilized expansionism. When it returns to the Old World in a state of decadence and decline akin to the frontier, the colonial template is imposed onto the enervated French. A visitor to Paris in 1889 named Pattie Miller Stocking claimed in the newspaper, "It was a little astonishing with what ease the cowboys always defeated the savages whenever they attacked a camp or a diligence, but I could see that triumph of virtue over vice made a due impression on the disciples of Zola, and scored one for the American cowboy."[71] After traveling from Washington, D.C., Stocking suggests that French viewers read Buffalo Bill's Wild West and its metaphors of civilizing savagery metaphorically as a "triumph of virtue over vice." She simultaneously created a metaphorical battle between the cowboy and the decadence that some critics associated with the naturalist literature of Émile Zola (1840–1902). Stocking implies that the modernism of Zola and his contemporaries signaled the debasing of culture akin to the Parisian debauchery about which many Americans complained. For Stocking, Buffalo Bill's Wild West could train and moralize the Parisian decadents.

Some commentators suggested that decadent French culture could be rejuvenated with the energy of the American West. Stocking also claimed that Buffalo Bill's Wild West "appeared to Parisians to be some fairy like tale of olden times; or perhaps better, the sudden embodiment of New World possibilities with Buffalo Bill, the cowboys, and the Indians for instantaneous and tangible illustration."[72] Contemporary discourse suggested that the "tangible illustration" was intended to reinvigorate an Old World inspired by displays of the American West. The character of the American West, as Turner codified it, invited a new social order, "in a large degree free from European precedents and forces." Turner celebrated how the frontiersman "looked at things independently and with small regard or appreciation for the best Old World experience." This alternative was characterized by "buoyant self-confidence and self-assertion."[73] By adopting the persona of the cowboy within these subtle mechanisms of cultural imperialism, French men could become stronger. Through the mechanisms of cultural imperialism, the adoption of American norms of masculinity transformed the European into an "American."[74]

Ambivalence and Questioning Taming

There was some resistance to this type of model in France, however, because the cowboy was so rugged. To some detractors, this so-called civilizing force seemed also wild. While Buffalo Bill and his troupe had many enthusiastic followers in France, some caricatures reveal a backlash against some of the ideals that his show exported. Attempts to civilize and alter France more broadly were registered in complaints about the Americanization of Paris through the rise of American models of business practice, obsession with financial success, and focus on efficiency.[75] For example, although the Eiffel Tower, built for the exposition of 1889, was designed by a Frenchman, some French contemporaries deemed the modern iron structure a mere "Yankee dream," indicative of the influx of American culture overseas.[76] American mass culture through posters and advertising also began to seep into the Parisian fabric, and some French critics registered anxieties about an influx of American culture. For instance, French critic Charles de Varigny (1829–99) began his exposé on American women with the ominous proclamation, "Europe is becoming Americanized."[77]

Buffalo Bill's Wild West in France triggered some of these anxieties. Indeed, this foreign incursion was not uncontested. As mentioned above, the French press noted the importance of wild horses for Cody's theme of taming. One cartoon from *L'Illustration* depicts two curious Parisians standing before Buffalo Bill sitting on a docile horse.[78] The caption asks, "And over time, do your horses remain always wild?" "Admittedly, we train them for this," came the imagined response.[79] This representation undercuts the assumed authenticity of the cowboys to tame wild horses. It implies that these animals were already tamed through time and repetition. Furthermore, it suggests that their wild character was merely cultivated. This cartoon appeared at the same time as a challenge that Cody received to tame wild French horses as proof of the authenticity of the show and the capability of his cowboys. In July 1889, members of a Paris jockey club asked Cody's cowboys to subdue one of their wild horses, and Cody included the challenge within the regular performance as proof of the authenticity of the taming.[80] In September, Rosa Bonheur initiated a similar challenge by inviting Cody's cowboys to tame mustangs that had been sent by John Arbuckle, of the Post Percheron Company, from the American West.[81] Both of the events—perhaps staged themselves—were avidly covered in the press.[82] This taming of horses allegorized Cody's larger refining of Paris but suggested that this cultural presence was not uncontested.

Though understood as a civilizing force in the context of indigenous America, the American cowboy was also sometimes denigrated as a primitive in French visual culture, as seen in a painting by French painter Félix Morel-Lamy in 1905 (Musée du Nouveau Monde, La Rochelle).[83] In this representation of one of Buffalo Bill's Wild West's cowboys during the 1905–1906 French tour, the artist emphasizes the cowboy's sneering direct gaze, raised eyebrow, and brown-checkered costume. Morel-Lamy underscores the figure's coarse character with rough brushwork. Cowboys constructed foreign stereotypes of the American man: rugged, virile, strong but also uncouth, and some observers critiqued them as being as "wild" as the Indians that they "civilized" over the course of the performance.[84] Similarly, a plaster bust made in 1905 by French sculptor Gustave-Louis Dussart (1875–1952; Musée du Nouveau Monde, La Rochelle) caricatured Buffalo Bill with his head turned to the side, his cowboy hat dramatically tilted as though being yanked off his head by a wind gust.[85] Dussart emphasizes Cody's crooked teeth and casual costume, which seems incompatible with the traditional format of the portrait bust. By caricaturing Cody rather than heroicizing him, Dussart highlights his brash entrepreneurship and mocks his displays of masculinity. Morel-Lamy and Dussart both draw attention to the performed nature of the cowboy's masculinity. Neither artist constructs the cowboy as a model to follow. Their caricatures implicitly challenge the American model that was otherwise becoming more accepted in France. These two objects by French artists are antithetical to the depictions of Cody and his cowboys in the official Buffalo Bill's Wild West imagery (fig. 6.5), which emphasize the militaristic prowess of the cowboy. In comparison, Morel-Lamy's and Dussart's images express curiosity about this masculine character but also ambivalence about the nature and impact of the Wild West ethos through caricature.

While historians have discussed the role of the frontier in the American imperial rhetoric of the 1890s, the role of this frontier mythology in France has been less thoroughly considered. Furthermore, the place of visual culture in the transatlantic imaginary of the frontier merits greater attention than it has received. An analysis of the depiction of cultural colonization in mass media allows a greater understanding of the interwoven discourses of masculinity and colonialism within Franco-American exchange. Conversations in late nineteenth-century Paris within the American artist community and within the responses to Buffalo Bill's Wild West together participated in a discourse in which the American frontier became a flexible metaphor that established the foreign capital as a frontier space ripe for taming.

Notes

Thanks to Frank Christianson, Monica Rico, Corey Dzenko, and my Auburn research assistant Michelle Mandarino for their feedback on this essay. For research assistance on Buffalo Bill's Wild West in France, I am grateful to Sylvestre Clapp and Alain Barnicaud, Archives de Palais du Roure, Avignon; Steve Friesen, Buffalo Bill Museum & Grave, Golden, Colorado; Mary Robinson, McCracken Research Library, Buffalo Bill Center of the West, Cody, Wyoming; Annick Notter and Evelyne Fazilleau, Musée du Nouveau Monde, La Rochelle; Mindy Besaw, Whitney Western Art Museum, Buffalo Bill Center of the West; and Linda Clark and Jeremy Johnston, William F. "Buffalo Bill" Cody Collection, Buffalo Bill Center of the West. This research has been supported by the Baird Society Resident Scholar Program, the Buffalo Bill Center of the West, the Metropolitan Museum of Art, the Smithsonian American Art Museum, the Terra Foundation for American Art, and the University of Nottingham.

1. On Buffalo Bill's Wild West in France, see Fiorentino, "'Those Red-Brick Faces'"; Jonnes, *Eiffel's Tower*, 107–13, 121–44; Kasson, *Buffalo Bill's Wild West*, 83–91;

Lefrançois *Les Indiens de Buffalo Bill et la Camargue*; Napier, "Across the Big Water"; Reddin, *Wild West Shows,* 96–102; Warren, *Buffalo Bill's America,* 344–57; and Zaretsky, *Cock & Bull Stories,* 61–84.

2. There is voluminous scholarship on this topic, but the most detailed considerations of the cultural context for and implications of the show are Kasson, *Buffalo Bill's Wild West,* and Warren, *Buffalo Bill's America.*
3. On the perceived historical veracity of these displays in France, see A. R., "Nos Gravures: Buffalo Bill," *L'Illustration,* June 8, 1889, 492; A. R., "Nos Gravures: La Troupe de Buffalo Bill," *L'Illustration,* June 22, 1889, 536; and Eugène Rastignac, "Courrier de Paris," *L'Illustration,* May 25, 1889, 438.
4. L. K., "At the Paris World's Fair," *New York Times,* June 23, 1889, 16.
5. Westermeier, "Buffalo Bill's Cowboys Abroad"; Rollins, *Cowboy*; Carlsen, *Cowboy Way.*
6. On American art study abroad, see Adler, Hirshler, and Weinberg, *Americans in Paris*; Weinberg, *Lure of Paris*; Fink, *American Art at the Nineteenth-Century Paris Salons*; McCullough, *Greater Journey*; Wiesinger et al., *Le voyage de Paris*; and Walton, *Internationalism, National Identities, and Study Abroad.*
7. Parker, "American Art Students in Paris," *Independent* (London), December 31, 1891, 6. On American identity defined through transatlantic encounter in the post–Civil War period, see Bradbury, *Dangerous Pilgrimages*; Portes, *Fascination and Misgivings*; and Méral, *Paris in American Literature.*
8. Bryce, *American Commonwealth,* 2:716.
9. Though Turner did not make his claim that the West had been closed until 1893, anxieties about the end of western expansion reverberated in the preceding decades. See Wrobel, *End of American Exceptionalism,* 4; Slotkin, *Fatal Environment*; and Slotkin, *Regeneration through Violence.*
10. On American imperialism in the late nineteenth century, see Lafeber, *New Empire*; McCoy and Saracano, *Colonial Crucible*; Brody, *Visualizing American Empire*; and McCartney, *Power and Progress.*
11. On American mass culture in Europe, see Endy, "Travel and World Power"; and Rydell and Kroes, *Buffalo Bill in Bologna.*
12. See Burns, "Old World Anew," 49.
13. On decline and decadence in 1890s France, see Fischer, "Constructing the 'American School' of 1900," 91–92; Fischer, "Declaration of Empire," 29–30; Leroi, "American Salon," 485; and Weber, *France: Fin de Siècle,* 9–50.
14. Burns, "Puritan Parisians."
15. The idea of Paris as a "savage" and "moral wasteland" can be traced to the earlier nineteenth century. See Higonnet, *Paris,* 77–78; and Prendergast, *Paris and the Nineteenth Century,* 87.
16. Catlin, *Adventures of the Ojibbeway and Ioway,* 2:320.
17. Scudder, "Childhood in Modern Literature and Art," 753.
18. Anonymous, "Shall Our Young Men Study in Paris?" 133.

19. Perdicaris, "Reminiscences of a Parisian Atélier," 644.
20. Shinn, "Art-Study at the Imperial School in Paris," 293.
21. On the Dreyfus Affair, see Burns, *Rural Society and French Politics*; and Harris, *Dreyfus.*
22. "Autobiographical Draft," Alexander Phimister Proctor Collection, MS 242, box 8, folder 13, p. 3, McCracken Research Library, Buffalo Bill Center of the West. On Proctor in Paris, see Hassrick, *Wildlife and Western Heroes*, 42–51.
23. Hassrick, *Wildlife and Western Heroes*, 4. The published autobiography omits the "Apache" metaphors. See Ebner, *Sculptor in Buckskin*, 129–30. The so-called wild Indians of the West were also used to describe working class unrest in the United States. See Slotkin, *Fatal Environment*, 338–42, 480–89.
24. See Kalifa, "Archéologie de l'Apachisme"; and Kalifa, *L'encre et le sang*, 10, 121, 152–61. Thanks to Vanessa Schwartz for suggesting Kalifa's work.
25. Shinn, "Art-Study in the Imperial School at Paris, No. V," 68.
26. Will Hicok Low, "The Primrose Way," typed autobiographical ms., p. 29, Will Hicok Low Papers, Albany Institute of History and Art.
27. As many scholars of American mythologies have argued, the American West had long been a central trope for the discovery of a national selfhood. See Goetzmann and Goetzmann, *West of the Imagination*; Hassrick, *American West*; Prown et al., *Discovered Lands, Invented Pasts*; and Smith, *Virgin Land.*
28. Turner, "Significance of the Frontier," 32. See Trachtenberg, *Shades of Hiawatha*, 35; and Huhndorf, *Going Native*, 56.
29. Turner, "Significance of the Frontier," 33–34.
30. "American Studio Talk," *International Studio* 7 (June 1899), xiv.
31. Davis, *About Paris*, 189.
32. Lubow, *Reporter Who Would Be King*, 102.
33. For an exploration of this question with regard to the American colony in Giverny, see Werth, "Long Entwined Effort," 57–58. See also Burns, "Old World Anew," 47–50.
34. See Faragher, *Rereading Frederick Jackson Turner*, 3, 8; Rydell and Kroes, *Buffalo Bill and Bologna*, 99–100; and Rosaldo, *Culture & Truth*, 83.
35. Oltean, "I Longed for a New World," 271. See Tornsey, "Translation and Transubstantiation," 40–43.
36. Rydell and Kroes, *Buffalo Bill and Bologna*, 101–2; Rainger, "Buffalo Bill," 245; and Martin, "'Grandest and Most Cosmopolitan Object Teacher,'" 96, 110, 116.
37. Warren, *Buffalo Bill's America*, 293.
38. Quésaco, "Buffalo Bill et C°," *Le Figaro de la Tour*, May 19, 1889, 2; and Rydell and Kroes, *Buffalo Bill in Bologna*, 114–15.
39. Huard, *Livre d'or*, 1:233; C. S. Reinhart, "Sketches from the Paris Exposition," *Harper's Weekly*, June 22, 1889, 492.
40. Bullet, "Our Show: At the Great Exhibition Opened in Paris," *Brooklyn Daily Eagle*, May 30, 1889, 3. On Bullet's time in Paris, see Bullet, *Autobiography of Emma Bullet.*

41. Boime, "Chocolate Venus," 71; Warren, *Buffalo Bill's America*, 348–49; Dixon, "Introduction," xxi; Rainger, "Buffalo Bill," 243–45; Burns, *Rural Society and French Politics*; and Irvine, *Boulanger Affair Reconsidered.*
42. "L'élection du 27 janvier: L'affichage sur les monuments publics pendant la période électorale," *L'Illustration*, January 26, 1889, cover.
43. "Déjà il s'est fait précéder dans Paris par des affiches gigantesques et multicolores . . . Ces annonces américaines enflamment déjà les curiosités de collégiens." Eugène Rastignac, "Courrier de Paris," *L'Illustration*, May 11, 1889, 394. See A. R., "Nos Gravures: Buffalo Bill," 492; "L'élection du 27 janvier: La manifestation de la place de la République," *L'Illustration*, February 2, 1889, 100; P. Artout, "Au Pays des Indiens," *L'Illustration*, June 15, 1889, 506; and Sears, "Bierstadt, Buffalo Bill," 9.
44. "La Semaine Comique," *L'Illustration,* September 7, 1889, supplement, np.
45. "J'entends, monsieur mon imprimeur, que vous donniez à mes affiches électorales le caractère artistique de celles-ci, en me représentant en train de tomber le gouvernement."
46. "Adieu, brave général / ton prestige est non plus / Nous prenons pour régal / Le héro du 'Wild West' / Tout est en décadence / Militaire et civil / Chantez, vive la France / et vive Buffalo Bill!" *New York Sunday News,* August 11, 1889; "Buffalo Bill's Laudation," *San Francisco Morning Call,* September 8, 1889, 1889 Scrapbook, William F. "Buffalo Bill" Cody Collection, McCracken Research Library, Buffalo Bill Center of the West (hereafter William F. "Buffalo Bill" Cody Collection). See Rainger, "Buffalo Bill," 243.
47. On the Shah of Persia's visit, see "Le Première visite du Schah de Perse à l'Exposition," *Le Figaro de la Tour,* August 1, 1889, 1. On the "courses des taureaux," see "Bull-Fighting in Paris," *Te Aroha News*, August 31, 1889, 6.
48. "Du haut de la Tour Eiffel, les trois actualités de l'année: le Schah de Perse, Buffalo et les Courses de taureaux accusent Boulanger d'avoir accaparé toute la réclame ces derniers temps et le condamnent à passer au second plan."
49. In French "Royalistes, Bonapartistes, Camelots et Mufles Sauvages."
50. See Blanchard et al., *Human Zoos*, as well as the exhibition catalog Blanchard et al., *Human Zoos: The Invention of the Savage.*
51. Rennert, *100 Posters*, 3. This image appeared in postcard format in 1905 (Armstrong Postcard Collections, Buffalo Bill Museum & Grave, Lookout Mountain, Golden, Colo.).
52. See Mizrahi, "La génie publicitaire américain," 14–19; Hovet, "America on Display"; and Klein, "When Buffalo Bill Caracoled"; and Delaney, "Advance Work."
53. Both the Buffalo Bill Museum & Grave in Golden, Colorado, and the Buffalo Bill Center of the West in Cody, Wyoming, have this poster. It can be seen online at ww1.prweb.com/prfiles/2016/08/30/13631087/1.69.169-WFC_famous_friends.jpg.
54. "Buffalo Bill à Dunkerque," *Le Phare du Nord* (Dunkerque), March 3, 1905, and "Buffalo-Bill's en France," *Le Phare du Nord* (Dunkerque), March 11, 1905, both

1905 Scrapbook, William F. "Buffalo Bill" Cody Collection. See Rydell and Kroes, *Buffalo Bill in Bologna*, 31.

55. Wawro, *Franco-Prussian War*, 48–49, 74. On trains in modern France, see Rubin, *Impressionism and the Modern Landscape*, 91–119; and Schivelbusch, *Railway Journey*.
56. Tucker, *Monet in the '90s*, 7.
57. Griffin, *Four Years in Europe*, 69. On the show and military planning, see Sears, "Bierstadt, Buffalo Bill," 9.
58. "Surprise in Paris," *New York Herald* (European ed.), April 4, 1889, 1; Rainger, "Buffalo Bill," 247; Rennert, *100 Posters*, 3; Kasson, *Buffalo Bill's Wild West*, 87–88; and Weber, *France: Fin de Siècle*, 112–13.
59. The Western History and Genealogy Library at the Denver Public Library holds the series of photographs from Bonheur's visit to Buffalo Bill's Wild West, and the Whitney Western Art Museum at the Buffalo Bill Center of the West holds Bonheur's portrait of Cody.
60. "Le Napolèon de la Prairie." Rastignac, "Courrier de Paris," May 25, 1889. "Ils sont tous colonels." Rastignac, "Courier de Paris," May 11, 1889.
61. See Jonnes, *Eiffel's Tower*, 130; "Col. Cody and His Band," *Chicago Tribune*, May 11, 1889, 2; and "Le Roi du Far-West," *Le Petit Parisien*, March 30, 1905, 1905 scrapbook, William F. "Buffalo Bill" Cody Collection.
62. On constructions of American masculinity, see Kimmel, *Manhood in America*; and Kasson, *Houdini, Tarzan and the Perfect Man*. I am grateful to Corey Dzenko for suggesting these references.
63. On Roosevelt and masculinity, see Testi, "Gender of Reform Politics"; Watts, *Rough Rider in the White House*; and Bederman, *Manliness & Civilization*, 170–216.
64. Portes, *Fascination and Misgivings*, 218–19. For example, see Duthoit, *Les idées du président Roosevelt*; Klein, *Au pays de "la vie intense"*; and Savine, *Roosevelt intime*.
65. "Les Cavaliers les plus hardis du monde," *Rough Riders* 8 (1905): 3.
66. "Se trouve un certain nombre de 'cowboys' américains, audacieux cavaliers des prairies américaines et avec eux environ 50 chevaux appelés 'maniacs' que l'on ne peut ni dresser, ni dompter." "Buffalo-Bill's en France," 1905 Scrapbook.
67. "Un des plus intéressants numéros parmi les attractions de Buffalo-Bill est le harnachement et la montée de ces chevaux qui présentent les plus grandes difficultés et doit se faire dans les conditions les plus dangereuses." "Buffalo-Bill's en France," William F. "Buffalo Bill" Cody Collection. See "Les Cowboys dans la vie réelle," *Rough Riders* 9 (1906): 6; and "L'homme à cheval," *Rough Riders* 9 (1906): 7.
68. Forth, *Dreyfus Affair*; Cryle and Forth, *Sexuality at the Fin de Siècle*; Forth and Accampo, *Confronting Modernity in Fin-de-Siècle France*; Forth and Taithe,

French Masculinities; Forth, *Masculinity in the Modern West*; and Nye, *Crime, Madness & Politics.*

69. Braun, *Picturing Time*, 67–69. I am grateful to Ting Chang for suggesting this reference.
70. "Il nous faut préparer une génération d'hommes vigoureux." "Chronique," *La Louveraineté*, August 6, 1889, 1889 Scrapbook, William F. "Buffalo Bill" Cody Collection. See Reddin, *Wild West Shows*, 101. On Buffalo Bill instructing "bored" Frenchmen "to ride in the American style," see "Light and Flippant," *New York Times*, July 7, 1889, 4.
71. Pattie Miller Stocking, "Big Show in Paris," *Washington Post*, October 6, 1889, 16. On Stocking, see Jonnes, *Eiffel's Tower*, 253.
72. Stocking, "Big Show in Paris," 16.
73. Turner, "Problem of the West," 66.
74. On French cowboys and their dialogue with Buffalo Bill's Wild West, see Rainger, "French Cowboys," 167–78.
75. Boime, "Chocolate Venus," 76–77; Rydell and Kroes, *Buffalo Bill in Bologna*, esp. 97–119.
76. "Tour de fer, rêve de Yankee." Coppée, "Sur la tour Eiffel, deuxième plateau," in Lemoine, *Tour de Monsieur Eiffel*, 103. See also Lemoine, *Tour de Monsieur Eiffel*, 55; and "La Protestation des Artistes," *Le Temps*, February 14, 1887, ibid., 99.
77. Varigny, *Women of the United States*, 1. See also Stead, *Americanization of the World*.
78. Draner, cartoon, *L'Illustration*, July 27, 1889, supplement, np.
79. "Et vos chevaux, depuis le temps, restent donc toujours sauvages?" "Certes, nous les dressons pour ça." See A. R., "Nos Gravures: Buffalo Bill," 492.
80. Jonnes, *Eiffel's Tower*, 173–74; and "Gossip from Gay Paris," *Chicago Tribune*, July 28, 1889, 26.
81. Jonnes, *Eiffel's Tower*, 245–46; and Ashton and Hare, *Rosa Bonheur*, 145–46, 157.
82. See Westermeier, "Buffalo Bill's Cowboys Abroad," 289–90. In 1889 Scrapbook, see the following items: "Buffalo Bill," *Le Parisien*, October 17, 1889; "Fontainebleau: Les Chevaux Sauvages de Mlle Rosa Bonheur," *Echo de la Brie Meaux*, October 6, 1889; *La Presse*, September 30, 1889; *l'Autorité*, September 30, 1889; and *Galignani's Messenger*, October 16, 1889. See also Dwyer, "Rosa Bonheur," 69; and Stanton, *Reminiscences of Rosa Bonheur*, 246. "Les chevaux américains," *Rough Riders* 9 (1906), explains the unique lineage of American wild horses. This emphasis on taming recurred in 1905. See Klein, "When Buffalo Bill Caracoled," 16–19.
83. On this painting, see Notter, *New World Museum*, 51; and Lefrançois, *Les Indiens de Buffalo Bill*, 150, cat. 17.
84. Boime, "Chocolate Venus," 85–86; and Warren, *Buffalo Bill's America*, 32. In 1889, *L'Illustration* emphasized the cowboy as a live manifestation of Cooper's and Aimard's novels, which showed "the accidental existence, the rude labors, the

dexterity, and the heroism of the cow-boys who have come from America for the *Exposition.*" ("Fenimore Cooper et Gustave Aymard [*sic*] sont eux-mêmes restés bien loin de la réalité en essayant de nous faire connaître, dans leur romains, l'existence accidentée, les rudes labeurs, l'adresse et l'héroïsme de ces cow-boys qui nous sont venus d'Amérique pour l'Exposition.") in A. R., "Nos Gravures: Buffalo Bill," 492.

85. See Lefrançois, *Les Indiens de Buffalo Bill*, 147, cat. 1.

7

"Painting the Town Red"

Buffalo Bill's Indians in the German Media

JULIA S. STETLER

For over two centuries, Germans have sustained a deep fascination with America's frontier, the people who settled in the West, and especially its Native inhabitants. This fascination has drawn generations of Germans to the American West—first as explorers, then as immigrants, and now as tourists. It has engaged the attention of German artists, writers, and scientists and has influenced both popular entertainment and scholarly studies. Ultimately, the appeal of the American West has helped shape the relationship between the United States and Germany from the formation and expansion of both countries to the present day.

While writers and artists built much of the foundation for the German perception of the American West and its Natives, showmen played an equally important role. Arguably the most famous of the showmen, and one of the main architects of the mythic construct that is the American West in the German imagination, was William F. "Buffalo Bill" Cody. He traveled to Germany with his Wild West entertainment in 1890 and again in 1905, a crucial time in the formation of a German national consciousness and adjustment to the changes of modernity. While the German audiences welcomed Buffalo Bill's Wild West with great excitement and lavished equally glowing reviews on the show and its creator, a more critical examination of the German response reveals that "America's National Entertainment" conveyed distinctly different meanings for Germans and Americans. This examination of how and why American and German audiences processed the Wild West show differently addresses questions about the process of cultural translation and the deeply ingrained concepts of identity, heritage, and national consciousness in both the United States and Germany.

Throughout the 1800s and early 1900s, the German public had been heavily inundated with a wide variety of information about the American West. Travelogues describing landscape, resources, and struggles with American Indians, along with boosterish reports of progress and town building, steadily supplied the German and European market. Such reports and travel accounts had been circulating in Europe starting with the early explorations of the North American continent; however, demand for information about the United States increased significantly toward the middle of the nineteenth century. Emigration societies actively recruited new settlers, and thousands of Europeans pondered the option of relocation, often drawing on travel reports to inform their decision. Journalists and travelers brought back tales of spectacular adventures and scenery, of vanishing Indian tribes, and of an abundance of free land and resources. The travelers were followed by immigrants, who sent back exuberant (and often vastly exaggerated) accounts of their economic success.

Moreover, novels set in the American West and featuring western characters began to flood the European market, vastly contributing to an ever-burgeoning body of literature on the American frontier. Early on, James Fenimore Cooper deeply inspired Germans' imaginations with his adventurous *Leatherstocking Tales,* or *Lederstrumpf.* The five volumes appeared between 1823 and 1841 and made Cooper the most translated American author in Germany. As in the United States, these books became a staple of youth literature and profoundly shaped German notions of Indians, America, and the developing frontier across the nineteenth century. Through the countless reproductions of Cooper's novels, the German fascination with American Indians intensified. Indeed, a series of German travel writers and novelists built on the success of those stories and created their own brand of "made in Germany" westerns. By writing about American Indians, in particular, they became best-selling authors during the remainder of the nineteenth century and well into the twentieth. The most prominent of these was Karl May, whose books have sold over two hundred million copies worldwide, about the same number as the most well-known American author of westerns, Louis L'Amour.[1] The American world, emerging between the pages of books, was complemented by visual impressions. Sketches and paintings of American landscapes illustrated the riveting stories published in journals and newspapers. Together, they created an image in Europeans' minds of adventure, opportunity, and romance in the far West.[2]

A second major element for the success of Buffalo Bill's Wild West in Germany was the German "love affair" with the American Indian, which had been a stable element of the German imagination even before the arrival of the Wild West. The Indian's rise to a status of cultural iconography was in part inspired and perpetuated by the traveling ethnographic exhibits that gained popularity in Europe and Germany in the second half of the nineteenth century. In their early incarnations, the shows featured one or two individuals from an "exotic" location.[3] Usually taken against their will and exhibited in a cage at local fairs, they were vulnerable to the oftentimes hostile or fearful responses of the paying audiences. During the course of the nineteenth century, this fair event of gawking at strangers morphed into proper "ethnographic exhibits," or *Völkerschauen,* as they were termed. These shows included a choreographed performance with fairly elaborate sets and a larger cast, which frequently consisted of a family unit or group of hunters. With the rise of colonial ambitions and therefore an increased interest in and exposure to "the other," the focus shifted from a "cabinet-of-horrors" to a "cabinet-of-curiosities" approach, and early showmen redesigned their exhibits accordingly. Aimed at education and entertainment rather than fear and shock, the new venue of the *Völkerschau* offered the visitor a glimpse of the life, customs, and manners of other cultures.

From 1874 until roughly 1931, these shows were a German mass phenomenon but also existed in other European countries. Toward the end of the nineteenth century, exhibits of "live specimens" from "exotic" places were gradually reframed in terms of science, especially physical anthropology and natural history, which were just emerging as scientific fields. Anthropologists frequently visited the shows to conduct scientific measurements or record languages and customs. This further legitimated the authenticity of the exhibits to the general public and elevated their respectability. Since they were also entertaining and often well-choreographed, the *Völkerschauen* were more easily consumable by a much wider audience than the previous fair exhibits. Buffalo Bill's Wild West therefore must be seen in the context of this tradition of ethnographic exhibits and as a continuation of this phenomenon. In fact, the 1893 edition of *Meyers Konversations-Lexikon* defined the American spectacle as the latest incarnation of "anthropological exhibitions" or "performances of representative foreign peoples for the satisfaction of visual pleasure and the dissemination of anthropological knowledge."

While several popular anthropological exhibits included American Indians before the Wild West's arrival, the majority consisted of peoples recruited from Africa and Oceania, and by the end of the century, German newspapers bemoaned an oversupply of these troupes, whose presence began to seem almost banal to German audiences. A reporter in Berlin articulated this growing fatigue, while at the same time expressing one of the reasons why Buffalo Bill's Wild West was met with such extraordinary success: "black skin color has become so ordinary and familiar that even the most exotic, thick-lipped, heathen, uncivilized, and rapacious Negro races can hardly arouse much interest with us anymore." However, he remarked, "there is something different about the Indian races and everything that has to do with Prairie life in North America. Today, despite the fact that steamships have already put North America on the map of even the most casual tourist, despite the fact that America no longer seems so distant, so exotic, so foreign to us, Indians and everything associated with them continue to exert a powerful, indescribable force of attraction."[4]

The roots of this force of attraction to the United States and its Native inhabitants reach deep into the very fabric of German cultural identity. In fact, the connection can be traced back as far as the first century to the writings of the Roman senator Cornelius Tacitus. In his work *Germania,* he portrayed Germans as a noble tribal people who lived in the forests of central Europe and who suffered at the hands of the Roman colonial civilization. As H. Glenn Penny argued in his study *Kindred by Choice,* Tacitus "wrote about Germans much in the same way German authors would later write about American Indians, as noble savages and formidable, violent warriors with painted faces, living in forest dwellings, whose most honorable qualities exposed the decadence and failings of the civilized world."[5]

Tacitus's work became an influential point of reference for Germans seeking to better understand themselves and their place in the world. The characterizations of Germans as brave, honest, loyal, and physically powerful offered a natural comparison to American Indians. As Penny further demonstrated, as early as the seventeenth century, "German writers conflated the ancient Teutons portrayed by Tacitus with contemporary American Indians, and by the middle of the nineteenth century such comparisons circulated widely."[6] American Indians were cast into a brotherly role, which laid the foundation for a mythical connection that blended their identities in the German perception. The German cultural imagination created and adopted an "ideal Indian" who embodied the elements of the noble savage (pure, uncorrupted, simple yet resourceful, one with nature) along with a host of dearly held German values with which every German could identify, such as Christianity, honesty, reliability, and bravery. In fact, German writer Karl May's literary creation of the Apache chief Winnetou is the personification of this imaginary cultural hybrid. Native American by birth, Winnetou assumed German values and became a symbol for the ideal combination of noble Native American heritage and the values that Germans had adopted for themselves. He remains one of the most powerful and enduring cultural icons in German cultural history.[7] Thus, at the close of the nineteenth century, Germans felt a strong romantic and nostalgic affection for peoples threatened by the march of civilization and identified with American Indians on a profound, cultural level.

The connection with the "noble savage" was also augmented by a feeling of loss of cultural bearings at a time when Germany was undergoing rapid industrial change and modernization. Nostalgia for a simpler life in the past sans uncertainties, the massive demographic and economic changes, and the acceleration of modern life caused many Germans to associate American Indians with notions of nature and simplicity, with a lifestyle less driven by the demands of modern life. They became a vessel for German longings and desires and assumed an idealized role in the German cultural imagination.

Thus, the stars for Buffalo Bill's arrival in Germany could not have been better aligned: Germans were more than ready to welcome this escapist utopia William Cody was offering, complete with adventure, romance, and American Indians, all packaged into a spectacular show. Additionally, to now see with their own eyes the Indians that they had previously encountered only in travel reports and in between the pages of books was spectacular for Germans. The first German tour started in Munich in April of 1890. Daily performances attracted more than five thousand spectators, and the show sold out consistently. In fact, the performances in Munich were extended eight days owing to high demand. King Ludwig of Bavaria and his court attended, and many camped out over night to get tickets. Wherever the show went, thousands of people had to be turned away at the doors, and those who did not manage to secure a ticket tried to catch a glimpse perched on top of nearby buildings or standing outside the periphery. The exhibition visited fifteen other locations in Germany in 1890 and 1891, including Frankfurt, Berlin, Dresden, Hamburg, and Cologne, repeating the tremendous success from Munich everywhere it went. The spectacular acts captured the German audience just as they had in other European countries and the United States.

However, it was not just the performance itself that awed visitors: the show grounds also included the camp, which encompassed the sleeping quarters of the cast members, the stockyards and corrals for the buffalo and horses, the kitchen and dining tents, and several exhibit tents. It was a part of the show that enhanced its authenticity and made it feel less a circus and more like a real-life microcosm of the actual frontier. Visitors had access to the camp, allowing them to peek into Indian teepees, watch the cowboys play cards, visit the kitchen tent and mess hall and talk to Annie Oakley, Buffalo Bill, or Buck Taylor, the "King of the Cowboys." It created the impression that the Wild West was not merely a show or some circus, but that these were authentic people from the frontier, giving a true demonstration of life as they had lived it. The modern technology and equipment elevated the performance to a spectacle, setting it apart from the previous *Völkerschauen* in choreography, cast size, and overall production values and scale.

The advertising machinery for the Wild West was sophisticated and operated on a massive scale, plastering cities and newspapers with colorful posters and announcements of the exhibition's arrival. Show organizers also secured the comfort of the audience by contracting with local vendors to erect champagne bars, cigar parlors, and establishments that offered confections and restaurant-quality meals on the grounds of the show. The spectacle of the performance, the access to the camp, combined with the massive advertising campaign and the fact that the company usually stayed in each city for an extended period of time (sometimes up to a month) during its first tour of continental Europe, generated extensive and detailed newspaper coverage of the show in each city it visited. This body of newspaper reports forms the primary source for understanding how the German audience responded to the Wild West.

Especially during this first tour, the longer stays afforded reporters the opportunity to visit the camp, to receive private tours—including visits to the stars' tents and interviews with Buffalo Bill and Annie Oakley—and to stroll around the camp at a leisurely pace to observe the customs of American

Indians, cowboys, and vaqueros, and even to acquaint themselves with the bucking horses and buffalo. The result is an abundance of eyewitness accounts, which were often lengthy or even serialized over several days to sustain the buzz the show created in each city. The accounts provide an invaluable record of genuine German reactions to the exhibition, which would otherwise be nearly impossible to ascertain, especially when considering that a significant portion of the coverage in the papers was based on promotional material disseminated by the production itself. The value of the eyewitness reports becomes yet clearer when comparing the news coverage generated by the two tours of the Wild West through Germany. By the time the show returned to Europe and Germany in 1905–1906, its nature had changed dramatically: Cody had partnered with the Barnum and Bailey Circus and had adopted a different production schedule. The exhibition stopped in each city for only a day. Consequently, newspaper reporters had only one opportunity to visit the performance and the camp, leading to a significantly smaller local record of the second tour of Germany. Most of the coverage for this later tour is based exclusively on the material provided to papers by Buffalo Bill's Wild West.

One of the most striking aspects of the German reaction to the Wild West is the way the German audiences adapted and refracted the underlying messages the Wild West spectacle was carrying with it. When William Cody created the show, he masterfully captured American hopes and anxieties at the time. He espoused Manifest Destiny and the superiority of white civilization through the battles with the Indians in the arena, who always attacked and always lost, in an ironic inverted version of conquest, as Richard White has argued.[8] The show was also imbued with manifestations of progress and celebrations of American national pride, such as the reenactment of a Pony Express stop, the prominent display of the American flag, or the endlessly embellished heroic tales of the show's participants in the accompanying program. Thus, Cody's interpretation of American history was shaped to perpetuate a positive national identity for Americans.[9]

The Wild West was also a success because it allowed the audience to "experience" frontier life exactly at the time when the census and historians were proclaiming the frontier days to be closed. By playing on frontier anxiety and using powerful icons of a vanishing American origin story, the message of the show attached itself to the core of American identity at the turn of the century.[10] In that sense, Cody's Wild West served the nation's construction of identity in creating a collective memory that sanitized the past, justified conquest, and unified Americans by stressing a common glorious past instead of an uncertain future. By erasing ambiguity and, instead, concentrating on a simplified and compelling narrative (such as overcoming savagery), the memory of the past became a repository for shared meanings in the modern world. Americans could experience the frontier vicariously from their seats in the show arena without risking the consequences of struggle and conflict. Even the Indians, who can perhaps be considered the quintessential trophy of conquest, got back up on their feet and waved to the audience after having been shot. Furthermore, the Wild West offered an escape into a past in which the march of civilization was inevitable and exciting (much more so than city life). No matter how dangerous the situation, Buffalo Bill would always save the day in the end. He was the stable element, always reliable and recognizable. Qualities and values that seemed to be disappearing in the modernizing world were found in abundance in the colorful, dramatic, and thrilling world of Buffalo Bill.[11]

The spectacle assumed a different meaning when it was transferred to the German cultural context. Audiences ignored or reinterpreted the cultural clues that American audiences responded to the most and instead attached a specifically German set of values. Germans applied a much more critical lens to the concept of Manifest Destiny, often rooting for the Indians, especially when they were faced with ruthless white "bandits" who used questionable moral tactics to attain their goals. Exactly because they were *not* Americans, the imagery in the Wild West did not elicit the same patriotic sentiments or feelings of cultural belonging as it did for Americans. Historian Eric Ames has argued that the success of the show in Germany was largely the result of a process of "vivification" of heroic literary characters, allowing German audiences to "take possession of the American entertainment and make it their own."[12] It is certainly true that the performers and acts in the arena gave life to these fictional characters that never existed in reality, and thus made many a spectator's childhood dream about participating in an adventure story come true. However, the nature of the German response to the American show was informed by more complex and inclusive contexts.

A practical illustration of the differences in the perception of Indians is the portrayal of a domestic scene from the Wild West in American and German newspapers. A German article from June 1890 featured a detailed description of the skills needed to assemble a teepee, the appearance of the camp, the dances and foot races, and the physical appearance of the Indians:

"The majority is almost naked, exposing the dense muscles of their upper body, arms and legs. The skin and faces are painted in bright red, yellow, and oranges, and around their wrists and ankles they are wearing brass or silver bands." The author further described the feathers and weapons worn by the Indians and the dances they performed: "This colorful bunch is starting to move according to the rhythm of three tambourines with short jumping steps that make the bells that are attached to them jingle, uttering abrupt yells while the drummers play their monotone ways." He closed his article with the comment that "the German audience would have liked to see more of these intimate scenes from the everyday life of the Indians."[13] The tone of this article is exceedingly positive and reflects a deep curiosity about domestic routines and cultural practices of American Indians.

In the United States, descriptions of the same scene belittled and mocked the Indians. Five years before the German article quoted above, the *Chicago Tribune* noted in 1885 that "the Indian dances were grotesque and funny, but rather tame. The warriors gathered in a circle, stamped their feet and jerked their bodies in time to the monotonous music from a couple of tum-tums, keeping up a continuous falsetto squeaking, and looking as hideous as possible."[14] Thirteen years later, descriptions of Indians in the United States had not altered significantly, and even the Wild West's program perpetuated the caricature: "Their paint and feathers, their hook-noses, serpent-like lips, cold, glittering black eyes and haughty port mark them as the genuine thing. Their war dances are enough to make one have bad dreams—the bowing, mowing figures; grinning gibbering faces, the gaudy, bird-like dresses—unsettling and eerie."[15]

German appropriation of "America's National Entertainment" extends well beyond the concepts of vivification and ethnological interest: Germans not only dismissed the elements that worked so well in the American context but also applied a dualistic framework to the representation of Native Americans in the show. The Indians they encountered inside the arena did not correspond with reality in the German estimation; their portrayal as adversaries to the American settlers was too belligerent and theatrical and did not reflect German stereotypes about the character of American Indians. Therefore, the acts that included Indians pitched directly against Americans, the very acts that were considered the highlights in the American reception, were almost dismissed by the German audiences as too staged and theatrically overdrawn. In contrast, whenever the Indians exited the arena and enjoyed "off-duty" time away from the show, perhaps with a German beer at a cultural event, every detail was relayed in the next day's papers. In those instances, the German romantic stereotypes were confirmed, and anthropological interests could be satisfied by observing the Indians in a more "natural" and "realistic" setting.

Evidence and an explanation for this dualistic view can be found in abundance in the German papers: during the show and inside the arena, the German audience did not find the Indians to be the most interesting and exciting act. Quite the opposite, many newspapers stressed that the trick riding was the highlight. For example, a Frankfurt newspaper asked, "what does the experienced Buffalo Bill show us? The poor Indians who were his friends all throughout his life, are just simple accessories to his show, the main attraction are the cowboys, his troupe, and he himself."[16]

This shift of focus for German audiences stems from their perception that the horsemanship demonstrations were the most *genuine* part of the show, much more so than the violent acts performed by the Native Americans. This reveals that the German public was indeed very aware of the theatricality and showmanship that permeated the show, and especially of those acts that were heavily scripted and cast the Indian in the role of the aggressor, such as the attacks on the Deadwood stagecoach and the emigrant train. A Berlin paper explained that "no matter how much the individual acts and the fights between redskins and whites excite you, no matter how much our fantasies of Indian stories from our youth are invoked, it is hard to deny that they only represent an illusion of authenticity and feel a little forced and theatrical." According to the reporter, this representation of the acts and the Indians within them even "slightly impedes the Romanticism of the wilderness and of prairie life that speaks from this performance."[17]

The Indian in the arena clearly did not correspond closely enough with the German image of the noble savage, who lived in harmony with nature and fit so easily into the German creation myth, and who deserved respect and sympathy. Instead, the Indian in the arena corresponded with American notions of a belligerent adversary who had to be conquered as part of a process of national self-realization. The element of struggle that was introduced by the Wild West was crucial to American ideology but did not at all serve the same purpose in the German perception; on the contrary, it corrupted the existing stereotypes of the noble Indian. In short, the feature that constituted the show's primary claim to authenticity elsewhere lost that authority in Germany because of the way it was presented.

Even in the descriptions of the violent struggles in the arena, German reporters were able to see beneath the superficial layer of savagery and wildness and dismissed the authenticity of the Indian portrayal. In the words of a Leipzig reporter, the Indians' "wildness is just painted on."[18] Instead of the Indians' ferocity, the report focused more strongly on ethnological elements: "their wild hair and the sparkling lances are decorated with feathers, their feet and hands are embellished with bells, and they are all bow-legged but wiry, with strong and well-developed upper bodies." They were "body-painted and move with a certain daintiness and lightness that reminds one of a dance."[19]

Whenever Indians were encountered outside the arena or talked about as a "concept," their image corresponded once more with the German imagination; they were perceived as significantly less antagonistic compared with how the show presented them. In fact, while Germans relived their childhood dreams of adventure in the Wild West, the spectacle prompted the audience to reflect critically on the situation of the Indians in America and on the reservations. The plight of the Indian generated significant sympathy in the papers, and when rumors about mistreatment surfaced while the show stayed in Hamburg in 1890, the German press responded with indignation and uproar.[20] A significant number of articles were very progressive when measured against the usual standards of the time; a Leipzig paper published a long essay on the wrongs committed against Indians by the American government and the terrible influence of civilization on the Indians, whose lifestyle was being "corrupted by alcohol, smallpox, and the teachings of the Mormon Church. The European influence causes degradation of nature's people, poisoning the very air the Indians breathe."[21] The reporter further explained that "civilization tools" such as forced farming, religious indoctrination, and Indian schools estranged the Indians from the land and corrupted their character, causing them "to develop the same fraudulent and dubious qualities as white Americans." Overall, German reporters were quite well-informed about conditions on the reservations and were not afraid to openly voice their opinions.

Indians were frequently seen in the cities, where they went to local stores, restaurants, cultural events such as theater and opera performances, and sightseeing destinations. This was of course part of the advertising for the show but also offered them the opportunity to escape the camp and experience the "host culture." They were an instant attraction and were soon surrounded and accompanied by throngs of curious people: "We saw the Indians downtown today. They caused a tremendous congestion, and women and children were warned to stay away for fear of being trampled. Of course, they were the ones in the first rows."[22] Most of the newspaper reports contained expressions of curiosity and awe, comments about the Indians' civilized behavior, and a touch of pride at having come into contact with these "most interesting specimens of humanity."[23] A Leipzig paper noted in detail the Indians' dress when they were seen shopping in the city and commented very positively on their "good taste in clothing" after they had bought "big cashmere plaids like our ladies wear traveling." Even though they neither spoke German, English, nor French, they "knew how to communicate with sign language very well. In order to understand the price of something, the chief took a handful of *Mark* coins and had the right amount counted out, knowing that one *Thaler* is worth three *Mark.*" When they left the store the crowd that had gathered outside cheered and applauded, which the "brown gentlemen received with dignity," as if it was "long-familiar homage."[24] According to the reporters, the "demeanor of these people was dignified and determined," they appeared "extraordinarily decent," and "it was very educational to meet them face to face."[25] Judging by the tone of these articles, the reporters regarded the Indians not at all as uneducated members of a lesser species but as resourceful travelers who graciously indulged a rather juvenile European admiration. Newspaper reports from other cities frequently corroborated these impressions.

Aside from shopping, the Indians and other cast members of the Wild West also participated in local cultural events. A Dresden paper reported that the *Concertgarten* at the *Cafe Imperial* was filled to capacity for its opera and waltz concert. Notably, the "complete Indian troupe was present and seated at a big table. The strange guests enjoyed beer and lemonade, and later also Colonel Cody and a few other gentlemen of the show appeared. The Indians raptly listened to the sounds of the band and applauded abundantly. A repeat is probable."[26] The article emphasized the show members' appreciation for the concert and the venue as a whole, suggesting a positive reception and acceptance of Indians and Americans in German society. They were not seen as savages but as civilized: since they were enjoying a sophisticated concert, they clearly had an appreciation for art and cultured entertainment, which in turn was incompatible with the notion of barbarity or savagery.

Other newspaper articles demonstrate not just the attention Indians received when moving around in the city but also their appreciation for the country's culinary specialties. In Dortmund, for example, they enjoyed a trip through the local breweries, eliciting the following comment: "Even though many people at first thought they were on the war path, the 'wild' Indians have acquired quite a tame attitude. It turned out that instead of thirsting for blood, they thirsted for beer because they were on the 'beer-path.' Cheers!"[27] Interestingly, it seemed not to have been a problem for the show's management to allow the consumption of alcohol in public, even though Cody was reportedly very concerned about his reputation as a "good steward" of the Indians and thus supposedly did not allow them to drink.[28] On the other hand, there are plenty of newspaper articles that give evidence that Indians frequented bars and beer halls and came to appreciate German brews.[29] It is nearly impossible that they could have done so behind Cody's back, and he therefore must have at least tolerated it. A newspaper reported that "a group of Indians visited the beer hall today and enjoyed the best brew of their lives. Their delight clearly showed on their dark faces."[30] Perhaps the Indians' consumption and appreciation of German beer heightened the German feeling of connection; since the Indians appreciated one of Germany's most cherished products, Germans could not help but feel flattered.

Overall, Indians were humanized through the numerous encounters with the German public. They were fascinating and romantic and utterly interesting because of their differences and their similarities in the German cultural imagination. Their appreciation of German products and their plight at home earned them the regard of the German audiences. The Indians' public appearances left lasting images in the German imagination and perpetuated the romantic stereotypes that had formed over time. As historian Paul Reddin noted, Indians were "seen less as bloody barbarians than as quiet and quite civilized individuals." In Germany especially, few newspapers mentioned the violent nature of the Indians but instead used "attributes such as 'romantic,' and 'nature's men'" and stressed "the demise of Indians and buffalo."[31]

Supporting the argument of a positive and romanticized perception of the Indian outside of the arena, an examination of the descriptions of the Indians in the newspapers further reveals that they were described in similar fashion as foreign royalty. In contrast to the show program that emphasized their natural belligerence, the chiefs especially were portrayed as proud, noble, and deliberate in interviews.[32] Rocky Bear, for example, who traveled with the Wild West in Europe between 1889 and 1892, was considered the representative and speaker for the different Indians in the troupe and greatly impressed the press with his noble, proud, and self-confident demeanor in his interactions with reporters, the nobility, politicians, and the general visitor. He was respectfully titled "medicine man" and "chief."[33] His assertive personality and air of authority seem to have generated feelings of nervousness and awe among the German reporters. It was Rocky Bear who appeared before the Anthropological Society of Berlin and gave an eloquent and riveting speech about the plight of Native Americans. Historian Eric Ames describes how Rocky Bear "took the podium with the *gravitas* of an elder statesman" and gave a performance that was "oratory, unrehearsed, and overtly political in content."[34] Augmenting his speech with hand movements that fascinated members of the audience, Rocky Bear openly challenged the US government. He finished his speech by appealing directly to the audience: "Look at my hand! It is black, but the heart in my breast beats like your heart, in feelings of friendship; our skin colors are different, our hearts are one."[35] Rocky Bear's rhetoric emphasized the affinity between German sentiments and the Indians, which transcended racial theories and created a lasting bond.

Other reporters described their personal experience with the Indians in the camp in similar, dignified terms that demonstrate respect and veneration for the Indians: "Our reporter visited the Indians during their break yesterday morning. Quiet, with dignity and unmoving facial features they were sitting there, leaning against the tents. One of the Cheyenne chiefs seemed to be especially dignified; his tribe is back on the war path."[36] Their nobility and graceful demeanor bespoke an important facet of Indian lore in the German imagination: the Indians might have been conquered, but they could not be subjugated. They were proud and noble despite their defeat.

The portrayal of the American Indian as bloodthirsty savages and the pitting of Indians against their conqueror in the show has been the subject of harsh criticism of Buffalo Bill and other Wild West show organizers. In the eyes of scholars such as Philip Deloria Jr., Cody can be justifiably accused of not representing the Indian adequately, as complex enough, differentiated enough, multidimensional enough, or even peaceful enough. Scholars rightly observe that Native American representation remained on the level of one-dimensional, simplified characters that reflected only the dichotomy between good and evil. Obviously, this was exactly the role that they needed to play and that was ascribed to them by Cody. Deloria also lamented that "Native peoples themselves have acquiesced to pictures made of them by others and now perceive of themselves in terms of such stereotypes."[37]

As much as this characterization might be true in the representation of the Indian in the show arena, it is only one half of the image that most Germans carried away from the stay of the Wild West in their town. The other and more significant half consisted of what they saw outside of the arena, which corresponded more with their own preconceptions and ideas and, consequently, was more easily absorbed into their existing mental world. Thus, even though Buffalo Bill's Indians in the arena represented the bloodthirsty adversary that the cowboys needed to reinforce the ideological message of civilization overcoming savagery, Buffalo Bill also perpetuated and reinforced the "positive" stereotypes about Indians in Germany. This dual view of Native Americans is crucial to understanding the German reception of the Wild West exhibition and supports the idea that Germans did not absorb the American ideology behind the show unequivocally and uncritically. Instead, they separated the representation of the Indians into two distinct entities, dismissing their representation in the arena as unrealistic and overdrawn and instead focusing on the ways in which the Indians propagated the positive stereotypes of nobility and brotherhood. Even though other nations in Europe were not uncritical, German reactions to this element of the exhibition certainly stand out.

That being said, some newspapers also printed critical or expressly negative views of the Indians. Despite the strength of the Indian myth in Germany, and keeping in mind that Germans were arguably more romantically infatuated with the Indian than other European nations and certainly their American counterparts were, Germans held views no less ethnocentric than their European neighbors. Theories of social Darwinism and the superiority of the white race certainly did influence German thinking, and examples of this kind of ambivalence in attitude toward Indians also occur in German newspapers. Some newspapers accentuated the Indians' uncivilized behavior, sometimes in quite degrading language. One reporter complained about the "ugly Indian custom" of dining out without paying, and then noted that "when considering that one of the main acts of the Indians in the show is the robbing and murder of a paleface, swindling appears as a comparatively innocent amusement."[38] Strikingly, this article references the Indian actions in the arena and the "barbarism" they portray there, which reinforces the dualistic image of the Indian.

One of the lengthiest and telling negative exposés about the stay of the Wild West in Germany appeared in a Dresden paper in June of 1890. Since over 100,000 people visited the "Indian company" in these two weeks, the reporter contemplated whether this American influence had been positive. He contended that the "Dark Men" have taught its citizens multiple "bad habits," ranging from lasso throwing among the youth—"during which, one must fear, our little ones could possibly choke each other"—to much more serious allegations among the adult population.[39] In fact, he suggested that an incidence of a murder was connected to the violent nature of the Wild West and its negative influence on the peaceful "members of a civilized nation." He further argued that the situation in the streets was virtually life threatening "whenever the Red Skins show themselves, due to the huge crowds that consist to a great part of women and our beloved school children." Lastly, he even stated his belief that the Indians were taking advantage of the inhabitants of Dresden, "extracting large sums of money from this city, more than from Vienna or Munich. The people of Dresden are very susceptible to performances. The Indians once again proved that."[40] There is no evidence for a particular "susceptibility" of the Dresden audience; the author's claims undoubtedly originate from his general uneasiness and ethnocentrism and are not grounded in verifiable fact.

The author of this article not only repeated the stereotypes of Indians as a negative and dangerous influence on a normally very civilized society but also feared damage to the women and children of Dresden owing to their exposure to this "barbaric lot." By warning his readership that the "wild people are in town," he hinted that no one could be safe while Buffalo Bill resided within the city walls. Even more tellingly, he ignored the fact that *white* Americans, and *not* the Indians, managed the show and reaped most of the profits from their performance in Dresden. Even though the reporter relied heavily on ethnocentric prejudices, it is nevertheless interesting that he granted the Indians a measure of authority they did not possess. In the eyes of this reporter, the Indians became a primary metonym for the West.

Criticism of a different kind was voiced by an article that appeared in Meitzen in June 1890. It demonstrates the permeation of German culture with Indian lore and the way stereotypes and expectations can distort perception. This comment also directly challenges the Wild West's claim to be an authentic and ethnological exhibition:

> It is an apparent flaw of the *Wild West* Company that they did not take more care to make this outer appearance of the Indian camp more interesting. Apart from beautiful scalps and other furs, they could have gathered a rich collection of old Indian weaponry and exhibited other Indian products, as we, mutatis mutandis, witnessed it during the exhibit of the Singhalese. Indian women make pretty pottery, and feather and pearl embroidery,

> and are highly appreciated in America as carpet weavers. Of all this, nothing is apparent in the *Wild West* and therefore it is missing the atmosphere that would effectively prepare the visitor for the Indian scenes.[41]

Other reports mention the fact that even during the performance, some spectators mocked the Indians, stating that they supposedly sounded like market criers praising their goods: "The chief's war cry in its long-drawn out sounds caused the misfortune of provoking the audience to holler back: 'Dutch herring!'"[42]

These alternative views demonstrate that the perception of Native Americans in Germany was not homogenous; Germany, and Europe by extension, was and is a complex conglomerate of cultures and values and cannot be regarded as a monolithic mass. As Robert Rydell and Rob Kroes note in *Buffalo Bill in Bologna*, culture and its interpretation has to be considered "along fluid, symbiotic, and dialectical lines, rather than in terms of mutually exclusive categories that decontextualize complex historical processes."[43] While many Germans shared the romantic nostalgia and attraction for Native Americans, scores of Germans rejected the romantic notions and instead adopted a more critical or dismissive stance toward American Indians.

Clearly, culture cannot be transferred into a different national context without experiencing some degree of transformation or reinterpretation. The process of transmission of one culture to another is not linear but rather a complex interchange of ideas, habits, information, symbols, and stereotypes that constantly reinterpret themselves and each other. Thus, meaning does not flow unilaterally from the point of production to its reception. Germans overwhelmingly disregarded the American expressions of national pride and Manifest Destiny central to American identity and instead took the Indians out of the context of the show, imbuing them with German notions of nobility and romantic nostalgia. When Buffalo Bill took his show to Europe, it surpassed his wildest dreams in terms of revenue and raising America's esteem in Europe; however, it did so in ways and for reasons that eluded even the visionary and entrepreneurial genius of William Cody. Continuing and expanding the tradition of ethnographic exhibits in Germany, Buffalo Bill's Wild West firmly planted a romanticized image of American Indians into the cultural iconography of the German imagination, where they remained well into the early decades of the twentieth century, and arguably still occupy a visible role today.

Notes

1. Despite being the best-selling German writer of all time, Karl May remains virtually unknown in the English-speaking world. His books have only recently been translated into readable English. The classics are *Winnetou,* vols. 1–3, and *The Oil Prince.*
2. In 1839, George Catlin toured Europe with his Indian Gallery, and even though he did not visit Germany, his work was reproduced in German media along with heavily romanticized descriptions of the vanishing Indian tribes.
3. *Exotic* meant places like the West Indies, Australia, Greenland, Africa, or the Amazon region of South America.
4. *Lokal-Anzeiger* (Berlin), July 24, 1890. This and all other German newspaper clippings cited in this chapter can be found in the William F. "Buffalo Bill" Cody Collection, MS 6, McCracken Research Library, Buffalo Bill Center of the West.
5. Penny's study explores the striking sense of affinity for American Indians that has permeated German culture for two centuries. It shows how those affinities stem from German polycentrism, notions of tribalism, a devotion to resistance, a longing for freedom, and a melancholy sense of shared fate. It also details the ways in which the Germans' fascination with the American West was connected both to their long-term interactions with the United States as well as the transnational world of German culture that spread across the Atlantic during the nineteenth century. Penny, *Kindred by Choice,* 30.
6. Ibid.
7. This phenomenon has been widely noted. See, for example, "In Germany, Wild for Winnetou." *New York Times,* September 12, 2007, or the remake of the 1964 *Winnetou* movies, which aired in Germany in time for Christmas in 2016 with the intent to "rekindle our sustained love for Winnetou and pass it on to a new generation of Germans."
8. White, "Frederick Jackson Turner and Buffalo Bill," 133.
9. The disruptions caused by the Civil War also extended to notions of American identity. Historians have argued that Buffalo Bill helped restore the nation's sense of continuity and history by providing a unifying, victorious, and sanitized version of American history that all Americans could identify with, no matter which side they had fought for in the war. The West served as neutral ground on which to rally and restore. See for example Deverell, "Redemptive West."
10. According to historian David Wrobel, the emergence of "frontier anxiety" had "affected the thinking of considerable numbers of Americans." Deeply ingrained beliefs in an agrarian Eden in the West were uprooted and replaced with a fear of an industrialism that would destroy the salutary effects of an unspoiled relationship between man and nature, the very relationship that had formed the exceptional character of the rugged frontiersmen in the West. The disappearance of free land would ultimately change society and caused a nostalgic wave to sweep over America. See Wrobel, *End of American Exceptionalism,* 25.

11. For a discussion about the convergence of fact and fiction and Buffalo Bill's impact on popular memory in the United States, see Joy Kasson, *Buffalo Bill's Wild West.*
12. Ames, "Seeing the Imaginary," 214.
13. *Dresden Journal*, Dresden, June 7, 1890, William F. "Buffalo Bill" Cody Collection.
14. *Chicago Tribune*, Chicago, May 18, 1885, William F. "Buffalo Bill" Cody Collection.
15. Show Program, 1898, William F. "Buffalo Bill" Cody Collection.
16. *Frankfurter Nachrichten,* October 1, 1890, William F. "Buffalo Bill" Cody Collection.
17. *Berliner Fremdenblatt,* July 25, 1890, William F. "Buffalo Bill" Cody Collection.
18. *Stadt- und Dorfanzeiger* (Leipzig), June 19, 1890, William F. "Buffalo Bill" Cody Collection.
19. Ibid.
20. The allegations against Cody garnered a significant amount of press coverage, and Cody traveled back to the United States to assuage the public. American newspapers commented on the events, as for example, "Explicit Denial of the Various Charges Made against 'Buffalo Bill.'" *New York Herald*, July 24, 1890, William F. "Buffalo Bill" Cody Collection.
21. No paper name noted, but the scrapbook location in the William F. "Buffalo Bill" Cody Collection indicates Leipzig, most likely June 21, 1890.
22. *Anzeiger* (Dresden), June 11, 1890, William F. "Buffalo Bill" Cody Collection.
23. Ibid.
24. *Stadt und Dorf-Anzeiger* (Leipzig), June 22, 1890, William F. "Buffalo Bill" Cody Collection.
25. *Tageblatt und Anzeiger* (Leipzig), June 19, 1890, William F. "Buffalo Bill" Cody Collection.
26. *Anzeiger* (Dresden), June 11, 1890, William F. "Buffalo Bill" Cody Collection.
27. *General Anzeiger* (Dortmund), May 5, 1891, William F. "Buffalo Bill" Cody Collection.
28. *Dresdner Journal,* June 4, 1890, William F. "Buffalo Bill" Cody Collection.
29. *Hamburger Nachrichten,* October 19, 1890, William F. "Buffalo Bill" Cody Collection.
30. Ibid.
31. Reddin, *Wild West Shows,* 111–12.
32. See also Moses, *Wild West Shows,* 226; 44, 56.
33. See, from the William F. "Buffalo Bill" Cody Collection, *Dresdner Journal,* June 3, 1890; *Hamburger Nachrichten,* August 28, 1890 and August 25, 1890; *Kölner Tageblatt,* September 16, 1890; *Dresdner Journal,* June 7, 1890. The frequency of the occurrence of the term may be explained by its inclusion in the show program.
34. *Hamburger Nachrichten,* August 25, 1890, William F. "Buffalo Bill" Cody Collection; Ames, "Seeing the Imaginary," 214, 222–23.
35. Ames, "Seeing the Imaginary," 223.
36. *Post* (Hannover), July 3, 1890, William F. "Buffalo Bill" Cody Collection.

37. See Deloria, *Playing Indian,* 125.
38. *Dresdner Tageblatt* (Dresden), June 15, 1890, William F. "Buffalo Bill" Cody Collection.
39. Several newspapers actually related stories of children sustaining injuries by throwing lassoes and even shooting each other while playing "Buffalo Bill."
40. *Tageblatt* (Dresden), June 15, 1890, William F. "Buffalo Bill" Cody Collection.
41. *Meitzener Tageblatt* (Meitzen), June 3, 1890, William F. "Buffalo Bill" Cody Collection.
42. *Stadt-Anzeiger der Kölnischen Zeitung,* May 10, 1891, William F. "Buffalo Bill" Cody Collection. Incidents like this also occurred in the United States. Reddin notes that sometimes audiences saw the dances as humorous and spectators shouted "such sallies as 'Rats!' 'Whoop'er up there, Jim!' and 'Dosy-do' at the most critical points of their performance," evoking "obvious disgust" from the Pawnees. Reddin, *Wild West Shows,* 79.
43. Rydell and Kroes, *Buffalo Bill in Bologna,* 6.

8

The "Black Legend" of Buffalo Bill in Barcelona

CHRIS DIXON

Buffalo Bill's Wild West undertook its first European tour in 1889, traveling from Paris to Lyons and Marseilles in the south of France, and then on to Spain, where the show made the single five-week stop in Barcelona that is the focus of this chapter, before proceeding through Italy, the Austro-Hungarian Empire, and Germany. Wherever it stopped, contemporary newspaper accounts not only spoke of the show's success but also provided evidence of an ongoing intercultural dialogue and exchange, with elements of the show being appropriated for various local purposes reflecting local concerns.

Although Buffalo Bill's Wild West had been lauded for bringing Britain and the United States together during the course of the 1887 English tour, the relationship between the United States and Spain in the first 115 years of the American Republic contained difficulties having unquestionably deeper roots than the relationship with its former colonial overlord. James W. Cortada quotes an "observant Spaniard" writing in 1821 that Americans "consider themselves superior to all the nations of Europe," and the dominant view of Spain in the United States at the time was of a backward, crude, and despotic country, permanently damned by the "Leyenda Negra," or "black legend," famously defined by Gibson as "the accumulated tradition of propaganda and Hispanophobia according to which Spanish imperialism is regarded as cruel, bigoted, exploitative and self-righteous in excess of reality."[1] In the face of such negative stereotypes, and given the fact that there had been serious difficulties in the relationship between the two nations in the previous century, bringing Spain and the United States together would doubtless represent a much greater challenge. Most previous studies of the visit suggest it was an insuperable one.

During the Revolutionary War, the United States and Spain had been "co-belligerents but not allies" against the British Empire. The 1795 Treaty of San Lorenzo, which defined the boundaries between the United States and the Spanish Empire's American colonies and was known in the United States as Pinkney's Treaty, appeared to have established a basis for good relations between the two countries.[2] Within ten years, however, the Louisiana Purchase of 1803, which was to be a fundamental driver of the western expansion of the United States, caused the situation to deteriorate until, in the words of historian Rodrigo Botero, they had become "unfriendly neighbors."[3] There were a number of diplomatic crises in the course of the century. As both countries sought self-definition—the United States within the Western Hemisphere and Spain in the context of its rapidly changing relationships with its former territories there—most of these crises were treaty or territorial disputes. A stronger adjective than "unfriendly" might reasonably apply to the relation between the two countries, who were at war twice in the first two decades of the nineteenth century. The conflict continued until the Adams-Onís Treaty was signed on February 22, 1819. The key provisions of the treaty were to cede Florida to the United States, to settle the boundary dispute along the Sabine River in Texas, and to establish the limits of US territorial claims through the Rocky Mountains and west to the Pacific Ocean. By its terms the United States also agreed to settle claims of $5 million that had been made by residents of the region against the Spanish Crown. The United States also renounced any claim on other Spanish territories, in particular eastern Texas beyond the Sabine River. This formally brought an end to the existence of the no-man's-land between Spanish Texas and the United States, which had been declared neutral in 1806.[4] Although the treaty arose directly from the conflict in Florida, it also reflected increasing tensions between the United States and Spain regarding territorial rights at a time of diminishing Spanish transatlantic power and increasing US self-confidence that would soon be expressed in both the Monroe Doctrine and the ideology of Manifest Destiny.

It was a generally held belief in Spain at the time that the United States aspired to control all of North and South America, and the independence movements in Latin America were viewed as proof of this.[5] Twenty-two years later, John L. O'Sullivan wrote of the United States' "manifest destiny to overspread the continent allotted by Providence for the free development of our yearly multiplying millions," giving rise to the phrase that came to characterize the nation's western expansion and further increasing Spanish distrust.[6]

Cortada has argued that the various points of conflict between Spain and the United States, although essentially political, were colored by fundamental cultural differences between the two nations. These differences created "a tradition of conflict of a generally unfriendly nature. By mid-century, a raft of problems, unfriendly negative images, and mutual suspicions over territorial ambitions existed between the two nations and it was these factors which characterized their relationships."[7] Although there were no further hostilities until 1898, the countries came close to war again in the 1860s when the United States was almost drawn into the Chincha Islands War between Spain and its former colonies of Peru and Chile.

In the midst of this negativity, American diplomat Horatio J. Perry also characterizes Spain in patronizing and condescending terms. "You must treat Spain as you would a pretty woman with a bad temper. Firm and constant and unyielding in your purpose, but flexible and always flattering in form—watching her moods—taking advantages of her prejudices and passions to modify her conduct towards you . . . logic and sound policy will not guide her unless you take good care of the region of her sentiments first."[8] The breadth of the appeal of Buffalo Bill's Wild West can undoubtedly be attributed to the factors that Perry mentions. It was certainly "flexible" and frequently revised its program to suit the venues in which it played; it was arguably "flattering in form" in view of the attention that was given to elaborate costumes, set design and musical performance; and it was unquestionably expert in "taking advantage of . . . prejudices and passions" in order to cater to the "sentiments" of its audiences in various parts of the world.[9] It therefore embodied the elements advised by Perry for the treatment of Spain. However, the audience it found in Barcelona was Catalan and would undoubtedly have rejected any suggestion that it was from a backward and underdeveloped country to which the negative Spanish stereotype might apply.

The Wild West in Catalonia

Josep Maria Fradera has characterized the period from 1865 to 1900 as one of "rural traditionalism and conservative nationalism" in Catalonia.[10] The conservative politician Francesc Rius i Taulet, who served four terms as mayor of Barcelona, thrived in that environment, and it was during his administration that the city staged the Universal Exhibition of 1888, the importance of which cannot be overestimated as a conditioning factor for the audiences that would see Buffalo Bill's Wild West there the following year. The Wild West's first visit to London had been as part of the American Exhibition; the first visit to Paris had been scheduled to coincide with Exposition Universelle; and the first visit to Spain would come in the wake of Barcelona's Universal Exhibition.

Towering 197 feet above the harbor is one of the iconic images associated with the city: a 24-foot tall bronze statue of a man pointing into the distance with his right hand while holding a scroll in his left. At the base of its Corinthian column is a plinth with the word *Tierra*—Spanish for "land"—inscribed on it. It stands close to the spot where on March 15, 1493, Christopher Columbus presented eleven of their "new subjects" to Queen Isabel and King Ferdinand on his return from the first of his four voyages to the New World. It marks the fact that Barcelona was the earliest port of entry for American Indian people coming to the Old World, and one of the portrait medallions on the monument's octagonal pedestal depicts the scene. The Indians, who thus discovered Europe, included the survivors of the six Tainos that Columbus kidnapped "in order that they might learn to speak" on October 12, 1492, the day he first made landfall on their home island of Guanahaní, which he renamed San Salvador—another scene that is portrayed on the base of the monument.[11]

The iconography of the monument encapsulates a number of key elements of how Spain memorialized its relationship with American Indian people. In addition to the two panels on the pedestal, two of the four statues around the base are of Captain Pedro Bertran i de Margarit, the military commander on Columbus's second journey to the Americas, and of Father Bernat de Boïl, the chaplain on that voyage.[12] Although these two figures from Columbus's second voyage may initially appear as anomalies in a monument to the first, they are significant in a number of ways.

First, these men were a Catalan and a Catalan-speaking Valencian, and their inclusion therefore ties in with a key aspect of the monument's design: it consistently emphasizes Catalan themes within the broader Spanish context. In this respect, the iconography of the monument clearly reflects what Josep Fradera has termed a "double patriotism," which is both Catalan and Spanish, a trait that art historian Oscar Vázquez has also found to be typical of Catalan art collections in the late 1880s.[13] More importantly, however, the inclusion of these two figures also encapsulates the prevalent Spanish view of the imperial expansion in the Americas, which was initiated by the voyages of Columbus. The sword and the cross were the twin instruments of civilization by which law and religion were brought to the Natives. The military commander and the chaplain are each presented with the figure of an Indian, apparently kneeling in humble submission to the civilizing and conquering Spaniard.

Within sixty years of Columbus's first voyage, the famous Valladolid debates between Bartolomé de las Casas and Juan Ginés de Sepúlveda established a basis for the treatment of American Indian people within the Spanish Empire by moving Spain's official position away from the dehumanizing implication of Columbus's journal entry claiming that the Natives lacked the power of speech. In 1550, Sepúlveda, a classical scholar, argued that Aristotle's principle of the natural slavery of some peoples justified Spain's violent conquest of the Indies, whereas Las Casas, the bishop of the Mexican province of Chiapas, took the position that the Indians were human beings with inherent rights and favored a benign conquest to ensure their conversion to Christianity. By modern standards, Sepúlveda's stance would be characterized as clearly racist, and that taken by Las Casas as more humane if somewhat paternalistic. It was the latter position that won the day, and regardless of the actual inequalities, exploitation, and violent outrages that Indian people suffered throughout Spain's subsequent involvement in the Western Hemisphere, the empire's official position, and the dominant social discourse relating to it, was typically that the Conquest was for the Indians' own good.[14] An unintended consequence of Las Casas's writings, in particular his fierce criticism of the early years of the Spanish Conquest in his 1552 work, *Brevísima Relación de la Destrucción de las Indias* or *Brief Account of the Destruction of the Indies*, was that it supported the development of the "black legend."[15]

According to its imperialist master narrative, Spain had offered the American Natives civilization by means of law and "true" religion; the myth presented by Buffalo Bill's Wild West was the inevitable triumph of superior technology, with the "vanishing American" giving way to civilization in the trans-Mississippi West. Neither of these constructs of conquest incorporates realities such as the setbacks the United States experienced at the hands of Arapaho, Cheyenne, and Lakota people in Wyoming's Powder River country, or those the Spaniards underwent when their incursions into northern Texas and Colorado were halted by fierce Apache and Comanche resistance.[16] Both do find a resonance in the Columbus monument, and it is hardly surprising that it features in some accounts of the Wild West's visit to Barcelona.

The monument is typically mentioned in relation to the company's arrival in port along the following lines:

> Burke, stirred to oratory by a crowd of Spanish journalists and by the historical associations of the quay on which he stood, pointed out that "on this very spot Christopher Columbus landed from his caravels upon his return from discovering America." He gestured dramatically toward the nearby statue of Columbus and declaimed, "There stands our advance agent, four hundred years ahead of us."
>
> "Damned bad day for us," one of the Indians remarked in cultivated tones, "when *he* discovered America."[17]

Even if the authenticity of this anecdote is questionable, it is understandable that the monument should appear in accounts of the Wild West's time in Barcelona. The proposal to erect it goes back to the middle of the nineteenth century in what historian Christopher Schmidt-Nowara has referred to as the period of "Colonofilia" or "Columbus worship," during which numerous projects commemorating the four-hundredth anniversary of 1492 were being undertaken in Spain and Spanish America.[18] The same phenomenon was occurring in the United States, with initiatives such as "Columbus Day" giving rise to the ritual that has become the daily pledge of allegiance in American schools.[19] Columbus was a figure who symbolically united Spain and the Americas. He was seen as representing progress and modernity, two themes that had a clear appeal to both Cody's enterprise and to the people of Barcelona.

The establishment of Barcelona's Chamber of Commerce—under the Spanish title of *Cámara de Comercio, Industria y Navegación,* which also encompasses industry and overseas trade—was a direct result of the committee's work, and its explicit objectives were to protect and develop Catalan business and to make the most of the opportunities that the exhibition might afford to develop international trade, in particular with the rest of Europe. Although Barcelona had been the principal port for trade with the colonies for ninety years prior to 1888, the Catalan economy had during that period always been focused largely on trade within Spain.[20] The Universal Exhibition was the first major step in the Europeanization of the Catalan economy.[21]

The Universal Exhibition ran from April 8 to December 9, 1888. It attracted at least 400,000 visitors from all over the world, with some estimates running between one and a half and two and one-quarter million.[22] At the opening, Rius i Taulet made to the Queen Regent a formal address that attempted to strike a delicate balance between catering to local interests and stressing Spanish national pride.[23] In writing of the event, Valero de Tornos hailed him as no great proponent of the Catalan cause and lauded him as the man who had done most for both Barcelona and for Catalonia in modern times.[24] In a lecture delivered during the exhibition, Antonio Cánovas del Castillo, the liberal conservative politician who served as Spain's prime minister on five occasions between 1874 and 1897, recognized the importance of the precedent that Barcelona had set for the rest of Spain and praised the great manifestation of energy that it represented.[25] The Madrid newspaper, *La Época,* waxed lyrical: "We have always believed that if some day Spain were to host a Universal Exhibition it would have to be in Barcelona. Its excellent climate, its beautiful location, the importance of its port and its products will certainly make it a success. The lower cost of living compared to other major cities, especially Madrid, its essentially industrial character, everything points to Barcelona for a success of this nature."[26] We can therefore see that there were many reasons for Cody and company to be optimistic about their trip to Barcelona despite the fact that the relationship between the United States and Spain was significantly more difficult than that with Britain or France.[27] It was clear that the show was going to a vibrant and growing city, one that had rapidly industrialized and undergone both a physical transformation and a cultural revival with a strongly nationalistic strand that had given rise to a dual patriotism that was prevalent among the upper echelons of society. It had recently staged the successful Universal Exhibition, which had heightened its international profile. It had a well-established bourgeoisie that provided a readership for the many newspapers and magazines, which could be used to publicize the visit, and it catered for the leisure interests of that key sector of its population with a lively café culture as well as numerous theatres and musical venues, which were well-attended. It also had numerous transatlantic commercial links, and there was clearly an interest in things American since it had both erected a Columbus monument featuring American Indian people in its iconography and sent numerous spectators to see the Wild West in Paris earlier in the year.

Rumors of a possible Wild West visit first surfaced in the Barcelona press in early October. *El Noticiero Universal* claimed on October 11, 1889, "We have heard that Buffalo Bill's great company which is currently in Paris is thinking of coming to Spain next year and that Barcelona will be the first major city they visit."[28] The story was picked up the following day by *La Dinastía,* which predicted, "Given the prior reports we have had of this great company from people returning from Paris, we can suppose that they will catch the attention of audiences in this city."[29] That very month, John M. Burke, the Wild West's general manager and chief publicist, traveled to Barcelona to make the preliminary arrangements and organize the publicity. He leased land for the show from prominent businessman Víctor Font in what is now the upper end of Barcelona's *Carrer Aribau, Carrer Còrsega,* and *Carrer Muntaner.*[30]

Burke's remit included dealing with the local bureaucracy to obtain the relevant permission. On October 29, 1889, he wrote to the borough council in Gràcia, describing himself with typical aplomb as the representative of "*La Gran Compañía del Buffalo Bill's Wild West*" and articulating the company's desire to "make known in this town the Great Exhibition of American Indian and Frontier Life which has so rightly been praised by all of the audiences in Paris and London before which it has appeared."[31] The purpose of the letter was a simple request for the closure of roads running through the grounds that had been leased for the show, and Burke argued for the necessary permission to be promptly granted due to the "educational nature" of the exhibition.[32] He also took the opportunity of emphasizing the link between Columbus, Barcelona, and Buffalo Bill's Wild West, stating how pleased the company was that its first appearance in Spain should be "in Barcelona the port where Christopher Columbus disembarked upon his return from the Americas, the native land of the Indians it features."[33] On November 9, *La Vanguardia* proclaimed, "It has now been confirmed that the show which caught the attention at the Universal Exhibition in Paris, Buffalo Bill's American Exhibition, will come to this city."[34]

The impending visit by the Wild West provided substantial business for Barcelona's merchants and public transport companies. With the former

Burke signed contracts for 880 kilos of grain, 2,000 kilos of alfalfa, and the same amount of straw daily, and with the latter he agreed a concession similar to that which had been in place for the previous year's Universal Exhibition.[35] On December 6, *La Vanguardia* announced that "on Sundays and holidays when there is a performance, the Tarragona to Barcelona and France Railway Company will run special services with reduced-price return fares, provided the ticket for the aforementioned show is purchased at the same time as the train ticket."[36] The Sarrià railway line, which ran from *Plaça de Catalunya* in the city center, also announced that it would open a new station at the bottom of *Carrer Rosselló,* very close to the show arena, and that it would sell tickets for the show along with train tickets.[37]

The *Palma*, a heavily laden steamer remembered years later by Annie Oakley as "a small tub they called a boat,"[38] sailed into Barcelona harbor with its 178 passengers, accompanied by 159 horses and 20 buffaloes. It weighed anchor at the port of entry at 11:20 a.m. on Wednesday, December 18, 1889.[39] After the compulsory health inspection of both people and animals and confirmation that the certificate from the port of origin stating that all passengers were in good health and not bringing the risk of any communicable disease to the local population was in order, the company was given permission to come ashore.[40] According to *La Dinastía,* Nathan Salsbury showed up on the quayside soon after the ship had tied up, as the company was waiting to disembark, and he was greeted by its members with enthusiastic cheers.[41] The Indians were first to leave the ship, followed by the horses and buffaloes. These they watched being unloaded, as they crouched, quietly smoking, wrapped in their blankets.[42] The ship's crane was used to lower the livestock to the ground one at a time, and they were then closed up in the wooden containers normally employed to transport bulls to the bullring. As predicted, the company's arrival was greeted by substantial crowds, and the police were in attendance to keep order.[43] By four o'clock in the afternoon, the unloading was complete. People had watched throughout as if it were the show itself. According to *El Barcelonés,* as the company left the docks, "the company's passage, all the way along the road to the hippodrome in Calle Aribau, was made almost impossible and the police had to intervene to enable them to continue on their way."[44]

At some stage during the disembarkation, John Crawford left the Sant Beltrán quay, made his way to the telegraph office in the *Rambla de Santa Mònica,* and submitted his dispatch to the *New York Herald Tribune.* His report included the following: "John Burke, encouraged to speak by a group of Spanish journalists and by the historical significance of the setting, noted: 'In this place Columbus disembarked when he returned from discovering the New World.' Pointing to the statue of Columbus he continued: 'Here is our agent, who arrived four hundred years in advance of us.' One of the Indians exclaimed: 'It was a bad day for us when he discovered America.'"[45] In addition to mentioning John M. Burke by name, Crawford's report has the Wild West's chief publicist's fingerprints all over it. Except for the comment by the unnamed Indian, Nate Salsbury's later description in his memoires of his arrival in Barcelona reproduces all of the key details mentioned in the report. He tells how "Burke suddenly jumped to his feet, and taking off his hat he fixed his enraptured gaze on the monument of Columbus."[46] There followed what he refers to as "a few minutes of pantomime," and then this exchange of dialogue between Burke and Salsbury:

> "It is possible that you see nothing to pay homage in that beautiful counterpart of your best friend in this country?"
>
> "My best Friend?" said I. "I see a fine statue of Columbus, nothing more."
>
> "Nothing more?" he shouted. "Nothing more? Damn this utilitarian age of money grubbers. Oh, man without a soul, you should go down on your knees in adoration of the man that statue typifies."
>
> "In the devil's name, why?" said I.
>
> "Why, Why, Why? Because he has been your ADVANCE AGENT FOR THE LAST FOUR HUNDRED YEARS, THAT'S WHY!!!!"[47]

Crawford's initial report was the longest to appear in any American newspaper while the Wild West was in Barcelona. The cost of sending a telegram from the city to the United States was one and one-quarter pesetas per word, which was an enormous price.[48] This was no doubt one factor that contributed to contemporary reports in the American press being so short.

The show's advertising had been running daily in the press since the December 7 announcement in *El Noticiero Universal*, although not in every newspaper every day. On the two days prior to the first performance, however, *El Barcelonés*, *El Diario de Barcelona*, *El Diario Universal*, *El Diluvio*, *La Dinastía*, *El Noticiero Universal*, *El Suplemento*, and *La Vanguardia* all carried advertisements that were nearly identical to the original notice.[49]

On December 19, a story stressing the authentic savagery of the Indians also appeared in *El Suplemento* and *El Noticiero Universal*. These stories were designed to reassure the public that, when the Indians left the Wild West camp, they would not be allowed to go around the city on their own but would be accompanied by a "person who could be trusted" at all times.[50] The stories also included warnings about the dangers of giving alcohol to the Indians, who when drunk were said to be capable of all sorts of crimes.

Frederic Pons, the acting mayor of Gràcia, signed the definitive authorization for the Wild West performances to go ahead on the morning of Saturday, December 21, 1889, just a few hours in advance of the 2:30 première.[51]

While no printed program from the Wild West's appearances in Barcelona has been located, the running order was documented in the detailed review of the first performance that appeared in *La Vanguardia* on Sunday, December 22, 1889. The article opens with a short introduction about the bison and then moves on to proclaim that "in 1493 Barcelona had the pleasure of seeing redskins of the great American family when Christopher Columbus returned from his first voyage and was welcomed by the *Reyes Católicos*."[52] There follows a statement that it is a novelty to see North American Indians perform in Barcelona, although many other races have appeared on stage in the city. Then comes a recognition that "North American Indians are somewhat different from those of Tierra del Fuego and South America, as indeed they are from the Toltecs of Central America."[53] This then leads to a strange observation about their language: "They belong for the most part to the Sioux tribes, and speak the Nakota language, which some scholars compare to the dialect of the Manchurian Tartars. A fact which could prove that in ancient times the sons of Asia invaded the plains of Alaska, passing over the Bering Strait."[54] The reviewer's overview of the Indians ends with a romanticized view of the "vanishing American" that is entirely in keeping with the master narrative of progress from savagery to civilization that was a key feature of Buffalo Bill's Wild West: "This race which has done us no harm and which was so welcoming to the first Europeans, causes real sadness to thinking men who see them destined to melt away before the rays of modern civilization which from day to day continues to extend its conquests towards the Far West."[55] Thereafter, the unnamed reviewer tells his readers that the program consisted of three different types of acts: "a presentation of the customs of the inhabitants of the West of the United States, horsemanship and shooting displays," and goes on to detail each of the numbers in turn, making reference to the printed program on three occasions.[56]

On the evening of December 28, 1889, the Equestrian Circus in the *Plaça de Catalunya* presented a parody of Buffalo Bill's Wild West entitled "Buffalo Bill at the Circus." Caricaturing the Wild West was not a new phenomenon in Europe, and in Barcelona it was the perceived lack of authenticity of the show, with very tame buffaloes and very civilized Indians, that was the focus of the parody.[57] All of the clowns and Arab dancers in the Equestrian Circus wore wigs and other elements of Indian costume. They acted out a mock opening parade, with considerable shouting and yelling; this was followed by a spoof of the buffalo-hunting scene, in which the buffalo were played by bull calves that the performers lassoed; finally, the Indians were attacked by pioneers in a volte-face of the Wild West's final scene. It was an outstanding success that ran until January 19, 1890.[58]

The Equestrian Circus parody is a clear indicator of the impact that the Wild West was having in the city. Similar instances of its penetration into popular culture can be found in the cartoons that appeared in *Esquella de la Torratxa* and *La Tramontana,* in Catalan wordplays punning on the name Buffalo Bill,[59] in the Indian-inspired hairstyles that were presented as the *nova moda* or new fashion,[60] in turkey feathers as the must-have fashion accessory for women,[61] and in the lampooning of the newly deposed mayor, Francesc Rius i Taulet, who is portrayed as turning up in blanket and feathers at the Wild West camp in *Carrer Muntaner.*[62] Each of these is adapting elements of the show, particularly American Indian iconography, for local purposes.

The Wild West received favorable press throughout its run. On December 31, 1889, for example, the weekly *La Ilustració Catalana,* carried a series of line drawings and three separate brief positive notices.[63] The first was a report that the stands were packed for the première;[64] the second also stated that there had been full houses[65] and then went on to say that the performance had caught the attention of the audience and won their applause;[66] the third was a brief but favorable comment in the theatre review section that the show has pleasantly surprised and pleased audiences.[67] That day would also bring to an end the first part of the run in Barcelona, as a change in the weather the following day led to performances being suspended for six days.

A period of sustained heavy rain began in Barcelona on New Year's Day 1890. The downpour continued almost without a letup for four days. In these circumstances, the company had no choice but to suspend performances, and on January 2, *El Diluvio* announced that "in view of the bad weather there will be no performances of the show until next Sunday."[68] The idea of restarting performances on Sunday January 5, 1890, the date scheduled for a special gala performance for the press and local dignitaries, proved to be overoptimistic. On Saturday it was announced,

> In view of the bad weather, Buffalo Bill's company has postponed their gala performance for the authorities and the press until next Tuesday.
>
> The arena will be specially decorated for the event and the audience will see some new acts.[69]

During the period when the company was not performing, Burke continued to feed stories to the press to maintain interest. One of the most striking was the report that a number of Indians went for a stroll around the *Plaça de la Universitat* and into the *Café Salò* where one of them took part in a game of a local form of billiards called *carambola* and displayed a good knowledge and remarkable talent for the game.[70]

The six days when there were no performances were, without doubt, the most difficult that the Wild West spent in Barcelona, not just because of the loss of revenue that the suspension of the show implied, but also because it was the period during which a mysterious illness afflicting the city—referred to as the "dengue" in contemporary accounts—appears to have touched the camp. In Jordi Marill Escudé's study of the Wild West's time in Barcelona, he outlines the following facts about this mysterious illness. From early December 1889, there is press coverage of an illness going around Barcelona. On December 31, the regional government had a joint meeting with the provincial health board. The meeting was rowdy at times, and the regional government officials were accused of not taking appropriate measures to deal with "the flu, the *dengue,* bronchitis or whatever this infection that was going around was called." The response of the regional government was clear: they had consulted officials of the health board, including the then-famous Doctor Robert, and these experts had found no characteristics of an epidemic and advised that there was no particular danger of the outbreak taking on the proportions of an epidemic. In the opinion of these experts, there was nothing to be done to limit the spread of the illness beyond normal good hygiene. Finally, the convener of the council, Señor Maluquer, brought the discussion to a close with the announcement that he would bring the concerns that had been raised to the attention of the civil governor, Luis Antúnez, and all resolved to take measures to calm the public, such as placing notices in the newspapers recommending basic principles of good hygiene.[71]

The announcements that the local health board ran in the press, calling for calm and good hygiene, were the only official statements on the outbreak. The notice that appeared in *La Vanguardia* on January 2 stressed that the illness "has been, and probably will continue being benign."[72] There is no record of any call for preventative public health measures such as isolation, quarantine, or sanitary cordons. There was a suggestion from theater owners that they should close temporarily from January 2, 1890, to limit the spread of the illness. The *Eldorado* theater, however, broke the voluntary embargo, and from January 3, all theaters were operating as normal and the scare was beginning to die down. *La Dinastía,* on January 4, was crediting the wet weather with turning the tide against the illness, and on the same day, *La Vanguardia* was praising the newly elected deputy mayor of Barcelona, Ignasi Pons, for getting the temporary hospital of *La Vinyeta* in *Hostafrancs* fitted out and up and running.[73] The situation was clearly improving, and the following day the new mayor, Fèlix Macià i Bonaplata, ordered the municipal band to restart its daily performances in the *Rambla de Santa Mònica.*[74]

Annie Oakley recalled, "We lost our orator, Frank Richmond, who always presented me to royalty and gave tone to the company."[75] His death occurred in the night of January 3–4, 1890, and she also gives the following additional details concerning it:

> Mr. B came in one night with all the symptoms of the disease. He had just left Frank Richmond. He had just been in bed an hour when Johnny Baker tapped on the door with the death tidings. Although Mr. B should have been in bed, he looked after all the arrangements for poor Frank, made arrangements to return his body to America, and all that. Then he took to his bed.
>
> He recovered and then the fight was on between me and the disease, but though they put me to bed I worked for an hour weakly trying to get into my costume and took my place in the arena that afternoon. Then I collapsed and had the flu in earnest.[76]

Frank Richmond was the stage name of New Yorker James Twitchell, the "orator" with Buffalo Bill's Wild West from its earliest days, whose voice was so powerful that it was the subject of an article in the *British Medical Journal* in 1887 while the show was appearing in London. The article referred to him as a "vocal athlete," pointed out that his commentary on the performance included more words than the part of Hamlet, and concluded that "the secret of his remarkable delivery lies more in the perfection with which he had learned to use his natural advantages than in any notable peculiarity of physical conformation."[77] According to one obituary, he was a lifelong friend of John M. Burke, who had been responsible for his employment with the Wild West, and during his stage career he was "one of the best Simon Legrees in *Uncle Tom's Cabin* that ever trod the boards."[78] Brown's *History of the New York Stage* indicates that by 1887, he was "appearing in cowboy stories" when not on the road with the Wild West.[79] Richmond's body was taken to the mortuary chapel of Barcelona's new cemetery, also known as the South Western Cemetery or the Montjuic Cemetery, where it was embalmed by Doctor Fraginals i Griñán, a well-known urologist, before being sent to the United States for burial.[80] Annie Oakley's account of his death and her husband's involvement in making the funeral arrangements suggests a special bond between Frank Richmond and the couple.

She also tells us, "One half of our people were down, but we lost only two more. They were Indians who died of smallpox."[81] On this point, she is mistaken, though there is a grain of truth in what she says that makes her error understandable. A number of Barcelona newspapers did report the death of an Indian on January 4 or 5, 1890, and the majority of studies of the visit that William F. Cody and his troupe made to Barcelona speak of Indian deaths in the city.[82] Given that we now have a participant stating that there were Indian deaths, this might at first glance appear to be compelling evidence that there were. Marill Escudé's research, however, makes it clear that this was not the case.

The Catalan scholar has shown that the Municipal Institute of Funeral Services in Barcelona have no records in their archive of any foreigners belonging to Buffalo Bill's Company having died in the period December 1, 1889, to January 31, 1890. He has also demonstrated that US records include neither any submission by the American Consulate in Barcelona, nor of the Spanish legation for the period from November 1889 to February 1890, mentioning the death of any member of the company.[83] His findings are in line with those of the subsequent study by L. G. Moses, as both are in agreement that the list of Indians who returned to the reservation in the custody of Cody and Salsbury can be reconciled with the list of those who departed. Taking into account the seven documented Indian deaths on the tour—none of which occurred in Spain—all of the Indian participants are accounted for.[84] The explanation for Annie Oakley's two Indian deaths is that both of the Lakota performers who were left behind in Marseilles died while the Wild West was in Barcelona, and two of the performers were left behind in hospital in the Catalan capital, although both recovered.

The twenty-six-year-old Oglala Lakota Cetan Sapa, or Black Hawk, took ill on January 1, 1890, his condition deteriorated until January 6, by which time it was so serious that he had to be admitted to the Santa Creu hospital, where he was diagnosed with smallpox and confined in a small isolation ward in the Santa Maria wing of the hospital.[85] At ten o'clock in the morning of the day that Black Hawk took ill, Swift Hawk died in the Hospital de la Conception in Marseilles. The news reached the Wild West camp three days later and is most probably the source of the Spanish newspaper reports of an Indian death. At four o'clock in the morning of the day that Black Hawk was admitted to the hospital, Featherman succumbed to his illness in southern France. Two weeks later, just before the Wild West troupe left for Italy, the nineteen-year-old Kangi Watakpe or Charging Crow broke out in smallpox pustules. He was confined alongside his compatriot Black Hawk in the same isolation ward in the Santa Maria wing of the Santa Creu hospital. The hospital records, which have their names as "Chorgen Croro" and "Blak Holck," show that both men were discharged from hospital on February 27, 1890, into the custody of Frederick Schenk, the American consul in Barcelona.[86] Consular records confirm that he made arrangements for them to travel by ship to Rome to rejoin the company.[87]

The show reopened January 7, 1890, with its gala performance for the press and local dignitaries. With improving weather and improving health in the city, the overall atmosphere in the newspapers of the time was much more optimistic. The following day, *El Suplemento* reported that the "performance was thoroughly crowded" and "the audience was, as ever, very well entertained and showed their appreciation through spontaneous, well-deserved rounds of applause to the troupe during the various scenes."[88] They also announced that "from today the show will begin at three o'clock in the afternoon, rather than two-thirty as has been the case until now."[89] The sun was setting later, and the extra daylight allowed for a later start.

The success of Buffalo Bill's Wild West was no longer news in Barcelona, and over the next ten days, advertising for the performances is the only coverage appearing in the Catalan press. Through January 1890, there was likewise little mention in the American press. On New Year's Day, the *Wichita Eagle* reported that "lots of people who wouldn't have recognized him when he lived in Kansas will be pleased to note that Buffalo Bill and his Wild West show have progressed on their European tour as far as Barcelona, Spain."[90] There were numerous brief mentions, such as that in the *News Herald* of Hillsboro, Ohio, which simply stated that "Buffalo Bill and his Wild West show are at Barcelona, Spain."[91]

On January 19, *La Vanguardia* announced arrangements for the company's departure: "Next Wednesday, the twenty-second, the steamer 'Bellver' which will take Buffalo Bill's Wild West Company to Naples will leave this port. For the departure, the 'Bellver' will be moored alongside the Sant Beltrán quay."[92] That same day, the Wild West put on a morning show and again played to a full house.[93] That evening, the Equestrian Circus presented its final performance of the Buffalo Bill parody. Thereafter, it packed up and headed for Valencia.[94]

Buffalo Bill's Wild West gave its final performance in its *Carrer Muntaner* arena on Tuesday, January 21, 1890. The last show was dedicated to the people of Barcelona, and tickets for the performance were half-price.[95] As with almost all of the shows of which we have a record, it was a sellout.[96] In addition to cutting prices for the audience, the company's management left a donation for the local police who had guarded the Wild West camp, protecting them from peddlers, hawkers, and thieves.[97] According to *La Vanguardia*, many members of the full-house audience hung around the Indian encampment until long after the final parade. The same report also stated that the weather was excellent and "the temperature so mild that many of the Indians appeared in the arena almost naked, or rather, dressed in their usual fashion."[98]

It should be clear from what has gone before that simplistic dismissals of the five weeks spent in Spain of the sort that are common in previous scholarship are not well-founded.[99] The contemporary evidence also has no trace of some of the more colorful stories associated with the Wild West's time in Barcelona. There is no indication that any Indians were accused of cannibalism, nor that William F. Cody had a run-in with the local bullfighters, nor indeed that he suffered toothache and had to have a tooth extracted during his time in the city. Unless further information comes to light, it therefore seems reasonable to dismiss these legends—along with the "black legend" of poor attendances, early closures, epidemics and quarantines, and Indian deaths that have featured in other studies touching on the subject of the Wild West's visit to the Catalan capital—and conclude that the visit was a success.

It seems reasonable to conclude both from the contemporary press coverage and from its obvious impact in the popular culture of the city that Buffalo Bill's Wild West was a qualified success in Barcelona. The company's takings may have been slightly down on what they had hoped for owing to the reduced number of performances, but it is difficult to believe that the gestures of having half-price tickets for the final show and of making a substantial donation to the local police would have been considered if the business had been experiencing severe losses.[100] It is an unfortunate coincidence that news of one of the many financial difficulties that beset Cody throughout the later part of his life broke in the American press while the company was in Barcelona. Some previous studies may therefore have been effectively conflating two otherwise unrelated issues and misinterpreting the financial aspects of the visit to Catalonia in the light of subsequent developments.[101]

The fact that the Wild West did not return to Spain during the 1906 European tour can be readily explained without having recourse to any suggestion that the 1889–1890 visit was a flop. Within the business model that the company followed for the second tour, with James A. Bailey, in spite of his failing health, taking responsibility for organizing travel and transportation, there were sound financial reasons for not returning to Spain.[102] The country's use of nonstandard railway lines would have constituted a minor complication that might have had cost implications,[103] but even more importantly Spain had not yet recovered from the economic depression that it experienced after its defeat in the war of 1898.[104] It would not therefore have represented an attractive potential venue for the exhibition for that reason alone. There were, however, numerous other reasons arising from the complete collapse of the relationship between the United States and Spain, the war this collapse led to, and the reactions to the outcome of the conflict in both countries.

Buffalo Bill's Wild West was credited with bringing Britain and the United States together with its 1887 and 1888 appearances in London, and the show would make great play of the close historical ties between the United States and France for its 1905–1906 tour.[105] But there was no "great rapprochement" in prospect for Spain and the United States at the time of the visit to Barcelona. By the time of the second tour, Spain's Philippine and Cuban colonies had rebelled—and a heroic martyr of each rebellion had written in glowing terms of Buffalo Bill's Wild West.[106] It would be overstating the case to suggest that either of these was in and of itself a key factor in the Wild West's decision not to return to Spain. Both cases do however illustrate how readily the ideology of Cody's master narrative could be aligned to the rebel cause and suggest the potential difficulties that it might have faced in resonating with a Spanish audience. A much more important factor was the absolute alignment of the Wild West with the anti-Spanish cause in its performance celebration of the *Resplendent Realism of Glorious War—Stupendous Spectacular Reproduction of the Battle of San Juan Hill.*

The contemporary record on both sides of the Atlantic clearly indicates that Buffalo Bill's Wild West was a success in Barcelona: the "black legend" that it was a failure can be dated to the events of 1898 and their aftermath.

Notes

1. Bennasser, *Spanish Character,* 250; Cortada, "Spain and the American Civil War," 9; Gibson, *Colonial Period in Latin American History,* 13–14.
2. Botero, *Ambivalent Embrace,* 1–18; Grant, "Treaty of San Lorenzo and Manifest Destiny"; Young, "Pinckney's Treaty."
3. Botero, *Ambivalent Embrace,* 19–50.
4. Haggard, "Neutral Ground between Louisiana and Texas," 1001–28.
5. Cortada, "Spain and the American Civil War," 5.
6. O'Sullivan, "Annexation," 5.
7. Cortada, "Spain and the American Civil War," 3.
8. Cited in ibid., 105.
9. Bridger, *Buffalo Bill and Sitting Bull,* 395–96, 402–5, 408; Joy S. Kasson, *Buffalo Bill's Wild West,* 5, 8, 41, 55–56, 61–68, 89, 93, 114, 119–21, 161–65; Russell, *Lives and Legends,* 267, 278–80, 298, 308, 322–28, 332, 338–39, 370–71, 376–82, 419–20, 442–50; Rydell and Kroes, *Buffalo Bill in Bologna,* 112; Warren, *Buffalo Bill's America,* xix, 39, 93, 104, 216–17, 224, 235, 264, 276–81, 292–96, 302, 366, 432, 434, 547.
10. Fradera, "Rural Traditionalism."
11. "Yo plaziendo a Nuestro Señor levaré de aquí al tiempo de mi partida para que deprendan fablar." Colón, *Textos y documentos completos,* 31. Modern translations often end this sentence with "speak our language." There is no reference to language in the original.
12. Fernández-Armesto, *Columbus,* 104, 106, 108, 110, 114, 138; Koning, *Columbus: His Enterprise,* 82–84, 120; Prunés, "Nuevos datos y observaciones."
13. Fradera, "The Empire, the Nation and the Homelands," 140; Vázquez, *Inventing the Art Collection,* 62.
14. Elliot, *Spain and its World,* 42–64; Green, *Spain and the Western Tradition,* 2:153–55; 3:35, 75, 90–91, 101, 299–300; 4:116; Losada, "Controversy between Sepúlveda and Las Casas," 279–309.

15. Las Casas, *A Brief Account.*
16. Carlisle, "Spanish Relations with the Apache Nations," 45–87, 130–63; Drury and Clalvin, *Heart of Everything,* 223–349; Fehrenbach, *Comanches,* 28, 63–64, 83–85, 155–56, 168–78, 183–87, 190–91, 199–208, 216–28, 230; Forbes, *Apache, Navaho, and Spaniard,* xviii; Hämäläinen, *Comanche Empire,* 3, 20, 32–36, 45, 71–76, 80, 119, 143, 179, 183–89, 205–7, 355; John, *Storms Brewed in Other Men's Worlds,* 36–37; McDermott, *Red Cloud's War*; Monnett, *Where a Hundred Soldiers Were Killed*; Wallace and Hoebel, *Comanches,* 3, 8, 11, 27; Worcester, *Apaches,* 8–9.
17. Burke, *Buffalo Bill: The Noblest Whiteskin,* 192.
18. Schmidt-Nowara, *Conquest of History,* 55–68.
19. Rydell and Kroes and Rydell, *Buffalo Bill in Bologna,* 58–60.
20. Delgado et al., *El comerç,* 111–19; Fernández-Armesto, *Barcelona,* 137–41; Fradera, "The Empire, the Nation," 139; McRoberts, *Nation Building without a State,* 92–94; Moreno Masó, *La Petjada dels catalans,* 29–52.
21. McRoberts, *Nation Building without a State,* 25.
22. Fernández-Armesto, *Barcelona,* 185; Hughes, *Barcelona,* 356.
23. Girona, *Memoria Sobre la Exposición Universal,* 61.
24. Tornos, *Cuarenta cartas,* 23. The actual phrase used by Tornos that I have translated as "no great proponent of the Catalan cause" was "no muy catalanista."
25. Bahamonde, *Historia de España Siglo XX,* 55–58; Cánovas del Castillo, "Discurso pronunciado por el Excmo," 15.
26. "Siempre hemos creído que si algún día había de celebrarse en España una Exposición Universal, debería realizarse en Barcelona. Su excelente clima, su hermosa tipografía, la importancia de su puerto y productos que hayan de figurar en el certamen, lo económico de la vida en relación a otras capitales y sobre todo Madrid, su espíritu esencialmente industrial, todo designa a Barcelona para un certamen de esta naturaleza." *La Época,* May 20, 1888. This and all other newspaper clippings cited in this chapter can be found in the William F. "Buffalo Bill" Cody Collection, MS 6, McCracken Research Library, Buffalo Bill Center of the West.
27. Gallop, *Buffalo Bill's British Wild West,* 7, 67–74, 114–18, 131, 176, 233, 263–66; Jonnes, *Eiffel's Tower,* 112, 142–44, 167–71, 173–75, 243–46, 257–58, 277–78, 298–99; *Punch,* May 7, 1887, William F. "Buffalo Bill" Cody Collection; Warren, *Buffalo Bill's America,* 302, 349–50.
28. "Según noticias, la gran compañía del Buffalo Bill's, que actualmente se encuentra en París, piensa venir a España en el año próximo, siendo Barcelona la primera capital que visitará." *El Noticiero Universal,* October 11, 1889, William F. "Buffalo Bill" Cody Collection.
29. "Dados los antecedentes que de esta gran compañía tenemos, por gente ya vuelta de París, llamará la atención del público de esta capital." *La Dinastía,* October 12, 1889, William F. "Buffalo Bill" Cody Collection.
30. Marill Escudé, *Aquell hivern,* 14.
31. "Dar a conocer en esta población la Gran Exhibition of American Indian and Frontier Life que tan justamente ha sido elogiada por todos los públicos de París

y Londres ante los que se ha presentado." Burke, To Gràcia (Barcelona) Civic Authorities, October 29, 1889, William F. "Buffalo Bill" Cody Collection.

32. The expression he—or more properly his unidentified Spanish translator—uses is "carácter instructivo."
33. "En Barcelona puerto donde desembarcó Cristóbal Colón en su regreso de las Américas pueblo de naturaleza de los indios que presenta."
34. "Es ya un hecho la venida a esta ciudad de un espectáculo que ha llamado la atención en la Exposición de París, la gran 'Exhibition americana del Buffalo Bill.'" *La Vanguardia,* November 9, 1889, William F. "Buffalo Bill" Cody Collection.
35. Marill Escudé, *Aquell hivern,* 15.
36. "Los domingos y días festivos en que haya exhibición, la compañía de los ferrocarriles de Tarragona á Barcelona y Francia, verificará un servicio especial de viajeros con billetes de ida y vuelta á precios reducidos, expendiendo al propio tiempo que el billete de ferrocarril, la entrada al referido espectáculo." *La Vanguardia,* December 6, 1889, William F. "Buffalo Bill" Cody Collection. Almost identical notices appeared on the same date in *La Dinastía* and in *El Noticiero Universal.*
37. Marill Escudé, *Aquell hivern,* 19.
38. Oakley, *Story of My Life,* 47.
39. *La Dinastía,* December 18, 1889, William F. "Buffalo Bill" Cody Collection.
40. Marill Escudé, *Aquell hivern,* 26.
41. "El director de la Compañía se presentó al poco rato, recibiéndole con gritos de júbilo los individuos que la componen." *La Dinastía,* December 19, 1889, William F. "Buffalo Bill" Cody Collection.
42. "Los indios desembarcaron en primer lugar, siendo desembarcados a seguida los caballos y búfalos. Los pieles-rojas iban envueltos en mantas y contemplaban las operaciones fumando con gran tranquilidad y sentados en cuclillas." Ibid.
43. "El público que acudió a presenciar el desembarque era muy numeroso, viéndose entre él muchos agentes de policía enviados para poner orden." Ibid.
44. "El paso de la comitiva hacia el hipódromo, situado en la Calle de Aribau, se hizo poco menos que imposible en todo el trayecto, teniendo que intervenir los agentes de la autoridad para dejar circular a la compañía." *El Barcelonés,* December 19, 1889, William F. "Buffalo Bill" Cody Collection.
45. *New York Herald Tribune,* December 21, 1889, William F. "Buffalo Bill" Cody Collection.
46. Nathan Salsbury Papers, MSS17, Beinecke Library, Yale University.
47. Ibid.
48. Marill Escudé, *Aquell hivern,* 31.
49. *El Barcelonés, El Diario de Barcelona, El Diario Universal, El Diluvio, La Dinastía, El Noticiero Universal, El Suplemento* and *La Vanguardia,* all December 19 and 20, 1889, in William F. "Buffalo Bill" Cody Collection.
50. *El Suplemento* and *El Noticiero Universal,* both December 19, 1889, in William F. "Buffalo Bill" Cody Collection. The term used in both stories is "persona de confianza."

51. Marill Escudé, *Aquell hivern,* 44.
52. "Barcelona tuvo el gusto de ver pieles-rojas de la gran familia americana en 1493 cuando Cristóbal Colón regresó de su primer viaje, siendo recibido en nuestra ciudad por los reyes católicos." *La Vanguardia,* December 22, 1889, William F. "Buffalo Bill" Cody Collection.
53. "Los indios de la América del Norte, algo distintos de los fueganos y sudamericanos, como también de los toltekas de la región central," *La Vanguardia,* December 22, 1889, William F. "Buffalo Bill" Cody Collection.
54. "Pertenecen en su mayoría a la tribu de los Siux, y hablan la lengua narcotah que algunos sabios comparan al dialecto de los tártaros manchues. Lo cual puede probar que en épocas remotas los hijos del Asia invadieron las llanuras del Alaska, pasando el estrecho de Bering." *La Vanguardia,* December 22, 1889, William F. "Buffalo Bill" Cody Collection.
55. "Esta raza que no nos ha hecho ningún mal y que tan bien acogió a los primeros europeos, causa verdadera tristeza a los hombres pensadores al verla destinada a fundirse ante los rayos de la civilización moderna que de día en día va extendiendo sus conquistas hacia el Lejano Oeste." *La Vanguardia,* December 22, 1889, William F. "Buffalo Bill" Cody Collection.
56. "Presentación de costumbres de los habitantes del Oeste de los Estados Unidos, Equitación y Ejercicios de tiro." *La Vanguardia,* December 22, 1889, William F. "Buffalo Bill" Cody Collection.
57. Warren, *Buffalo Bill's America,* 349–50.
58. *El Noticiero Universal,* December 29, 1889, William F. "Buffalo Bill" Cody Collection.
59. *Esquella de la Torratxa,* December 27, 1889, William F. "Buffalo Bill" Cody Collection. See List of Illustrations, fig. 10.
60. Ibid. See List of Illustrations, fig. 9.
61. *Esquella de la Torratxa,* January 10, 1890, William F. "Buffalo Bill" Cody Collection. See List of Illustrations, fig. 16.
62. *La Tramontana,* December 27, 1889, William F. "Buffalo Bill" Cody Collection. See List of Illustrations, fig. 8.
63. See List of Illustrations, figs. 11–14.
64. "El primer dia omplí de gom a gom lo lloch destinat als espectadors." *La Ilustració Catalana,* December 31, 1889, William F. "Buffalo Bill" Cody Collection.
65. "Plé s'ha vist aquests dies l'espayós local hont actúa." *La Ilustració Catalana,* December 31, 1889, William F. "Buffalo Bill" Cody Collection.
66. "S'ha guanyat l'interès i l'aplauso de la concurrencia." *La Ilustració Catalana,* December 31, 1889, William F. "Buffalo Bill" Cody Collection.
67. "Ha sorprès agradablement al nostre publich i li ha plagut." *La Ilustració Catalana,* December 31, 1889, William F. "Buffalo Bill" Cody Collection.
68. *El Diluvio,* January 2, 1890, William F. "Buffalo Bill" Cody Collection.
69. *El Diluvio,* January 4, 1890, William F. "Buffalo Bill" Cody Collection.
70. *La Dinastía,* January 3, 1890, William F. "Buffalo Bill" Cody Collection.

71. Marill Escudé, *Aquell hivern,* 86–87.
72. "Ha sido, y probablemente continuará siendo benigna," *La Vanguardia,* January 2, 1890, William F. "Buffalo Bill" Cody Collection.
73. *La Dinastía* and *La Vanguardia,* both January 4, 1890, in William F. "Buffalo Bill" Cody Collection.
74. *El Suplemento,* January 5, 1890, William F. "Buffalo Bill" Cody Collection.
75. Oakley, *Story of My Life,* 48.
76. Ibid.
77. "A Marvellous Voice," *British Medical Journal,* 1887, 2:732.
78. *Richmond Dispatch,* January 7, 1890, William F. "Buffalo Bill" Cody Collection.
79. Brown, *History of the New York Stage,* 2:318.
80. *La Publicidad,* January 5, 1890, William F. "Buffalo Bill" Cody Collection; Marill Escudé, *Aquell hivern,* 92.
81. Oakley, *Story of My Life,* 47.
82. Bridger, *Buffalo Bill and Sitting Bull,* 354; Burke, *Buffalo Bill: The Noblest Whiteskin,* 192; Carter, *Buffalo Bill Cody,* 333; Croft-Cooke and Meadmore, *Buffalo Bill,* 194; Rivarola, *Buffalo Bill,* 156; Rosa and May, *Buffalo Bill and His Wild West,* 144; Russell, *Lives and Legends,* 352; Warren, *Buffalo Bill's America,* 344; *La Vanguardia, Diario de Barcelona* and *El Suplemento,* January 4, 1890, William F. "Buffalo Bill" Cody Collection; *La Dinastía* and *El Diluvio,* January 5, 1890, William F. "Buffalo Bill" Cody Collection.
83. Marill Escudé, *Aquell hivern,* 87–90.
84. Moses, *Wild West Shows,* 92–94, 127.
85. Maddra, *Hostiles,* 66; Marchena, *Buffalo Bill,* 10–11; Marill Escudé, *Aquell hivern,* 94; Moses, *Wild West Shows,* 94; Moses, "Wild West Shows, Reformers," 203; and Warren, *Buffalo Bill's America,* 370.
86. Marchena, *Buffalo Bill,* 18–19.
87. Marill Escudé, *Aquell hivern,* 90.
88. "El público quedó, como siempre, sumamente complacido del espectáculo y tributó justos y espontáneos aplausos a la *troupe* en los diversos ejercicios." *El Suplemento,* January 8, 1890, William F. "Buffalo Bill" Cody Collection.
89. "Desde hoy se empiezan los espectáculos a las tres de la tarde, en vez de las dos y media en que han comenzado hasta ahora." *El Suplemento,* January 8, 1890, William F. "Buffalo Bill" Cody Collection.
90. *Wichita Eagle,* January 1, 1890, William F. "Buffalo Bill" Cody Collection.
91. *The News-Herald* (Hillsboro, Ohio), January 16, 1890, William F. "Buffalo Bill" Cody Collection.
92. "El próximo miércoles, día 22, saldrá de este puerto el vapor «Bellver» que conducirá á Nápoles la Compañía Buffalo Bíll's Wild West. Para el embarco atracará el «Bellver» de costado al muelle de Sant Beltrán." *La Vanguardia,* January 19, 1890, William F. "Buffalo Bill" Cody Collection.
93. *El Barcelonés, La Dinastía, El Noticiero Universal* and *La Vanguardia,* all January 20, 1890, in William F. "Buffalo Bill" Cody Collection.

94. Marill Escudé, *Aquell hivern,* 98.
95. *La Dinastía,* January 19, 1890, William F. "Buffalo Bill" Cody Collection.
96. *El Barcelonés, Diario de Barcelona, La Dinastía, El Noticiero Universal, El Suplemento* and *La Vanguardia,* all January 21, 1890, in William F. "Buffalo Bill" Cody Collection.
97. Marill Escudé, *Aquell hivern,* 100.
98. "Era tan templada la temperatura, que muchos indios salieron a la arena casi desnudos o por mejor decir, vestidos a su usanza." *La Vanguardia,* January 21, 1890, William F. "Buffalo Bill" Cody Collection.
99. Blackstone, *Buckskins, Bullets and Business,* 24; Bridger, *Buffalo Bill and Sitting Bull,* 354–55; Burke, *Buffalo Bill: The Noblest Whiteskin,* 192–93; Carter, *Buffalo Bill Cody,* 333; Croft-Cooke and Meadmore, *Buffalo Bill,* 194; Portes, *Buffalo Bill,* 177–78; Rosa and May, *Buffalo Bill and His Wild West,* 144; Russell, *Lives and Legends,* 352; Sell and Weybright, *Buffalo Bill and the Wild West,* 181; Warren, *Buffalo Bill's America,* 344.
100. *El Barcelonés, Diario de Barcelona, La Dinastía, El Noticiero Universal, El Suplemento* and *La Vanguardia,* all January 21, 1890, in William F. "Buffalo Bill" Cody Collection; Marill Escudé, *Aquell hivern,* 100.
101. Blackstone, *Buckskins, Bullets and Business,* 15, 17, 27, 29–35, 96; Bonner, *William F. Cody's Wyoming Empire,* 170, 216, 222, 236, 246–47, 251; Carter, *Buffalo Bill Cody,* 378–84; Kasson, *Buffalo Bill's Wild West,* 141–58; *New York Times,* December 15, 1889, William F. "Buffalo Bill" Cody Collection; Russell, *Lives and Legends,* 378–85; Sorg, *Buffalo Bill,* 61–69, 77–82; and Warren, *Buffalo Bill's America,* 421, 444, 468–71.
102. Blackstone, *Buckskins, Bullets and Business,* 27; Bridger, *Buffalo Bill and Sitting Bull,* 408–10; Carter, *Buffalo Bill Cody,* 380–81; Joy S. Kasson, *Buffalo Bill's Wild West,*141–51; Russell, *Lives and Legends,* 378–82; Sorg, *Buffalo Bill,* 61–87; Warren, *Buffalo Bill's America,* 494.
103. Domènech, *Los Caminos de la Era Industrial,* 47–54; Puffert, *Tracks Across Continents,* 36–37, 181–82, 192.
104. Balfour, "'The Lion and the Pig'"; Carr, *Modern Spain,* 23–30, and *Spain,* 473–97; Esdaile, *Spain in the Liberal Age,* 194–216; Payne, *Spain,* 155–60; Mary Vincent, *Spain 1833–2002,* 87–98.
105. Burk, *Old World, New World,* 189–275; Griffin, *Four Years in Europe,* xxiv, xxxiv, 69–92; Perkins, *Great Rapprochement*; and Perkins, "The Great Rapprochement," *The Times,* November 1, 1887, William F. "Buffalo Bill" Cody Collection.
106. Conway, "José Martí frente," 129–42; Delmendo, *Star-Entangled Banner,* 26–29; Guerrero, *First Filipino,* 130; Lomas, *Translating Empire,* 216–17; Martí, "William F. Cody," 168–70 and "¡Magnífico espectáculo!" 678–87; Zaide and Zaide, *Jose Rizal,* 136–38.

9

"Buffalo Bill, the Italian Hero of the Prairies"

A Fascist Twist on Americanization in Italy

RENEE M. LAEGREID

In 1939, the Florentine publishing house G. Nerbini introduced the series "Buffalo Bill: The Italian Hero of the Prairies." Other than the designation of Buffalo Bill as an Italian, there is nothing unusual about yet another Buffalo Bill series in Italy. William F. Cody's first Wild West tour through Italy in 1890 sparked a fascination with the frontiersman and his adventures in the Far West. The first story published in Italian that featured Cody, a translation of an American dime novel, appeared in 1890; in 1904, Emilio Salgari published the first series on Buffalo Bill written by an Italian.[1] Shortly after Cody's 1906 European tour, publishing houses in Milan and then in Florence began translating US dime novels to sell in Italy, as well as publishing stories by Italian authors.[2] In 1939, Cody had been a popular icon for half a century; perhaps it seemed natural to include him as part of the Italian family. Certainly the image of Buffalo Bill on the cover of the first issue, with shoulder-length black hair and a dark goatee, appeared more Italian than the blond Colonel Cody of earlier series illustrations.

The construction of Buffalo Bill as Italian seems an obvious example of Americanization, defined by Robert W. Rydell and Rob Kroes as the "export and reception of American mass cultural forms in a transatlantic context."[3] Placing the "Buffalo Bill: The Italian Hero of the Prairies" series within the context of a new state confronting the challenges of modernity also fits well within Rydell and Kroes's admonishment to explore the process of what they call "creolization—the shaping or hybridization of American mass culture forms into the countries on the receiving end."[4] A solid understanding of the historical processes in Italy and the factors shaping the reception and translation of American iconography from Buffalo Bill's Wild West between 1890 and 1939 illuminates their responses to Buffalo Bill. Rather than following a straightforward process of Americanization, his memory over the course of nearly fifty years of internal concerns was embraced, rebuffed, and reconfigured. In 1939, the Fascist regime co-opted the familiar hero, Buffalo Bill, into the service of Italian nationalism, appropriating his contributions to the US colonization of the frontier West and applying them to further the Italian imperialist agenda.

Italy and the United States shared similar national experiences in the mid-nineteenth century that set the stage for the Italian usurpation of Buffalo Bill. Both countries had experienced a long and bloody civil war, and both faced the postwar challenges of a rapid adjustment to modernity.[5] William F. Cody began his Wild West performances after the US Civil War. He tapped into the American public's fascination with frontier war stories and helped reconfigure painful memories of the Civil War through the "fiction and drama" of his shows. As the nation underwent the process of "memorialization and reconciliation," frontier themes helped shift attention from Civil War political ideology and national division to individual traits: honor, self-sacrifice, noble motives, and moral character.[6] Cody focused his shows on the people whose skills, integrity, and fortitude helped bring the lands and indigenous people of the frontier West under US control.[7] While a popular reminder of the country's premodern past, his Wild West coincided with the era of rapid industrial and commercial growth in the United States. Rydell and Kroes note, "the show was as much a display of the products of nineteenth-century industrialized civilization as it was of the savage life of the frontier."[8] Indeed, his first commercial Wild West show, which opened in Omaha, Nebraska, in 1883, straddled the disconcerting reality of a region won through the benefits of the same modern technologies that simultaneously threatened to take away that region's defining characteristics.

Italians also experienced the uneasy confluence of postwar experience and emerging modernity. Italy emerged as a unified state in 1861; in 1870, twenty years prior to Cody's first tour, the state further consolidated its power by reducing the Vatican's holdings to its current, much-reduced size. As the leaders of the new country turned their attentions from war to issues of state, they had ambivalent feelings about embracing modernity. While recognizing the benefits, if not outright necessity, of the entire country entering the industrial age, elites balked at changes that would disrupt Italy's traditional social structure and remained opposed to the concept of modern corporations. Therefore, Italy lagged behind the United States and other European countries in developing a middle-class citizenry of sufficient numbers to develop large-scale leisure activities.[9] While villages and cities certainly enjoyed cultural and social events that included fairs, carnivals, and religious celebrations, these forms of entertainment retained characteristics rooted in tradition and locality.

In their respective postwar eras, both the United States and Italy also sought to create a sense of national unity in their countries. Even before the Civil War, the United States brought into play "economic, technical, political, and religious forces that foster[ed] the search for and development of a national culture that would override local and regional cultural loyalties."[10] After the Civil War, the emergence of a premodern icon, the cowboy, helped serve this function. Cody played a significant role in remaking the reputation of the cowhand—who, he lamented, had been "greatly despised" and "sneeringly referred to" by the general public—into a celebrated American hero.[11] During his first show in 1883, the program included an article entitled "The Cow Boy," which implored patrons to give cowhands recognition and respect for the hard work they had accomplished helping "extend American civilization" into the West.[12] The 1902 publication of Owen Wister's book *The Virginian: Horseman of the Plains* further promoted the image of the cowboy as a hero for the nation.[13] Wister constructed the protagonist, a poor, uneducated young man from the South, who found the opportunity to realize his potential while working as a cowboy in the West. The southern-born cowhand, known only by his nickname "The Virginian," ultimately wins the hand of an educated schoolteacher from the East and becomes a wealthy landowner in Wyoming, deftly tying together the three sections of the United States while promoting the cowboy as a uniquely American symbol of the American Dream.

After unification, Italian elites sought to develop a national culture that would both override centuries of local and regional affiliations and deal with "the anxieties and malaise induced by modernism."[14] To do so, Italians also reached back to a rural past. "Young intellectuals in Florence," notes Walter Adamson, sought a common denominator rooted in the preindustrial past to build "a culture of sufficient spiritual depth to offset, or at least complement, a social life based increasingly on industrialization, urbanization, science, and technology."[15] While the US and Italian elites both employed a common means—celebrating premodern workers—they had very different ends in mind. The image of a cowboy in the United States meant to highlight the importance of individual character and initiative. As a national icon, the cowboy stood as a metaphor for a young, vigorous society, thriving and powerful, free from age-old domination by a rigid social hierarchy. Italian intellectuals, on the other hand, valorized rural peasants as a whole. They did not recognize the Italian cowboy, or *buttero,* as a symbol of individual ingenuity or upward mobility. Instead, the buttero figured as only one part of an overall rural peasantry, thus reinforcing social traditions and class stability.

When Buffalo Bill arrived in 1890, his Wild West performances in Naples, Rome, Florence, Bologna, Milan, and Verona represented both a window into America's exciting frontier past and a harbinger of modern industrial society.[16] Louis Warren argues that aside from the novelty of the American West traveling to their doorstep, Europeans flocked to see Cody's shows "because of the way it spoke to European desires and anxieties" as countries approached modernity.[17] For example, during the decade of the 1880s, the city of Turin hosted an industrial exposition to stimulate industrialization in the city. The expo hosted "14,237 exhibitors, including 14,014 Italians," and "2,934,332 visitors."[18] By 1888 the city had installed electricity to support manufacturing growth and provide residents with modern conveniences.[19] But these advances brought worrisome change, especially in terms of rural-to-urban migration. During the early years of 1900, Turin experienced the first wave of immigration as thousands of villagers from the Piedmont countryside, attracted by Italy's first industrial revolution, poured into the city.[20] Such migration shifts occurred throughout Italy, contributing to the sense of social unease at all levels of society.

Along with industrialism and demographic changes, modernity included imperialism as nations sought to establish colonial holdings. When the "scramble for Africa" began in 1882, Italian intellectuals and politicians engaged in heated controversy over establishing colonies, providing, as Mark Choate argues, "a crucial debate in foreign policy and societal vision" from 1890 through World War II.[21] Prime Minister Francesco Crispi, the principal architect for Italy's African empire, initiated the first settler colony in 1890, part of a two-fold solution for both emigration and the rising threat of socialism (a by-product of rapid social and economic changes).[22] Preparing for his first European tour, Cody addressed the anxieties felt by European countries as they reached out to extend their own national frontiers by making "the story of the American West merge within the story of European expansion."[23] Cody's visit to Italy in 1890 came during Crispi's push for creating a "Greater Italy" in Africa. While Crispi may have appreciated Cody, the icon of imperialism, in Italy during his push for imperial colonies, so too did his opponents. Anti-imperialist critics depicted Cody and Crispi together in political cartoons, lampooning both men and the supposed benefits of expansion.[24]

When Cody returned to Italy in 1906, he performed to welcoming audiences and invigorated the country's enthusiasm for the American West. Although he did not spend as much time in each city as in the 1890 tour—only days instead of weeks—he expanded the number of cities where the show performed from six to thirty-four.[25] Taking the show into the smaller cities around Italy allowed Cody to dig deeper into the Italian citizenry and to expose more spectators to the story of his role in conquering the West. In the sixteen years since his previous tour, Italian industrialization had grown, as had the population in cities, as rural peasants sought factory work. Although unified as a country in name, Italian social and cultural life still remained centered in localities—city, town, village—and aligned by region. Each of the cities, unsurprisingly, recalled or focused on a specific memory associated with Cody's visit. For example, during his 1890 stay south of Rome, this had happened with the event known as *La Sfida,* the bucking contest between Buffalo Bill's cowboys and the Italian cowboys or *butteri.* Cody claimed his cowboys had won, stating the Italian riders exceeded the time limit; Italians disagreed, and the butteri made national news for their victory over Cody's cowboys for a brief time before slipping back into obscurity. While forgotten outside of their region, their victory against Cody's cowboys remained—and still remains—an important part of the local lore of the region.[26] During his 1906 tour, then, while the Wild West shows followed a well-scripted format, spectators recalled both an overall reaction to the performance and a specific memory of Cody's earlier visit to their particular city. The people in the region around Rome thus remembered his poor sportsmanship during La Sfida, as Cody announced his cowboys as winners on a technicality; Venetians, on the other hand, remembered Cody for his admiration of the city's architecture; and in Turin his memory was captured within the city's cultural whirlwind as rural people immigrated into the city, bringing with them oral storytelling traditions.[27] "The best memory alive in Turin is from a *piole* (local song)," writes Milo Julini.[28] "But, to be honest," he continues, "it does not seem very nice. Unlike Venetians and Romans, we Turin remember Buffalo Bill for the story of an unfaithful wife and a cuckolded husband."[29]

Each town held carefully its own specific memory of Cody, perpetuated for generations. Piergiorgio Balocco recalled hearing about Buffalo Bill from his grandmother: "[She] told us how she had been a witness of his coming to Turin, the magnificence of the event, how the city had been involved, and for how long one talked about it."[30] Silvio Rutteri attended the 1906 Wild West show in Trieste, Italy. Interviewed in 1966 as the city celebrated the sixtieth anniversary of Cody's visit, Rutteri recalled,

> Buffalo Bill took us to the world of the cowboy, the Indian tribes—the red skins— . . . It was a whole new world for us that we would eventually see reflected in the pages of adventure writers, like [the author Emilio] Salgari, and here [his show] formed a wonderful reality, because it brought before us a fantastic world and that was superbly coming true in absolute naturalness corresponding to the real habits of the people of the West.[31]

Cody's shows exposed Italians to the people and values of the newly conquered region through adventures on the American frontier; the memories of his show became part of a complex and multilayered imprint in Italian culture that persisted for generations. From personal recollections of Cody and his show, reading stories based on Cody's "true" adventures, or both, Cody's two brief tours through Italy left a deep and pervasive impact.

Rutteri's mention of the Italian adventure writer Emilio Salgari brings up an important point. Through mass-marketing technology and the publication of Buffalo Bill stories in Italy, the memory of Buffalo Bill became codified.[32] Readers familiar with Cody's Wild West show eagerly bought the stories, keeping alive the adventures brought to life in the arena. Authors based their stories on the "reflection" of the "reality" presented by Buffalo Bill's Wild West show and on translated dime novels rather than on actual experience with or knowledge of the American West. In doing so, they reified themes related to imperial conquest: patriotism, self-sacrifice, military adventure, violence, and racial attitudes toward indigenous peoples. Mass-marketed images of Buffalo Bill's Wild West show thus existed alongside local memories and personal recollections of Cody, the man who inspired works of music—both great opera and tawdry ballads—or loved architecture, or exhibited bad sportsmanship, or introduced spectators to popcorn.[33] The various ways in which he was remembered—either personally or through mass-marketed stories—extended the fascination of Buffalo Bill and his adventures on the frontier across generations, although in an increasingly standardized format.

In an example of fortuitous timing, the mass marketing of Buffalo Bill stories occurred as more Italians could read. After unification, Italy embraced the drive for universal literacy, as had most European countries between the 1860s and the beginning of the First World War.[34] Bringing Italy's literacy rates in line with other countries served as one motivation; developing a sense of national unity provided an even more compelling rationale. Frank Coppa explains that "in Italy, liberalism—removal of the various princes and the union of their principalities in a single state—was associated with nationalism, and liberals advocated education as a means to generate a sense of citizenry in the new country."[35] They had created a country; "it was now necessary to make Italians."[36] Liberal politicians envisioned elementary schools and adult literacy programs operating to "create a national culture and a sense of national belonging that would erode regional loyalties," undercutting local dialects by enforcing a standard Italian language, and teaching patriotism to the new country with civics and national history classes.[37] Literacy gaps existed, depending on gender, class, urban or rural location, but the 1910 census indicated significant advancements throughout the population. Male illiteracy dropped from a countrywide average of 65 percent in 1860 to 25 percent in 1910. During the same period, illiteracy for women dropped from 85 percent to 40 percent.[38]

While apathy from Italians and lack of enforcement from politicians kept literacy rates low during the early decades after unification, Linda Reeder demonstrates a correlation between dropping illiteracy rates, emigration to the United States, and an emerging sense of Italian nationalism.[39] Beginning in the 1880s, Italy entered into an era of unprecedented transatlantic mass migration, as "millions of Italians left their country" to find work.[40] Nearly 900,000 emigrated to the United States.[41] Emigrants leaving for the United States may still have self-identified by their home village or family—despite the Italian government's efforts—but upon arrival in the United States they found themselves cast under the unifying umbrella of Italian. As Reeder argues, "To the customs agents waiting at Ellis Island, the passport he clutched labeled him a citizen of Italy. To non-Italians in the new world his look, language and gestures made it clear he was Italian. . . . Daily life in the Americas strengthened an individual's identification with the Italian nation state."[42] When emigrants returned home, as many did, they brought with them a sense of identity with Italy.

This metamorphosis from illiterate and locally oriented to literate and patriotic continued to gain momentum during the early twentieth century. When placed in the context of Buffalo Bill's role in the Americanization of Italy, two trends are worth noting. First, Italians had an interest in learning about the country where so many of their friends and family members had emigrated. Second, the increasing number of children and adults who learned to read during the era of Buffalo Bill's tours through Italy meant that large numbers of Italians of all ages read about Buffalo Bill in newspapers during his tour. In effect, the rise of literacy and Cody's popularity worked hand in hand, creating a demand for the mass-produced stories that featured him in a popular form of publication called *fumetti*. Widespread readership worked as a socializing instrument, encouraging cultural literacy based on Buffalo Bill's Wild West adventures.

The term *fumetti* translates roughly into English as "comics," although as Luca Somigli points out, the translation does not adequately address "both the parameters of the genre [nor] its origins."[43] The fumetti that emerged in 1904 reflected an older form of the genre based on illustrated narratives. According to Somigli, "thanks to innovations in printing and in the technology for reproduction of images, throughout the nineteenth century publishers experimented with publications for children and adolescents, both books and periodicals, in which illustrations had a crucial role."[44] Similar to the dime novels published in the United States, fumetti had an illustrated cover depicting the main character involved in an action representing the theme of the story, followed by sixteen to twenty pages of text.

Italian writer Emilio Salgari created the first story based on the adventures of Buffalo Bill in the fumetti tradition.[45] As a reporter for a Veronese newspaper, he covered Cody's 1890 Wild West and participated as a stagecoach passenger in the show. Salgari wrote one book on Buffalo Bill, *The Sovereign of the Gold Field*. First published as an installment in a Geona weekly magazine, *Per Terra e per Mare* [*For Land and Sea*], in 1904, the story appeared in book form the following year.[46] "And then," writes Felice Pozzo, came "all the rest, an ocean of paper," based on the exploits of Buffalo Bill.[47] The number of fumetti, both translated American stories and stories by Italian authors, is stunning. Up to the year 1911, the publishing house Editorial Milanese had a series with 150 issues; a second series, with 39 issues, appeared in 1912. Casa Editrice Americana di Milano took over publication of Buffalo Bill stories in 1913, printing both American and Italian authors.

The First World War and its aftermath disrupted publishing houses throughout Italy. Production of Buffalo Bill adventure stories did not pick up until the publishing house G. Nerbini purchased the publication rights from Casa Editrice Americana di Milano in 1919.[48] Several years later, in 1922, G. Nerbini began reprinting the first one hundred issues originally published from 1908; in 1927, the publishing house released reprints from the 1913 issues onward, two hundred issues in all. Cristofori Franco and Alberto Menarini write that in this later production, "Not all two hundred [issues] . . . came from the previously published editions," and they list the episodes that "were definitely written by Emilio Fancelli, as well as probably many others [i.e., issues] that are not reflected in the original American edition."[49] In 1922 the Glorious House of Milan added American- and Italian-authored issues, reprints, and "other sporadic initiatives."[50] G. Nerbini introduced another new series in 1931 while also keeping up sales with reprints. Adding to this plethora, in 1934 the demand for Buffalo Bill stories encouraged Fernando Bellini, editor of the Illustrated Editions of Rome, to author and publish a thirty-issue series entitled "Life and Adventures of Buffalo Bill" under the pseudonym George H. Driwson. During that same year Ciancimino Calogero di Sciacca invented "The Son of Buffalo Bill," creating three series of twelve issues each, as well as another series entitled "The Nemesis of Buffalo Bill," published in book form. As more Italian authors wrote stories, loosely based on reflections of Cody's life if not outright fabrications, memories of Buffalo Bill that began with spectators witnessing his Wild West shows settled more broadly and firmly into the Italian population. Publication of fumetti played an important role by redirecting locally specific memories of Cody into a mass-produced image that focused on his role in "conquering" the frontier.

At this point it is worth reflecting on the admonition, "A truly historical project must be attentive to the ways in which 'memory' is not a generic term of analysis, but itself an object appropriated and politicized."[51] Editorial houses had a subtle political agenda in disseminating popular works at a good price and with pro-republican and anticlerical leanings—Buffalo Bill's adventure fit the bill well. The politics of publishing became less subtle when Benito Mussolini took control of the Italian government in 1922.[52] Immediately after he assumed the role of dictator, Mussolini instituted a policy of "Italy for Italians" in order to emphasize the works of Italian authors, artists, and film producers—a policy that quite likely factored into the increasing number of Buffalo Bill stories by Italian authors. Although Fascist censorship never held absolute control over artistic works, the publishing industry experienced a distinctive shift as the number of books celebrating the people, culture, and heritage of Italy increased.[53] For example, Italian cowboys, the butteri, who had disappeared into obscurity within weeks after defeating Buffalo Bill's cowboys in 1890, emerged in print as the honorable horsemen of the marshlands. The poem "Settembre," by Gabriele D'Annunzio, celebrating the courage and fortitude of the cowboys tending their herds, became a national hit. People in homes and bars throughout the Tuscan region sang "Maramma Mia," the sad song of a young bride watching her new husband ride after the cattle, perhaps never to return from the malaria-infested swamps along the western coast of Italy. Even Italians who emigrated found a champion: Ugo E. Imperatori, renowned emigration scholar, published numerous books on Italians around the world and their contributions to the social and cultural development in the countries where they settled.[54]

Nerbini and his sons, while strong supporters of the Fascist government, continued to publish fumetti featuring American characters such as Mickey Mouse, Nick Carter, Flash Gordon, and Buffalo Bill. However, shortly after Mussolini signed the Pact of Steel with Hitler in 1939, thereby solidifying German and Italian alignment against capitalism and communism, the *Washington Post* ran the following headline: "'Buffalo Bill's Life' banned by Fascists." Along with the "works of many writers, including many Jews . . . [the] Life and Adventure of Buffalo Bill . . . were condemned today as unsuited for fascists."[55] Mario Bussoni notes that "during the fascist regime, the publisher Nerbini had to adapt to the new state rules to tell only homegrown and edifying stories, and during the Second World War, to ignore people who either originated from or dealt with countries with which Italy was at war."[56] G. Nerbini immediately ceased publication of all banned fumetti, as required. Later that year, however, the publisher introduced a new *fumetto,* "Buffalo Bill: The Italian Hero of the Prairies."[57]

When set into the context of Italy's imperialist agenda, the new fumetto functions better as a strategy for encouraging support for Mussolini's troubled

FIGURE 9.1. Cover of *Le avventure di Buffalo Bill: L'eroe italiano della prateria* (Buffalo Bill: The Italian Hero of the Prairies), Firenze: G. Nerbini, 1939.

colonies in Ethiopia rather than as a curious flouting of Fascist policy. Italian forces invaded Ethiopia in 1935, and by 1936 they had control of the country.[58] As planned, the Italian government established agricultural colonization projects. Two factors complicated the situation. First, enticing farmers to move to the new settlements proved difficult, and second, Ethiopians continued to resist Italian control. By 1939, with the Second World War looming, Mussolini's government found itself in the position of scrambling for both settlers and military recruits to maintain its hold on the country. What better model of patriotism and self-sacrifice on the frontier for the Italian people than Buffalo Bill?

The illustrated cover of the first installment of the series, published ca. 1939, depicts a swarthy Buffalo Bill astride a rearing horse, under the heading, "Buffalo Bill: The Italian Hero of the Prairie." The subject of the issue, "Il Piccolo Corriere" (The Little Courier), tells the story of his family on the plains and the death of his father. No mention is made of Buffalo Bill's Italian heritage during the entire story. Instead, a full-page editorial essay at the end of the issue provides the explanation for this amazing discovery under the headline "How the Italian Domenico Tambini Came to Be Buffalo Bill."[59] The essay begins with a simple yet powerful sentence: "As recalled by Ugo E. Imperatori in his recent article, Buffalo Bill, the heroic protagonist of many adventurous enterprises on American soil, was Italian, and his real name was Domenico Tambini."[60] Rumors that Buffalo Bill had been born in Italy with the surname Tambini emerged shortly after Cody's death in 1917.[61] Associating this discovery with the weight of Imperatori's reputation as a scholar was meant to turn rumor into fact.

The next sentence, albeit covering three topics, is also instructive: "Born in the countryside of Faenza, emigrated with his father and with his mother to America to reunite with an older brother who was there for a few years, and the painful events that afflicted him in his youth, led him to become a naturalized son of the land and to voluntarily enroll in the troops of the North American Union."[62] Having established the credibility of Buffalo Bill's Italian origins, the editor reveals Cody's place of birth, "the countryside of Faenza," not coincidently also the birthplace of Benito Mussolini. Placing his origins in the countryside rather than in a city reinforced Mussolini's "back to the land" programs and his ideology that all that is good and true in Italy came from the simple life of rural people. Reference to emigration to reunite with a family resonated with readers. Italians constituted the largest and last immigrant group before the United States instituted restrictive immigration policies, and they often shared the experience of chain migration, with one family member venturing to the United States to find work before sending for others. The reference to "the painful events" relate to the difficulties of emigration and the death of his father during Cody's youth, providing a rationale for why he did not return to his homeland.

The following third of the essay lists Cody's exploits and adventures, highlighting his character and courage as a US soldier in the Civil War, then as he conquered the frontier West for settlers. The essay then shifts to his Wild West business, explaining that "in his mature age, Cody the entrepreneur, was always in search of new business combinations."[63] His business adventures included taking his show abroad "as a manager of a company of which the Red Skins displayed various exercises of skill against groups of scouts and cowboys." Although adventurous in his youth, later in life Cody demonstrated practical wisdom by making the transition from real-life frontiersman to businessman performing his past exploits. Although engaging in a more stable life in order to care for his family, Cody refused to abandon the physical, demanding work that had played such a strong role in developing his character.

The editor continues with Cody's development as a politician: "You should know, however, that during his Europe trip he had a hidden political purpose, and that the colonel was instructed by his government to draw America closer to Europe in order to start trade negotiations of the utmost importance between the new and the old world. He was received by the sovereigns of the several States and Queen Victoria of the UK . . . [for which] the UK distinguished him with high honor."[64] The sections on business and politics created links between Cody and Mussolini that Italians would have easily recognized. Both men shared lowly origins, both demonstrated strong character and embraced violence to advance the frontiers of their respected countries, and both served their governments as they engaged with the leaders of European states. No mention is made of a political assignment for Cody in Italy; the editor suggests he traveled there, "perhaps attracted by the desire to see again the land of Romagna, the land of his birth," as someone who, after venturing afar, wished to see his "family" once again.[65]

The editorial concludes with a description of how Buffalo Bill's "true" Italian heritage came to light: "Buffalo Bill died in Philadelphia in 1910, not rich, but well-off. After his death, the practices of succession revealed and vindicated the Italian origin of the hero from the prairie. We will see in this first episode, when Domenico Tambini, though changed in name and nationality, always remains a good Italian in character, and a true blood Romagnaian."[66] While only the cover of this first issue carries the title "Buffalo Bill: The Italian Hero of the Prairie," the heading remains on the interior title page for all seventy-six issues; his Italian origin is only briefly revisited in the third issue, describing his mother's death. No further mention of Italy or his Italian heritage appears in the remaining issues. However, the editorial essay in this first issue ends with the publisher's encouragement to stay tuned: "The wonderful adventures of William Cody that have so enthused readers around the world . . . are collected in this new series of installments, each with 16 pages, a color cover and a complete story!"[67] Readers did indeed stay tuned, with 500,000 copies sold over the course of the series' publication.

There is no point in worrying over the factual errors in the editor's essay—there are so very, very many. Rather, it is far more useful as an example of Americanization appropriated by the Italian government. Rydell and Kroes argue that American cultural forms are seldom passively accepted by the receiving country; rather, they are "creolized" or adapted to cultural or political norms.[68] Mussolini's cultural office encouraged the use of popular culture that served "a propagandistic purpose, with the intent of creating consent through the dissemination of recurring works and images that would serve to glorify the Fascist empire and deify its leader."[69] By appropriating the popular American character, Buffalo Bill, the government used the widespread affection for the frontiersman for its own purposes. In a savvy twist, they "respond[ed] to popular tastes and interests": the heroic Buffalo Bill became Italian, his virtues representing those of his "countrymen," and his patriotic support for imperialism now aligning with those of the Italian government.[70]

Then, seventy-two weeks after publication of the first installment, the fumetto ended as inexplicitly as it had begun. On the last page, in the space usually reserved for a teaser for the upcoming issue, bold type announced that the series had come to an end. The timing makes sense, however, when placed in the context of Italy's struggle to maintain the Ethiopian territory. In June 1940, when Italy entered World War II aligned with Hitler, its hold on Ethiopia faced increasing military pressure from Ethiopians, who now had Allied advisors and help from British, free French, and Belgian forces. In November of 1941, British forces, along with Ethiopian fighters, liberated the country, ending Italian imperial control.

Rydell and Kroes argue that "far from being monolithic monoculture, mass culture is pluralistic and, in the hands of the oppressed, can be selectively appropriated and refashioned into weapons of the weak." However, mass culture can also be appropriated by those in power to support a national agenda.[71] With the addition of one word, "Italian," Buffalo Bill became a foil to advance Fascist support for their imperial aims by co-opting the skills, adventures on the frontier, and the commitment to patriotism Buffalo Bill exhibited as he brought the US West under US control. All of Buffalo Bill's good qualities became, by association, the qualities of all Italians, and in particular their leader: moral character, patriotism, and participating in imperialism for the good of country. American cultural forms, Rydell and Kroes note, "were hardly value free." By creating an alternative genealogy for Buffalo Bill, the values represented by the hero of the American West became inextricably linked with Mussolini.

It is difficult to know how or if many readers subjected to mass-cultural forms absorbed their ideological messages, if, as Rydell and Kroes ponder, culture industries such as the ones designed and implemented by Mussolini's Fascist regime could become "all-powerful and their audiences passive sponges . . . or if audiences [remained] more resilient and creative than we often think."[72] It is difficult to know if or how Italians accepted the revelation of Buffalo Bill's Italian origin. Did the people who witnessed Cody's Wild West performances in their towns, who recalled not only the memories of the show, but of Cody's particular imprint on their local history, accept the Fascist storyline? Would their memories and the memories handed down across generations have created a buffer of sorts from the revelation in G. Nerbini's new series? Perhaps the passage of time since his last tour and the reification of Cody and other characters in fumetti made the assertion seem more plausable. Ferruccio Alessandri, an Italian interviewed for a blog dedicated to remembering World War II atrocities, recollected that "during the time of fascism I was in elementary school, and like all of my schoolmates, I was subjected to total propaganda. Just to give you an idea, I read . . . the stories of Buffalo Bill entitled, 'Buffalo Bill, the Italian Hero of the Plains.'" Reflecting on the effects of propaganda when mass culture is controlled to the point that the people have no other point of reference, Alessandri continues, "we didn't know anything else. . . . It takes generations to break free from 'ways of thinking' instilled by a controlling state—or culture industries."[73]

Americanization can be complicated, uneven, and contested. Teasing out the political and cultural complexity of the country on the receiving end of the process is essential in order to grasp the rich subtleties—or ironies—that emerge as individual countries adapted or reconfigured aspects of American mass culture for their own nationalistic purposes. Nothing captures this better than Cody's alternative genealogy in Nerbini's fumetti. Indeed, the legacy of Cody's Wild West offers a case study for mass culture and nationalism in Italy. Buffalo Bill's Wild West performances in Italy certainly factor into the process of Americanization in that country. And yet the impact of his shows and long-term influence on the Italian people becomes historically more meaningful when placed into the context of Italy, a new country, responding to the demands of modernity. Literacy and emigration worked in tandem to create a sense of Italian patriotism, useful for a government engaging in imperial expansion; mass marketing and increasing literacy contributed to Buffalo Bill's popularity nationwide; and Italian familiarity with the stories of Buffalo Bill and the values he represented in subduing indigenous peoples proved useful in 1939, when the regime sought public support in the fight to keep their Ethiopian colony.[74] Joy Kasson writes that in the United States, "American identity was founded in the Western Experience: triumphant conquest of wilderness through virtue, skill, and firepower," and violence.[75] These are the qualities that Italians had associated with Buffalo Bill for nearly a half-century, qualities that aligned with Mussolini's ideology and hopes for his country as well.

Notes

1. Pozzo, "Buffalo Bill eroe da romanzo popolare," 97.
2. Biscàro, *Buffalo Bill* è *Arrivato a Torino,* 84n33.
3. Rydell and Kroes, *Buffalo Bill in Bologna,* introduction.
4. Ibid., 5–6.
5. Shugaar, "Italy's Own Lost Cause," *New York Times,* May 2, 2012, opinion page: "In the same eventful spring of 1861 that marked the outbreak of the American Civil War, Italy declared its existence as a united kingdom. In fact, just as the bombardment of an island fortress in Charleston, S.C., riveted the attention of a nation plunging into civil war, the kingdom of southern Italy made a last-ditch stand against northern Italian bombardment of a waterfront fortress midway between Rome and Naples. The two sieges, of Fort Sumter and of Gaeta, came only weeks apart."
6. Joy Kasson, *Buffalo Bill's Wild West,* 242, 236–38.
7. Quote from Wild West reproduction poster in author's possession.
8. Rydell and Kroes, *Buffalo Bill in Bologna,* 113.
9. On the development of leisure and the middle class, see Levine, *Highbrow/ Lowbrow*; Kammen, *American Culture, American Tastes*; Braden, *Leisure and Entertainment in America*; and Nasaw, *Going Out.*
10. Rydell and Kroes, *Buffalo Bill in Bologna,* 10.
11. Buffalo Bill Program, p. 25, found in the William F. "Buffalo Bill" Cody Collection, McCracken Research Library, Buffalo Bill Center of the West.
12. Reddin, *Wild West Shows,* 69.
13. Wister, *Virginian.*
14. Adamson, *Avant-Garde Florence,* 2.
15. Ibid., 2.
16. Reddin, *Wild West Shows,* 103.

17. Warren, *Buffalo Bill's America*, 302.
18. Biscàro, *Buffalo Bill è Arrivato a Torino*, 17.
19. Ibid.
20. Ibid.
21. Choate, *Emigrant Nation*, 9.
22. Ibid., 9, 15.
23. Rydell and Kroes, *Buffalo Bill in Bologna*, 111.
24. These and other cartoons from Italian newspapers can be found in the William F. "Buffalo Bill" Cody Collection, MS 6, McCracken Research Library, Buffalo Bill Center of the West.
25. *Griffin, Four Years in Europe*, 151–52.
26. American sources include Urban's essay, "When the 'Wild West' Went to Florence" (the earliest scholarly publication on La Sfida I have found to date); Redding, *Wild West Shows* (although he inexplicably misspells butteri throughout his discussion); Rosa and May, *Buffalo Bill and His Wild West*; Rydel and Kroes, *Buffalo Bill in Bologna*; Warren, *Buffalo Bill's America*; and American newspaper coverage from March 5–27, 1890, in William F. "Buffalo Bill" Cody Collection.
27. For details on the public response to Buffalo Bill's Wild West in over twenty cities, see Bussoni, *Buffalo Bill in Italia*.
28. Julini, preface to *Buffalo Bill è Arrivato a Torino*, by Andrea Biscàro, 11.
29. Ibid., 8.
30. Balocco, introduction to *Buffalo Bill è Arrivato a Torino*, by Andrea Biscàro, 7.
31. Rutteri quoted in Stern, *Buffalo Bill a Trieste*, 17.
32. Pozzo, "Buffalo Bill."
33. Bussoni, *Buffalo Bill in Italia*, 98.
34. David Vincent, "Progress of Literacy," 414. See also, Tortella, "Patterns of Economic Retardation and Recovery"; and Alhearn, "Qualifying Quantitative Literacy."
35. Coppa, "From Liberalism to Fascism," 137.
36. Ibid., 138.
37. Reeder, "Women in the Classroom," 113.
38. David Vincent, "Progress of Literacy," 413–14.
39. Reeder, "Women in the Classroom," 102, 111.
40. Choate, *Emigrant Nation*, 23.
41. Laegreid, "Italians," 237–38.
42. Reeder, "Women in the Classroom," 111.
43. Somigli, "Fumetti," 789.
44. Ibid., 787.
45. Pozzo, "Buffalo Bill," 96–97.
46. Ibid., 97.
47. Ibid., 101. Pozzo writes, "Cristofori Franco and Alberto Menarini have carefully listed the various series of installments that have appeared in Italy since 1908."
48. De Berti, *Dallo Schermo alla Carta*, 12.

49. Pozzo, "Buffalo Bill," 102.
50. Ibid., 103.
51. Matsuda, *Memory of the Modern,* 6.
52. The liberal government that ruled after unification did not survive the First World War, and the succeeding attempts at socialism failed to address postwar issues.
53. Reich, "Mussolini at the Movies," 6.
54. Imperatori, *Italiani Fuori.*
55. "'Buffalo Bill's Life' banned by Fascists," *Washington Post,* August 5, 1939.
56. Bussoni, *Buffalo Bill in Italia.*
57. Chiarelli, *Mamma Italia.*
58. Sbacchi, "Italian Colonization in Ethiopia," 504. Prime Minister Crispi tried unsuccessfully to take control of the African state in 1896.
59. Nerbini editore (publishing house), *Le Avventure di Buffalo Bill: L'eroe Italiano della Prateria*, 16.
60. Ibid.
61. Bussoni, *Buffalo Bill in Italia*, 96.
62. Nerbini editore, *Le Avventure di Buffalo Bill,* 16.
63. Ibid.
64. Nerbini editore, *Le Avventure di Buffalo Bill,* 16.
65. Ibid.
66. Ibid.
67. Ibid.
68. Rydell and Kroes, *Buffalo Bill in Bologna.*
69. Reich, "Mussolini at the Movies," 6.
70. Rydell and Kroes, *Buffalo Bill in Bologna*, 5.
71. Rydell and Kroes, *Buffalo Bill in Bologna*, introduction.
72. Ibid., 7–9.
73. Ferruccio Alessandri, "27 Gennaio 2012, Per Non Dimenticare," *Cartoonist globale* (blog), January 27, 2012, http://lucaboschi.nova100.ilsole24ore.com/2012/01/27/27-gennaio-2012-per-non-dimenticare/.
74. Rydell and Kroes, *Buffalo Bill in Bologna,* 7–9.
75. Kasson, *Buffalo Bill's Wild West,* 265–66. See the works by Slotkin on violence in the West, in particular his *Regeneration through Violence.*

Epilogue

The Special Relationship in Popular Culture
The Legacy of 1887

FRANK CHRISTIANSON

South Kensington's lustre is waning,
The Westminster fun's getting stale;
The star of the Battenberg's setting,
The Parnellite comet grows pale.
The Crawford-Dilke scandal's
forgotten,
The Law Court sensations are nil;
Society needs a new tonic,—
So come along, Buffalo Bill.

Referee, 1887

During a brief visit in the summer of 2013, I began tracing the marks of Buffalo Bill's Wild West on the palimpsest of London's cityscape. It started with Earls Court Exhibition Centre in the Borough of Kensington and Chelsea, built near the site where the American Exhibition was originally staged in 1887. I had seen reference to some archival materials held there and hoped to access primary documents not available elsewhere. I was disappointed to discover that, aside from a wall placard commemorating the May 9 "Grand

Opening" of the Wild West exhibition, most of their actual holdings consisted of more recent material from the various exhibitions and performances hosted in the current Earls Court Building. I did, however, locate an institutional history of the site, written by a former director, John Glanfield, and titled *Earls Court and Olympia: From Buffalo Bill to the 'Brits.'* As the title indicates, Glanfield identified the American Exhibition, and the Wild West show in particular, as an inaugural event that had consecrated that space ever after as a showground. It was part of the tradition that began with open-air arenas staging spectaculars, followed by the enclosed exhibition spaces of Earls Court One and Earls Court Two, as well as the Olympia events complex.

On this same visit, I learned that the Earls Court Exhibition Centre was slated for demolition in 2015 to make way for new housing units. Constructed in 1937, long after the first Wild West tour, the centre had accommodated everything from rock concerts to Olympic competitions to dog shows. For 128 years, Earls Court had served as an enduring monument to the culture of mass spectacle embodied by the Wild West. But even as one marker was slated for erasure, other traces of the Wild West's European transit remained. That same summer I came across more signs of the exhibition's passage through Britain: a Wild West show program in the Victorian wing of the Museum of London; a burial marker in Brompton Cemetery for Long Wolf, a Lakota Sioux performer who died of pneumonia in 1892; street signs in Salford, Manchester, with names such as "Buffalo Court," "Cody Court," and "Kansas Avenue," indicating where the exhibition encamped and performed during the winter of 1887 and 1888;[1] a bronze Buffalo Bill statue in Glasgow's east end; and a saddle displayed in the castle at St. Michael's Mount, which Cody gave to the Baron St. Levan in 1904 during the Wild West's farewell tour of England. These were but some pieces of public memory preserved and displayed in locations prominent and obscure; and they, in turn, were supplemented by the thousands of items—newspapers, periodicals, dime novels, postcards, illustrations, art, sheet music, and photographs—stowed in various archives across the country, including the British Library.

Physical evidence of the Wild West's European history is more apparent in Britain than other parts of Europe. The exhibition began its first and final European tours in England, where it spent more time than in any other country outside the United States. Like Buffalo Bill's Wild West, this volume ends where it began, with a consideration of the British tour as a template for the broader phenomenon of the international Wild West. The British experience of the Wild West has a prominent place in this volume, in part because England played a determining role within the broader history of American cultural exportation. Because of its relative linguistic and cultural affinity with the United States, England was the natural port of entry to Europe for the Wild West and functioned as a proof of concept for Cody and his partners. Thus, with success in England, the fundamental patterns and practices the Wild West established there would persist for the most part throughout the subsequent international tours. Emboldened by their success after nearly a year in England, the exhibition organizers returned to the United States to regroup and prepare for a much more extensive continental run the following year. Intermittently until 1906, they would repeat the circuit with extended multiyear tours across the continent.

In his study of post–WWII Americanization in Britain, H. L. Malchow argues that "viewing the special relationship as popular culture" offers a demotic but rich means of exploring how culture moves across national boundaries in shaping both "public policy and private subjectivity."[2] The essays in this volume illustrate the value of this proposition for an earlier moment in north Atlantic history, even as they broaden the inquiry beyond the Anglo-American framework. In 1887, Cody and his team saw an opportunity, through the spectacle of the Wild West exhibition, to reimagine the relationship between the United States and Britain. An opportunity that was at the same time a business venture with its commercial potential bound up in these same political and cultural subtexts. In calling Buffalo Bill's Wild West "the most important commercial vehicle for the fabrication and transmission of the Myth of the Frontier" in the late nineteenth century, Richard Slotkin points to both the geographic scope and the audience size as evidence of the reach of the tours between 1885 and 1905. Slotkin's frontier trilogy, beginning with *Regeneration through Violence*, helped establish a cultural historiography that critically examined the processes of popularization in the development of cultural nationalism. That work has influenced countless other scholars who have sought to account for the ways *frontier* history, broadly speaking, became integral to an ideology of American exceptionalism. Joy Kasson offered a more focused treatment of Slotkin's thesis by using the exhibition as a case study for understanding the mutually informing functions of modern celebrity and public memory. Her work shows how the Buffalo Bill phenomenon "*created* American memory through the medium of popular entertainment" and "heralded the opening of a new age in mass communication."[3] This particular medium, Kasson argues, would come to wield both political and economic authority in demonstrating the "power of the mass media to . . . sell a product, and shape popular perceptions."[4]

The mass media environment Kasson describes presages Malchow's account of how the American culture industry generated content for the British public. A half-century before the Cold War, and before American Studies programs were appearing in Europe to perform their own version of Americanization, many of the factors on which Malchow bases his study were already emerging. Indeed, his characterization of the postwar context that made "American culture and its agents central to any narrative of Britain" could aptly describe the environment that ushered the Wild West *east* to Europe at the fin de siècle: a "vast increase in contact" transmitted American culture via "tourist and professional cross-traffic" and an "unparalleled growth in the density of transatlantic media."[5] The quantitative and qualitative transformation of a transatlantic media culture in particular, as Joel Wiener has shown, was a hallmark of the Victorian and Edwardian eras. The media revolution he details is another unifying thread interweaving the studies in this collection. It requires a transatlantic frame because it was in significant measure a *product* of the interaction between American and British institutions responding to the possibilities of mass circulation.[6]

The epigraph to this chapter, from an anonymous poem published in *Referee* magazine before Buffalo Bill's London debut, suggests the mass-mediated environment that awaited the exhibition in the early months of 1887. The litany reads like a headline summary of several months of London newspapers; from politics to law to society scandals, it evokes the public's relentless appetite for distraction and entertainment. From the time the exhibition arrived in port, the media coverage of the Wild West's London season was as insatiable as the poetic invitation implies. And that coverage was, in turn, central to how the exhibition represented itself across media platforms, including in its own marketing materials. Cody's own account of the first international tour places newspaper stories at the center of the narrative as a way of validating his self-promotional claims and expressing, through an ostensibly local voice, the political subtext of the performance. The 1888 edition of Cody's autobiography references the new media epoch in its direct attention to the press as well as its own narrative voice.[7] Incorporating the international experience within the larger nationalist project, the centerpiece of Cody's account is a carefully orchestrated staging—on showground and in the pages of the book—of the

Wild West's command performance for Queen Victoria, a performance that coincided with the celebration of her Jubilee.[8] The queen's patronage of the Wild West was an integral part of the broader ritual commemoration of her fifty-year reign: the Wild West as one (of many) expressions of Britain's imperial legacy; part of the proliferation of narratives that charted the Anglo-settler explosion of the eighteenth and nineteenth centuries; the concurrent performances working in the mutual interest of national self-definition. Certainly, the British public and press embraced the Wild West in ways that go beyond the sheer entertainment and exoticism of the show. Joy Kasson observes that "the Wild West displayed American military and cultural adventurism" in a way that should have seemed familiar to British audiences "at the high tide of imperialism."[9] And Kate Flint goes further in suggesting that the Wild West, as it performed before audiences in Earls Court, referenced US territorial ambitions that would increasingly look like a form of imperialism "that actually threatened British interests" as the century came to an end.[10] Although these political subtexts were not openly expressed in the writing of the time, including press accounts and Wild West promotional material, the story of empire was clearly the master narrative that organized both exhibitions—the Wild West and the Jubilee—in the summer of 1887.

Cody's description of the command performance takes on an overtly patriotic tone in depicting the queen and her nobles bowing before the American flag. Cody uses the scene as the foundation for all his success claims for the Wild West show both as a business venture and as a cultural emissary. Of course, Cody's account of the event operates under the burden of a larger irony. Just as he has cast the queen in his moment of becoming "America's National Entertainment," he and his entire enterprise are literally engaged in a command performance for the queen. During the summer of 1887, the British press made much of the queen's gradual renewal of her public role as head of state. She had spent the last twenty-five years in mourning and extreme privacy after the death of Prince Albert. The Wild West was among the first of her public appearances leading up to the Jubilee, which constituted a reassumption of her role as a truly public figurehead. Given this context, the command performance becomes a kind of commentary on the nature of publicity as one performance is staged *within* another and the routes of interests served become difficult to trace.

The queen's own journal account of the event pays less attention to the political context in favor of the exotic personnel, especially the "Red Indians," whom she describes in detail. The queen's distinction of the *Red* Indians reminds us that she knew of other Indians within her range of global subjects. It also suggests that the Wild West's iconography of empire would have been all too familiar to Victoria at this stage of her reign. Taken in the full context of the cultural reaffirmation of the English monarchy, the Wild West becomes one episode in a much larger display of British national pageantry, one that incorporated the American story into a broader history of Anglo-Saxon imperialism embodied in the figure of Victoria herself.

A version of this dynamic helps explain why cultural nationalism of the period is hyperconscious of its European—and in particular British—roots, counterparts, or competitors. In her study of antebellum Anglophone relations, Elisa Tamarkin describes a "more intricate culture of American response" that moves beyond a straightforward story of "influence": one that exhibits what Tamarkin calls a devotion or Anglophilia that does not "depend on prior ties or ethnic sympathies with Britain but, rather, exploits a complex of American attitudes toward history, sociability, and the emotional terrain of nationalism itself."[11] Tamarkin's conception indicates a much wider engagement in American society, with the legacies of British history and culture that would remain "an index to a particular experience of being American" throughout the nineteenth century.[12] What Tamarkin sees as devotion, we might broaden to a form of attention to another culture that might just as readily evoke feelings of estrangement as of affinity, with the result that Anglophilia and Anglophobia might simultaneously be expressions of the same nationalist impulses.

The autobiography repeatedly represents this ambiguous relationship in its concluding chapters. While most of the narrative details the exhibition's time in London, Cody devotes a few pages to the final weeks of the tour in Manchester. The shift in scene affords Cody the opportunity to make a brief study of the contrasts between the cultural center in the south and the capital of manufacturing in the north. In surveying the VIPs in attendance at one of the opening performances, Cody notes the absence of "dynastic royalty"—the very people he had celebrated earlier in the narrative—and, instead, points to the "sublimer royalty of commerce, of invention, of fire and steel" that represent the social elite of "Cottonopolis." Cody asserts a different kind of kinship, a "closer resemblance to the natural dignity of the American citizen" in the "self-made millionaires" whose accomplishments are "held in more esteem than long descent or the glamors of inherited wealth."[13] Cody repeatedly invokes such standard republican sentiments in these closing chapters as he anticipates the Wild West's return to the United States. The closing lines of his account make sentimental reference to the "old flag" as an emblem he cherishes above all the honors from abroad. Once again Cody's patriotism takes its meaning from his expatriate experience as the exhibition began an extended run in New York, and the marketing of "America's National Entertainment" found new resonance in the interplay of the domestic and the international dimensions of the exhibition.

While four of the chapters in this collection are concerned with aspects of *the* special relationship, other chapters show how continental Europeans found their own relationship to the frontier narrative on display in the Wild West's arena. In doing so they suggest how the inherent nationalistic strains within mass culture find some of their most concentrated formal expression in the Wild West. They also explain how a form of hyperspectacle that availed itself of the wider resources of an increasingly dynamic media landscape could exert itself on local cultures in unprecedented ways. The essays in this volume have taken up the question of how a myth of national exceptionalism translates in a context that is "national in character and yet held beyond the limits of the national territory." This description, drawn from the official program of the 1887 American Exhibition in London, concisely formulates the nationalist logic of the international Wild West. The national *character* of the exhibition emerged in relation to the so-called limits it transcended. Even as these studies address the nature and impact of that boundary crossing, they point to the potential for further study. This volume both addresses and calls for more attention to a number of issues foregrounded by the Wild West's European history. Indeed, further attention could productively engage how the various features of the exhibition—its logistics, its marketing, its performance—shaped European perceptions of the United States. An expanded inquiry would also address how individual countries or regions appropriated aspects of the exhibition—before, during, and after its tours—in the service of their own regional or national interests, whether political or cultural. This scholarship could offer an ever-more-nuanced treatment of how the exhibition registered movements toward globalism, even as it enacted a ritual of high nationalism. It could also account more fully for how notions of gender, ethnicity, race, and class translated within the text of the performance, which could claim for itself a radical egalitarianism while promoting a racialized narrative of western expansionism and conquest. Collectively, a more linear history of the Wild West's evolution should reveal how an increasingly internationalized Wild West—most notably in the addition of the Rough Riders of the World, with its cosmopolitan fraternity of horsemanship and militarism—was understood by American audiences with a nostalgia-driven appetite for the vanishing American frontier. Further study of these issues would run a parallel course with the ongoing editorial work of the Papers of William F. Cody, which continues to discover and publish the documentary record of the Wild West's European tours. These mutually enabling efforts will continue to trace out the ways this most ephemeral form of culture left its mark on the people and places of turn-of-the-century Europe.

Notes

Epigraph: Quoted in Cody, *The Wild West in England.*

1. In his autobiographical account of the 1887–88 English tour, Cody includes a letter from the Mayor of Salford informing him that several streets would be built in honor of his visit. The plan called for three streets named "Cody Street," "Buffalo Street," and "Bill Street."
2. Malchow, *Special Relations*, 1.
3. Kasson, *Buffalo Bill's Wild West*, 265.
4. Ibid.
5. Malchow, *Special Relations*, 1–2.
6. Wiener, *The Americanization of the British Press*, 4.
7. The similarities between the narrative voice in *The Wild West in England* and other promotional writing generated for the Wild West has led some to conclude that the autobiography was ghost written by Cody's press agent, John Burke.
8. See my introduction to *The Wild West in England.*
9. Kasson, *Buffalo Bill's Wild West*, 66.
10. Flint, *The Transatlantic Indian*, 7.
11. Tamarkin, *Anglophilia*, xxvi.
12. Ibid.
13. Ibid., 110–11.

Bibliography

1889 Scrapbook. William F. "Buffalo Bill" Cody Collection, MS 6, McCracken Research Library, Buffalo Bill Center of the West.

1905 Scrapbook. William F. "Buffalo Bill" Cody Collection, MS 6, McCracken Research Library, Buffalo Bill Center of the West.

Abate, Michelle Ann. *Tomboys: A Literary and Cultural History.* Philadelphia: Temple University Press, 2008.

Adams, Amanda. *Performing Authorship in the Nineteenth-Century Transatlantic Lecture Tour.* Burlington: Ashgate, 2014.

Adamson, Walter L. *Avant-Garde Florence: From Modernism to Fascism.* Cambridge, MA: Harvard University Press, 1993.

Adler, Kathleen, et al. *Americans in Paris, 1860–1900.* London: National Gallery Company Limited, 2006.

Alford, Norman W. "Oscar Wilde in Texas." *Texas Quarterly* 10 (1967): 193–98.

Alhearn, Brian. "Qualifying Quantitative Literacy." *Journal of Economic History* 69, no. 3 (September 2009): 783–808.

American Exhibition, London, 1887: Official Catalogue of the Exhibition, with an Illustrated History of the United States, Their Origin and Growth, A Century of Progress. New York and London: J. J. Garnett, and B. W. Dinsmore & Co., 1887.

"American Studio Talk." *International Studio* 7 (June 1899): xiii–xvi.

Ames, Eric. "Seeing the Imaginary: On the Popular Reception of Wild West Shows in Germany, 1885–1910." In *I Like America: Fictions of the Wild West,* 213–29. Edited by Pamela Kort and Max Hollein. Frankfurt am Main: Schirn Kunsthalle, 2006.

Anderson, Nancy Fix. *Woman against Women in Victorian England: A Life of Eliza Lynn Linton*. Bloomington: Indiana University Press, 1987.

Annie Oakley Scrapbooks. William F. "Buffalo Bill" Cody Collection, MS 6, McCracken Research Library, Buffalo Bill Center of the West.

Anonymous. *Girls and Their Ways, by One Who Has Known Them*. London: James Hogg, 1881.

Anonymous. "Shall Our Young Men Study in Paris? Written by an American Girl after Two Years of Parisian Art Study." *Arena* 8, no. 1 (June 1895): 131–34.

Armigate, Shelley. "Rawhide Heroines: The Evolution of the Cowgirl and the Myth of America." In *The American Self: Myth, Ideology, and Popular Culture*, 166–81. Edited by Sam B. Girgus. Albuquerque: University of New Mexico Press, 1981.

Aron, Stephen. "Returning the West to the World." In *America on the World Stage: A Global Approach to U.S. History*, 85–98. Edited by Gary W. Reichard and Ted Dickson. Urbana: University of Illinois Press, 2008.

Ashton, Dore, and Denise Browne Hare. *Rosa Bonheur: A Life and a Legend*. New York: Viking Press, 1981.

Assael, Brenda. *The Circus and Victorian Society*. Charlottesville: University of Virginia Press, 2005.

Baden-Powell, Agnes. *The Handbook for Girl Guides or How Girls Can Help Build the Empire*. London: Thomas Nelson, 1912.

Bahamonde, Angel, ed. *Historia de España Siglo XX: 1875–1939*. Madrid: Cátedra, 2000.

Balfour, Sebastian. "'The Lion and the Pig:' Nationalism and National Identity in *Fin-de-Siècle* Spain." In *Nationalism and the Nation in the Iberian Peninsula. Competing and Conflicting Identities*, 107–18. Edited by Clare Mar-Molinero and Angel Smith. Washington, DC: Berg, 1996.

Balocco, Piergiorgio. Introduction ("Presentazione") to *Buffalo Bill è Arrivato a Torino: Storie di Piole, Amore e Selvaggio West*, by Andrea Biscàro, 6–9. Rivoli: Neos Edizioni, 2010.

Barringer, Tim. *Opulence and Anxiety: Landscape Paintings from the Royal Academy of Arts*. Warkwickshire: Compton Verney, 2007.

Bederman, Gail. *Manliness & Civilization: A Cultural History of Gender and Race in the United States, 1880–1917*. Chicago: University of Chicago Press, 1995.

Belich, James. *Replenishing the Earth: The Settler Revolution and the Rise of the Anglo World, 1783–1939*. New York: Oxford University Press, 2010.

Bender, Thomas, ed. *Rethinking American History in a Global Age*. Berkeley: University of California Press, 2002.

Bennasser, Bartolomé. *The Spanish Character: Attitudes and Mentalities from the Sixteenth to the Nineteenth Century*. Translated by Benjamin Keen. Berkeley: University of California Press, 1979.

Bennet, Estelline. *Old Deadwood Days*. Lincoln: University of Nebraska Press, 1982. First published 1928 by J. H. Sears.

Berti, Raffaele De. *Dallo Schermo alla Carta: Romanzi, Fotoromanzi, Rotocalchi Cinematographici: Il film e I suoi paratesti*. Milano: Fratelli Treves, 2000.

Bilston, Sarah. *The Awkward Age in Women's Popular Fiction, 1850–1900: Girls and the Transition to Womanhood.* Oxford: Oxford University Press, 2004.

Bird, Isabella L. *A Lady's Life in the Rocky Mountains.* New York: G. P. Putnam's Sons, 1879.

Biscàro, Andrea. *Buffalo Bill è Arrivato a Torino: Storie di Piole, Amore e Selvaggio West.* Rivoli: Neos Edizioni, 2010.

Bishop, Joseph Bucklin. *Theodore Roosevelt and His Time: Shown in His Own Letters.* Vol. 2. New York: Charles Scribner's Son's, 1920.

Blackstone, Sarah J. *Buckskins, Bullets and Business: A History of Buffalo Bill's Wild West.* Westport, CT: Greenwood Press, 1986.

Blanchard, Pascal, Gilles Boëtsch, and Nanette Jacomijn Snoep, eds. *Human Zoos: The Invention of the Savage.* Paris: Musée du Quai Branly, 2011.

Blanchard, Pascal, Nicolas Bancel, Gilles Boëtsch, Eric Deroo, Sandrine Lemaire, and Charles Forsdick, eds. *Human Zoos: Science and Spectacle in the Age of Colonial Empires.* Liverpool: Liverpool University Press, 2008.

Boime, Albert. "The Chocolate Venus, 'Tainted' Pork, the Wine Blight, and the Tariff. Franco-American Stew at the Fair." In *Paris 1889: American Artists at the Universal Exposition,* 67–91. Edited by Annette Blaugrund et al. Philadelphia: Pennsylvania Academy of the Fine Arts, 1989.

Bolton, Herbert Eugene. *The Spanish Borderlands: A Chronicle of Old Florida and the Southwest.* New Haven, CT: Yale University Press, 1921. Reprint, Albuquerque: University of New Mexico Press, 1996.

Bonner, Robert E. *William F. Cody's Wyoming Empire: The Buffalo Bill Nobody Knows.* Norman: University of Oklahoma Press, 2007.

Botero, Rodrigo. *Ambivalent Embrace: America's Troubled Relationship with Spain from the Revolutionary War to the Cold War.* Westport, CT: Greenwood Press: 2001.

Bradbury, Malcolm. *Dangerous Pilgrimages: Trans-Atlantic Mythologies & the Novel.* London: Secker & Warburg, 1995.

Braden, Donna R. *Leisure and Entertainment in America.* Dearborn, MI: Henry Ford Museum, 1988.

Brantlinger, Patrick. *Rule of Darkness: British Literature and Imperialism, 1830–1914.* Ithaca: Cornell University Press, 1988.

Braun, Marta. *Picturing Time: The Work of Etienne-Jules Marey (1830–1940).* Chicago: University of Chicago Press, 1992.

Bridger, Bobby. *Buffalo Bill and Sitting Bull: Inventing the Wild West.* Austin: University of Texas Press, 2002.

Brody, David. *Visualizing American Empire: Orientalism and Imperialism in the Philippines.* Chicago: University of Chicago Press, 2010.

Browder, Ann. *Her Best Shot: Women and Guns in America.* Chapel Hill: University of North Carolina Press, 2006.

Brown, Thomas A. *History of the New York Stage from 1732 to 1901.* 3 vols. New York: Benjamin Blom, 1903.

Bryce, James. *The American Commonwealth*. Volume 2. London: MacMillan and Co., 1889.

Bullet, Emma. *The Autobiography of Emma Bullet: Twenty-Five Years Paris Correspondent of the Brooklyn Daily Eagle*. New York: Eagle Press, 1906.

Bülow, Bernhard. *The Memoirs of Prince von Bülow*. Translated by F. A. Voigt. 4 vols. Boston: Little, Brown, and Company, 1931–32.

Burk, Kathleen. *Old World, New World: Great Britain and America from the Beginning*. New York: Atlantic Monthly Press, 2008.

Burke, John M. *Buffalo Bill: From Prairie to Palace*. Chicago: Rand, McNally, 1893.

———. *Buffalo Bill: The Noblest Whiteskin*. New York: G. P. Putnam's Sons/Capricorn Books, 1973.

Burnand, F. C. *The Colonel: A Comedy in Three Acts. The Nineteenth-Century Marteau*. Edited by Anton Kirchhofer. Cologne, Germany: Pierre Marteau, 2004. First published 1881.

Burns, Emily. "The Old World Anew: The Atlantic as the Liminal Site of Expectations." In *Framing the Ocean, 1700 to the Present: Envisaging the Sea as Social Space*, 37–54. Edited by Tricia Cusack. Aldershot, UK: Ashgate, 2014.

———. "Puritan Parisians: American Art Students in Late Nineteenth-Century Paris." In *A Seamless Web: Transatlantic Art in the Nineteenth Century*, 123–46. Edited by Marian Wardle and Cheryll May. Newcastle upon Tyne, UK: Cambridge Press Scholars, 2014.

Burns, Michael. *Rural Society and French Politics: Boulangism and the Dreyfus Affair, 1886–1900*. Princeton: Princeton University Press, 1984.

Burr, Martha. "The American Cowgirl: History and Iconography, 1860–Present." PhD diss., New York University, 1998.

Burton, Richard Francis. *The City of the Saints, and Across the Rocky Mountains to California*. Edited by Fawn Brodie. New York: Alfred A. Knopf, 1963. Reprint, Santa Barbara, CA: Narrative Press, 2003.

Bussoni, Mario. *Buffalo Bill in Italia: L'Epopea del Wild West Show*. 1885. Reprint, Fidenza: Mattioli, 2011.

Carlisle, Jeffrey D. "Spanish Relations with the Apache Nations East of the Rio Grande." PhD diss., University of North Texas, 2001.

Carlsen, Paul H., ed. *The Cowboy Way: An Exploration of History and Culture*. Lubbock: Texas Tech University Press, 2000.

Carr, Raymond. *Modern Spain, 1875–1980*. Oxford: Oxford University Press, 2002.

———. *Spain 1808–1939*. Oxford: Oxford at the Clarendon Press, 1966.

Carter, Robert A. *Buffalo Bill Cody: The Man Behind the Legend*. New York: Wiley, 2002.

Castle, Gregory. "Misrecognising Wilde: Media and Performance on the American Tour of 1882." In *Wilde Discoveries: Traditions, Histories, Archives*, 85–117. Edited by Joseph Bristow. Toronto: University of Toronto Press, 2013.

Catlin, George. *Adventures of the Ojibbeway and Ioway Indians in England, France and Belgium: Being Notes of Eight Years Residence in Europe with the North American Indian Collection*. 2 vols., 3rd edition. London: printed by author, 1852.

Chiarelli, Riccardo. *Mamma Italia: Romanzo*. Firenze: G. Nerbini, 1939.

Choate, Mark. *Emigrant Nation: The Making of Italy Abroad*. Cambridge, MA: Harvard University Press, 2008.

Christianson, Frank. Introduction to *The Wild West in England*, by William Cody, xiii–xxxv. Lincoln: University of Nebraska Press, 2012.

Clemens, Samuel Langhorne (Mark Twain). *Following the Equator: A Journey Around the World*. Hartford, CT: American Publishing Company, 1897.

Cody, William F. *The Wild West in England*. Edited with an introduction by Frank Christianson. Lincoln: University of Nebraska Press, 2012.

Cody, W. F., and Nate Salsbury. *Buffalo Bill's Wild West. America's National Entertainment, an Illustrated Treatise of Historical Facts and Sketches*. London: Allen, Scott & Co., 1887.

Cogan, Frances B. *All-American Girl: The Ideal of Real Womanhood in Mid-Nineteenth-Century America*. Athens: University of Georgia Press, 1989.

Colón, Cristóbal. *Textos y documentos completos*. Edited and with a prologue and notes by Consuelo Varela. Madrid: Alianza-Universidad, 1982.

Conway, Christopher. "José Martí frente al Wild West de Buffalo Bill: Frontera, raza y arte en la civilización y barbarie norteamericana." *Hispanic Journal* 19, no. 1 (1998): 129–42.

Cooper, Courtney Ryley. *Under the Big Top*. Boston: Little, Brown, and Company, 1947.

Coppa, Frank J. "From Liberalism to Fascism: The Church-State Conflict over Italy's Schools." *The History Teacher* 28, no. 2 (February 1995): 135–48.

Cortada, James W. "Spain and the American Civil War: Relations at Mid-century, 1855–1868." *Transactions of the American Philosophical Society* 70, no. 4 (1980): 1–121.

Croft-Cooke, Rupert, and W. S. Meadmore. *Buffalo Bill: The Legend, the Man of Action, the Showman*. London: Corgi, 1957.

Cryle, Peter, and Christopher Forth, eds. *Sexuality at the Fin de Siècle: The Makings of a "Central Problem."* Newark: University of Delaware Press, 2008.

Cunningham, Tom. *Your Fathers the Ghosts*. Edinburgh: Black and White Publishing Ltd., 2007.

Davis, Richard Harding. *About Paris*. New York: Harper & Brothers Publishers, 1895.

Davis, Tracy C. *Actresses as Working Women: Their Social Identity in Victorian Culture*. New York: Routledge, 1991.

———. "Shotgun Wedlock: Annie Oakley's Power Politics in the Wild West." In *Gender in Performance: The Presentation of Difference in the Performing Arts*, 141–57. Edited by Laurence Senelick. Hanover, NH: University Press of New England, 1992.

Delaney, Michelle. "Advance Work: Art and Advertising in Buffalo Bill's Wild West, 1883–1916." PhD diss., University of Strathclyde, in progress.

Del Castillo, Antonio Cánovas. "Discurso pronunciado por el Excmo. Sr. D. Antonio Cánovas del Castillo en la tarde del 16 octubre de 1888." In *Estudios Sobre La Exposición Universal de Barcelona inaugurada en 20 de Mayo y Cerrada en 9 de Diciembre de 1888*. Edited by José M. Serrate. Barcelona: Establecimiento Tipográfico del Diario Mercantil, 1888.

Delgado, Jose M. et al. *El comerç entre Catalunya i América (segles XVIII i XIX).* Barcelona: L'Avenc, 1986.

Delmendo, Sharon. *The Star-Entangled Banner: One Hundred Years of America in the Philippines.* New Brunswick, NJ: Rutgers University Press, 2004.

Deloria, Philip J. *Playing Indian.* New Haven, CT: Yale University Press, 1998.

D'Estournelles de Constant, Paul Henri Benjamin. *Les Etats-Unis d'Amerique.* Paris: Colin, 1913.

Deverell, William. "The Redemptive West: Nationhood and Healing in the Post-Civil War American West." NEH seminar. Huntington Library, 2005. http://college.usc.edu/huntington/private/NEH_Syllabus_Final.doc

Dixon, Christopher. Introduction to *Four Years in Europe with Buffalo Bill,* by Charles Eldredge Griffin, xiii–xxvi. Lincoln: University of Nebraska Press, 2010. First published 1908 by Stage Publishing.

Domènech, Pascual i. *Los Caminos de la Era Industrial: La Construcción y Financiación de la Red Ferroviaria Catalana (1843–1898).* Barcelona: Publicacions de la Universitat de Barcelona, 1999.

Drury, Bob, and Tom Clavin, *The Heart of Everything That Is: The Untold Story of Red Cloud, an American Legend.* New York: Simon and Schuster, 2013.

Duthoit, Emile. *Les idées du président Roosevelt.* Lille: A. Amorel, 1903.

Dwyer, Britta C. "Rosa Bonheur and Her Companion-Artist: What Made Anna Klumpke Special?" In *Rosa Bonheur: All Nature's Children,* 63–78. New York: Dahesh Museum, 1998.

Ebner, Katherine C., ed. *Sculptor in Buckskin: The Autobiography of Alexander Phimister Proctor.* Norman: University of Oklahoma Press, 2009.

Elliot, John H. *Spain and Its World, 1500–1700.* New Haven, CT: Yale University Press, 1989.

Endy, Christopher. "Travel and World Power: Americans in Europe, 1890–1917." *Diplomatic History* 22 (1998): 565–94.

Esdaile, Charles S. *Spain in the Liberal Age: From Constitution to Civil War, 1808–1939.* New York: Wiley-Blackwell, 2000.

Eubank, Keith. *Paul Cambon: Master Diplomat.* Norman: University of Oklahoma Press, 1960.

Faragher, John Mack, ed. *Rereading Frederick Jackson Turner: "The Significance of the Frontier in American History" and Other Essays.* Revised ed. New Haven, CT: Yale University Press, 1999.

Fehrenbach, T. R. *Comanches: The History of a People.* London: Vintage Books, 2007.

Fernández-Armesto, Felipe. *Barcelona: A Thousand Years of the City's Past.* Oxford: Oxford University Press, 1992.

———. *Columbus.* Oxford: Oxford University Press, 1991.

Fink, Lois Marie. *American Art at the Nineteenth-Century Paris Salons.* Washington, DC: National Museum of American Art, Smithsonian Institution, 1990.

Fiorentino, Daniele. "'Those Red-Brick Faces': European Press Reactions to the Indians of Buffalo Bill's Wild West Show." In *Indians and Europe: An Interdisciplinary*

Collection of Essays, 403–13. Edited by Christian F. Feest. Lincoln: University of Nebraska Press, 1999.

Fischer, Diane P. "Constructing the 'American School' of 1900." In *Paris 1900: The "American School" at the Universal Exposition*, 1–94. Edited by Diane P. Fischer. New Brunswick, NJ: Rutgers University Press, 1999.

———. "Declaration of Empire: The United States National Pavilion at the Paris Exposition of 1900." In *Twenty-First-Century Perspectives on Nineteenth-Century Art: Essays in Honor of Gabriel P. Weisberg*, 29–38. Edited by Petra ten-Doesschate Chu and Laurinda S. Dixon. Newark: University of Delaware Press, 2008.

Flint, Kate. *The Transatlantic Indian, 1776–1930*. Princeton: Princeton University Press, 2009.

Florence, Ronald. *Lawrence and Aaronsohn: T. E. Lawrence, Aaron Aaronsohn, and the Seeds of the Arab-Israeli Conflict*. New York: Viking Press, 2007.

Forbes, Jack D. *Apache, Navaho, and Spaniard*. Norman: University of Oklahoma Press, 1994.

Forth, Christopher. *The Dreyfus Affair and the Crisis of French Manhood*. Baltimore: Johns Hopkins University Press, 2006.

Forth, Christopher, ed. *Masculinity in the Modern West: Gender, Civilization, and the Body*. Basingstroke: Palgrave MacMillan, 2009.

Forth, Christopher, and Bertrand Taithe, eds. *French Masculinities: History, Culture, Politics*. Basinstroke: Palgrave MacMillan, 2007.

Forth, Christopher, and Elinor Accampo, eds. *Confronting Modernity in Fin-de-Siècle France: Bodies, Minds, and Gender*. Basingstroke: Palgrave MacMillan, 2010.

Fradera, Josep M. "The Empire, the Nation and the Homelands: Nineteenth-Century Spain's National Idea." In *Region and State in Nineteenth-Century Europe: Nation Building, Identities and Separatism*, 131–48. Edited by Joost Augusteijn and Eric Storm. Basingstoke, UK: Palgrave MacMillan, 2012

———. "Rural Traditionalism and Conservative Nationalism in Catalonia 1865–1900." *Critique of Anthropology* 10 (1990): 51–72.

France 1905 Scrapbook. William F. "Buffalo Bill" Cody Collection, MS 6, McCracken Research Library, Buffalo Bill Center of the West.

Friedman, David M. *Wilde in America: Oscar Wilde and the Invention of Modern Celebrity*. New York: W. W. Norton, 2014.

Gagnier, Regenia. *Idylls of the Marketplace: Oscar Wilde and the Victorian Public*. Stanford: Stanford University Press, 1986.

Gallup, Alan. *Buffalo Bill's British Wild West*. Gloucestershire, UK: Sutton, 2001.

Gerstäcker, Friedrich. *Narrative of a Journey Round the World, Comprising a Winter Passage Across the Andes to Chili, with a Visit to the Gold Regions of California and Australia, the South Sea Islands, Java, &c*. New York: Harper and Brothers, 1853.

Gibson, Charles. *The Colonial Period in Latin American History*. Washington, DC: Service Center for Teachers of History, 1958.

Giles, Paul. *Atlantic Republic: The American Tradition of English Literature*. Oxford: Oxford University Press, 2006.

———. *Virtual Americas: Transnational Fictions and the Transatlantic Imaginary.* Durham, NC: Duke University Press, 2002.

Girona, Manuel. *Memoria Sobre la Exposición Universal de Barcelona de 1888 que presenta al Gobierno el Excmo. Sr. D. Manuel Girona comisario regio de la misma en cumplimiento de lo dispuesto en el artículo 6.0 del Real Decreto—Instrucción de 11 noviembre de 1888.* Barcelona: Imprenta de Henrich y Compà En Comandita, 1889.

Goetzmann, William H., and William N. Goetzmann. *The West of the Imagination.* Norman: University of Oklahoma Press, 2009.

Grant, Ethan. "The Treaty of San Lorenzo and Manifest Destiny." *Gulf Coast Historical Review* 12, no. 2 (1997): 44–57.

Green, Otis H. *Spain and the Western Tradition: The Castilian Mind in Literature from El Cid to Calderón.* 4 vols. Madison: University of Wisconsin Press, 1965.

Griffin, Charles Eldridge. *Four Years in Europe with Buffalo Bill.* Edited and with an introduction by Chris Dixon. Lincoln: University of Nebraska Press, 2000.

Guerrero, León Ma. *The First Filipino.* Manilla, Philippines: Guerrero, 2007.

Haggard, John V. "The Neutral Ground between Louisiana and Texas." *Louisiana Historical Quarterly* 28 (1945): 1001–28.

Hämäläinen, Pekka. *The Comanche Empire.* New Haven, CT: Yale University Press, 2008.

Harris, Ruth. *Dreyfus: Politics, Emotion, and the Scandal of the Century.* New York: Henry Holt and Co., 2010.

Hassrick, Peter. *American West: Out of Myth, into Reality.* Washington, DC: Trust for Museum Exhibitions, in association with the Mississippi Museum of Art, 2000.

———. *Wildlife and Western Heroes: Alexander Phimister Proctor, Sculptor.* Fort Worth: Amon Carter Museum, 2003.

Higonnet, Patrice. *Paris: Capital of the World.* Translated by Arthur Goldhammer. Cambridge: The Belknap Press of Harvard University Press, 2002.

Hovet, Ted. "America on Display: Constructing and Containing Images of the United States." *19: Interdisciplinary Studies in the Long Nineteenth Century* 9 (2009): doi:10.16995/ntn.508.

Hoxie, W. J. *How Girls Can Help Their Country: The 1913 Handbook for Girl Scouts.* Sixtieth anniversary facsimile edition. Washington, DC: Girl Scouts of America, 1972.

Huard, Lucien. *Livre d'or de la Exposition.* 2 vols. Paris: L. Boulanger, 1889.

Hughes, Robert. *Barcelona.* New York: Alfred A. Knopf, 1992.

Huhndorf, Shari. *Going Native: Indians in the American Cultural Imagination.* Ithaca: Cornell University Press, 2003.

Huxley, David. "Buffalo Bill and William Gladstone: The 'Champion Scalper' and the 'G.O.M.' in Moonshine Magazine, April–November 1887." *Early Popular Visual Culture* 9, no. 4 (2011): 353–62.

Hyde, Anne. *Empires, Nations and Families: A History of the North American West, 1800–1860.* Lincoln: University of Nebraska Press, 2011.

Igler, David. *The Great Ocean: Pacific Worlds from Captain Cook to the Gold Rush.* New York: Oxford University Press, 2013.

Imperatori, Ugo E. *Italiani Fuori d'Italia: Sentisi del Contributo Italiano allo Sviluppo Sociale d'Ogni Paese.* Milano: Oberzan Zucchi, 1937.

Irvine, William D. *The Boulanger Affair Reconsidered, Royalism, Boulangism, and the Origins of the Radical Right in France.* Oxford: Oxford University Press, 1989.

Johannsen, Albert. *The House of Beadle and Adams in Its Dime and Nickel Novels: The Story of a Vanished Literature.* Norman: University of Oklahoma Press, 1950.

John, Elizabeth A. H. *Storms Brewed in Other Men's Worlds: The Confrontation of Indians, Spanish, and French in the Southwest, 1540–1795.* Norman: University of Oklahoma Press, 1996.

Jonnes, Jill. *Eiffel's Tower and the World's Fair Where Buffalo Bill Beguiled Paris, the Artists Quarreled, and Thomas Edison Became a Count.* New York: Viking Press, 2009.

Julini, Milo. Preface ("Prefazione") to *Buffalo Bill è Arrivato a Torino: Storie di Piole, Amore e Selvaggio West,* by Andrea Biscàro, 10–1.3 Rivoli: Neos Edizioni, 2010.

Kalifa, Dominique. *L'encre et le sang: Récits de crimes et société à la Belle Epoque.* Paris: Fayard, 1995.

———. "Archéologie de l'Apachisme. Les representations des Peaux-Rouge dans la France du XIXe siècle." *Revue d'histoire de l'enfance irrégulière 4 (2002): 19–37.*

Kammen, Michael. *American Culture, American Tastes: Social Change and the Twentieth Century.* New York: Alfred A. Knopf, 1999.

Kasper, Shirl. *Annie Oakley.* Norman: University of Oklahoma Press, 1992.

Kasson, John F. *Houdini, Tarzan and the Perfect Man: The White Male Body and the Challenging of Modernity in America.* New York: Hill and Wang, 2001.

Kasson, Joy S. *Buffalo Bill's Wild West: Celebrity, Memory, and Popular History.* New York: Hill and Wang, 2000.

Kellar, Kenneth C. *Seth Bullock Frontier Marshall.* Aberdeen, SD: North Plains Press, 1972.

Kennan, George. *Tent Life in Siberia and Adventures among the Koraks and Other Tribes in Kamchatka and Northern Asia.* New York: G. P. Putnam's Sons; London: Sampson Low, Son, and Marston, 1870.

Kimmel, Michael S. *Manhood in America: A Cultural History.* New York: Free Press, 1996.

Klein, Abbé Félix. *Au pays de "la vie intense."* Paris: Plon, 1904.

Klein, Pierre. "When Buffalo Bill Caracoled in Nancy (France): Cody's and the American Shows through the Local Press (1902–1905)." PhD diss., Université de Nancy 2, 2004.

Kocks, Katinka. *Indianer im Kaiserreich. Völkerschauen und Wild West Shows zwischen 1880 und 1914.* Gerolzhofen: Spiegel & Co, 2004.

Koning, Hans. *Columbus: His Enterprise: Exploding the Myth.* New York: Monthly Review Press, 1992.

Laegreid, Renee. "Italians." In *Encyclopedia of the Great Plains,* 237–38. Edited by David J. Wishart. Lincoln: University of Nebraska Press, 2004.

LaFeber, Walter. *The New Empire: An Interpretation of American Expansion, 1860–1898.* Ithaca, NY: American Historical Association and Cornell University Press, 1963.

Lamar, Howard, and Leonard Thompson. *The Frontier in History: North America and South Africa Compared.* New Haven, CT: Yale University Press, 1981.

Las Casas, Bartolomé de. *A Brief Account of the Destruction of the Indies.* London: Penguin, 1999.

Lawrence, T. E. *Lawrence of Arabia: The Selected Letters.* Edited by Malcom Brown. London: Little Books, 2005.

Lears, T. J. Jackson. *No Place of Grace: Antimodernism and the Transformation of American Culture, 1880–1920.* New York: Pantheon Books, 1981.

Lefrançois, Thierry. *Les Indiens de Buffalo Bill et la Camargue.* La Rochelle: Musée du Nouveau Monde, 1994.

Lemoine, Bertrand. *Tour de Monsieur Eiffel.* Paris: Gallimard, 1989.

Leroi, Paul. "The American Salon." *Magazine of Art* 9 (June 1886): 485–87.

Levine, Lawrence. *Highbrow/Lowbrow: The Emergence of Cultural Hiearchy in America.* Cambridge, MA: Harvard University Press, 1999.

Limerick, Patricia Nelson. "Going West and Ending Up Global." *Western Historical Quarterly* 32 (Spring 2001): 5–23.

———. *The Legacy of Conquest: The Unbroken Past of the American West.* New York: W. W. Norton, 1987.

Linton, E. Lynn. *The Girl of the Period and Other Social Essays.* Vol. 1. London: Richard Bentley & Son, 1883.

Lomas, Laura. *Translating Empire: José Martí, Migrant Latino Subjects, and American Modernities.* Durham, NC: Duke University Press, 2009.

Losada, Angel. "Controversy between Sepúlveda and Las Casas." In *Bartolomé de las Casas in History: Toward an Understanding of the Man and his Work.* Edited by Juan Freide and Benjamin Keen, 279–309. DeKalb: Northern Illinois University Press, 1971.

Lowe, Charles. *Four National Exhibitions in London and Their Organiser.* London: T. Fisher Unwinn, 1892.

Lubow, Arthur. *The Reporter Who Would Be King: A Biography of Richard Harding Davis.* New York: Charles Scribner's Sons, 1992.

MacInerney, Dorothy McLeod, William Warren Rogers, and Robert David Ward. "Oscar Wilde Lectures in Texas, 1882." *Southwestern Historical Quarterly* 106, no. 4 (2003): 550–73.

Maddra, Sam A. *Hostiles? The Lakota Ghost Dance and Buffalo Bill's Wild West.* Norman: University of Oklahoma Press, 2006.

Malchow, H. L. *Special Relations: The Americanization of Britain?* Stanford: Stanford University Press, 2011.

Marchena, Domingo. *Buffalo Bill. Del Oeste al Eixample.* Barcelona: Colección 'Periodismo de Vanguardia,' 2010.

Marill Escudé, Jordi. *Aquell hivern . . . L'espectacle de Buffalo Bill a Barcelona.* Palma de Mallorca: Hesperus, 1998.

Marsh, Jan. *Back to the Land: The Pastoral Impulse in England, from 1880 to 1914*. London: Quartet Books, 1982.

Martí, José. "William F. Cody—Buffalo Bill." In *Obras Completas de José Martí*, Vol. 2, pp. 168–70. Edited by Jorge Quintana. Caracas: Litho-Tip C. A., 1964.

———. "¡Magnífico espectáculo!" In *Obras Completas de José Martí*, Vol. 2, pp. 678–87. Edited by Jorge Quintana. Caracas: Litho-Tip C. A., 1964.

Martin, Jonathan D. "'The Grandest and Most Cosmopolitan Object Teacher': *Buffalo Bill's Wild West* and the Politics of American Identity, 1883–1899." *Radical History Review* 66 (1996): 96–123.

Matsuda, Matt K. *The Memory of the Modern*. New York: Oxford University Press, 1996.

May, Karl. *The Oil Prince*. Translated by Herbert Windolf. Pullman: Washington State University Press, 2003.

———. *Winnetou, the Chief of the Apache: The Winnetou Trilogy in One Volume*. Translated by Thomas A. Mary. Liverpool: CTPDC Publishing, 2014.

McCartney, Paul. *Power and Progress: American National Identity, the War of 1898, and the Rise of American Imperialism*. Baton Rouge: Louisiana State University Press, 2006.

McCoy, Alfred W., and Francisco A. Saracano, eds. *Colonial Crucible: Empire in the Making of the Modern American State*. Madison: University of Wisconsin Press, 2009.

McCoy, Tim. *Tim McCoy Remembers the West*. Lincoln: University of Nebraska Press, 1988.

McCullough, David. *The Greater Journey: Americans in Paris*. New York: Simon & Schuster, 2011.

McDermott, John D. *Red Cloud's War: The Bozeman Trail, 1866–1868*. 2 vols. Norman: Arthur C. Clark, 2010.

McLaird, James D. *Calamity Jane: The Woman and the Legend*. Norman: University of Oklahoma Press, 2005.

McNenly, Laura Scarangella. *Native Performers in Wild West Shows: From Buffalo Bill to Euro Disney*. Norman: University of Oklahoma Press, 2015.

McRoberts, Kenneth. *Catalonia: Nation Building without a State*. Cambridge: Oxford University Press, 2001.

Meisel, Perry. *The Cowboy and the Dandy: Crossing Over from Romanticism to Rock and Roll*. Oxford: Oxford University Press, 1999.

Mendelssohn, Michèle. *Henry James, Oscar Wilde and Aesthetic Culture*. Edinburgh: Edinburgh University Press, 2007.

Méral, Jean. *Paris in American Literature*. Translated by Laurette Long. Chapel Hill: University of North Carolina Press, 1989.

Mitchell, Sally. *The New Girl: Girls' Culture in England, 1880–1915*. New York: Columbia University Press, 1995.

Mizrahi, Claire. "Le génie publicitaire américain." In *The Wild West: Buffalo Bill à Marseilles*, 14–19. By Soulage Rizoulières, Patrick Boulanger, Pierre Echinard, and Claire Mizrahi. Marseilles: Musée d'histoire de Marseilles, 2008.

Monnett, John H. *Where a Hundred Soldiers Were Killed: The Struggle for the Powder River Country in 1866 and the Making of the Fetterman Myth*. Albuquerque: University of New Mexico Press, 2008.

Moor, Daniel G. *Log of a Twentieth Century Cowboy*. Tucson: University of Arizona Press, 1965.

Moreno Masó. *La Petjada dels catalans a Cuba: Assaig sobre la presencia catalana a Cuba durant la primera meitat del segle XIX*. Barcelona: Generalitat de Catalunya, Comissio America i Catalunya, 1992.

Morgan, Benjamin. "Oscar Wilde's Un-American Tour: Aestheticism, Mormonism, and Transnational Resonance." *American Literary History* 26, no. 4 (2014): 664–92.

Moses, L. G. *Wild West Shows and the Images of American Indians, 1883–1933*. Albuquerque: University of New Mexico Press, 1996.

———. "Wild West Shows, Reformers and the Image of the American Indian," *South Dakota History* 14, no. 3 (1984): 193–221.

Napier, Rita G. "Across the Big Water: American Indians' Perceptions of Europe and Europeans, 1887–1906." In *Indians and Europe: An Interdisciplinary Collection of Essays*, 383–401. Edited by Christian F. Feest. Lincoln: University of Nebraska Press, 1999.

Nasaw, David. *Going Out: The Rise and Fall of Public Amusements*. Cambridge, MA: Harvard University Press, 1999.

Nash, Gerald D. "European Images of America: The West in Historical Perspective." *Montana: The Magazine of Western History* 42, no. 2 (Spring 1992): 2–16.

Nathan Salsbury Papers. MSS17. Beinecke Library, Yale University.

Nead, Lynda. "The Secret of England's Greatness." *Journal of Victorian Culture* 19, no. 2 (2014): 161–82.

Nerbini editore (publishing house). *Le Avventure di Buffalo Bill, L'eroe Italiano della Prateria*. Florence: G. Nerbini, c. 1939.

Notter, Annick. *The New World Museum: Visitor's Guide*. La Rochelle: Imprimerie Rochelaise, 2009.

Novak, Daniel A. "Performing the 'Wilde West': Victorian Afterlives, Sexual Performance, and the American West." *Victorian Studies* 54, no. 3 (Spring 2012): 451–63.

Nugent, Walter. "Comparing Wests and Frontiers." In *The Oxford History of the American West*, 803–33. Edited by Clyde A. Milner II, Carol A. O'Connor, and Martha Sandweiss. New York: Oxford University Press, 1994.

———. *Crossings: The Great Transatlantic Migrations, 1870–1914*. Bloomington: Indiana University Press, 1992.

———. *Habits of Empire: A History of American Expansion*. New York: Knopf, 2008.

Nye, Bill [Edgar Wilson]. "Apostrophe to Oscar Wilde." In *Forty Liars, and Other Lies*, 274–75. Chicago: Belford Clarke, 1882.

Nye, Robert. *Crime, Madness & Politics in Modern France*. Princeton: Princeton University Press, 1984.

Oakley, Annie. *The Autobiography of Annie Oakley*. Edited by Marilyn Robbins. Greenville, OH: Darke County Historical Society, 2006.

———. *The Story of My Life*. Unpublished manuscript, 1926. William F. "Buffalo Bill" Cody Collection, MS 6, McCracken Research Library, Buffalo Bill Center of the West.

Oltean, Roxana. "'I Longed for a New World': Colonial Hysteria, *The American*, and Henry James's Paris." *Henry James Review* 24, no. 3 (Fall 2003): 269–80.

O'Sullivan, John L. "Annexation." *United States Magazine and Democratic Review* 17, no. 1 (July–August, 1845): 5–10.

Parker, Lew. *Odd People I Have Met*. N.p., n.d.

Payne, Stanley G. *Spain: A Unique History*. Madison: University of Wisconsin Press, 2011.

Peck, Gunther. *Reinventing Free Labor: Padrones and Immigrant Workers in the North American West, 1880–1930*. Cambridge: Cambridge University Press, 2000.

Penny, H. Glenn. *Kindred by Choice: Germans and American Indians since 1800*. Chapel Hill: University of North Carolina Press, 2015.

Perdicaris, Ion. "Reminiscences of a Parisian Atélier." *Galaxy*, March 15, 1867, 644–53.

Perkins, Bradford. *The Great Rapprochement: England and the United States, 1895–1914*. New York: Scribners' Sons, 1968.

Peyser, Thomas. *Utopia and Cosmopolis*. Durham, NC: Duke University Press, 1998.

Portes, Jacques. *Buffalo Bill*. Paris: Fayard, 2002.

———. *Fascination and Misgivings: The United States in French Opinion, 1870–1914*. Translated by Elbourg Forster. Cambridge: Cambridge University Press, 2000.

Powell, Kerry. *Acting Wilde: Victorian Sexuality, Theatre, and Oscar Wilde*. Cambridge: Cambridge University Press, 2011.

Pozzo, Felice. "Buffalo Bill eroe da romanzo popolare Il primate Italiano di Salgari." In *Almanaccca Piemontese*. Asti: Viglongo, 2006.

Prendergast, Charles. *Paris and the Nineteenth Century*. Oxford: Blackwell, 1992.

Prown, Jules, Nancy K. Anderson, William Cronon, Brian W. Dippie, Martha A. Sandweiss, Susan Prendergast Schoelwer, and Howard R. Lamar. *Discovered Lands, Invented Pasts: Transforming Visions of the American West*. New Haven, CT: Yale University Press and Yale University Art Gallery, 1992. Exhibition catalog.

Prunés, Josep M. "Nuevos datos y observaciones para la biografía de fray Bernardo Boyl." *Bollettino Ufficiale dell'Ordine dei Minimi* 49 (2003): 555–74.

Puffert, Douglas J. *Tracks across Continents, Paths through History*. Chicago: University of Chicago Press, 2009.

Rainger, Judy Greaves. "Buffalo Bill, Boulanger, and Bonheur: Trans-Atlantic Cultural Exchanges in the Fin-de-Siècle." In *Proceedings of the Western Society for French History: Selected Papers of the 1998 Annual Meeting*, 243–52. Greeley: University Press of Colorado, 2000.

———. "French Cowboys: The Guardians of the Camargue and Buffalo Bill." In *Cowboy Way: An Exploration of History and Culture*, 167–78. Edited by Paul H. Carlson. Lubbock: Texas Tech University Press, 2000.

Reddin, Paul. *Wild West Shows*. Urbana: University of Illinois Press, 1999.

Reeder, Linda. "Women in the Classroom: Mass Migration, Literacy, and the Nationalization of Sicilian Women at the Turn of the Century." *Journal of Social History* 32, no. 1 (Autumn, 1998): 101–24.

Reich, Jacqueline. "Mussolini at the Movies: Fascism, Film, and Culture." In *Re-Viewing Fascism: Italian Cinema, 1922–1943*, 3–29. Edited by Jacqueline Reich and Piero Garofalo. Bloomington: Indiana University Press, 2002.

Rennert, Jack. *100 Posters of Buffalo Bill's Wild West*. New York: Darien House, 1976.

Rico, Monica. *Nature's Noblemen: Transatlantic Masculinities and the Nineteenth-Century American West*. New Haven, CT: Yale University Press, 2013.

Riley, Glenda. *The Life and Legacy of Annie Oakley*. Norman: University of Oklahoma Press, 2002.

Rivarola, Guiseppe. *Buffalo Bill: Vero e falso*. Genova: Delecasa Editore, 1968.

Rollins, Philip Ashton. *The Cowboy: His Characteristics, His Equipment, and His Part in the Development of the West*. New York: Skyhorse, 2007.

Roosevelt, Theodore. *African and European Addresses*. New York: G. P. Putnam's Sons, 1910.

———. *Cowboys and Kings: Three Great Letters by Theodore Roosevelt*. Edited by Elting E. Morison. Cambridge, MA: Harvard University Press, 1954.

———. *Letters and Speeches*. Edited by Louis Auchincloss. New York: Literary Classics of the United States, Inc., 2004.

———. *The Letters of Theodore Roosevelt*. Edited by Elting Morison. 8 vols. Cambridge, MA: Harvard University Press, 1954.

———. *The Works of Theodore Roosevelt*. Edited by Herman Hagedorn. 24 vols. New York: Charles Scribner's Sons, 1923–26.

Rosa, Joseph G. *They Called Him Wild Bill: The Life and Adventures of James Butler Hickok*. Norman: University of Oklahoma Press, 1974.

Rosa, Joseph G., and Robin May. *Buffalo Bill and His Wild West: A Pictorial Biography*. Lawrence: University Press of Kansas, 1989.

Rosaldo, Renato. *Culture & Truth: The Remaking of Cultural Analysis*. Boston: Beacon Press, 1993.

Rowe, John Carlos, ed. *Post-Nationalist American Studies*. Berkeley: University of California Press, 2000.

Rubin, James H. *Impressionism and the Modern Landscape: Productivity, Technology, and Urbanization from Manet to Van Gogh*. Berkeley: University of California Press, 2008.

Russell, Don. *The Lives and Legends of Buffalo Bill*. Norman: University of Oklahoma Press, 1979.

Russell, Henry S. Undated, untitled document. Sartain Family Papers, 1795–1944. Microfilm roll 4564. Archives of American Art. Smithsonian Institution.

Rydell, Robert W. "Buffalo Bill's 'Wild West': The Racialisation of the Cosmopolitan Imagination." In *Colonial Advertising & Commodity Racism*, 97–118. Edited by Wulf D. Hund et al. Zurich: LIT Verlag, 2013.

———. "London's American Exhibition of 1887: How a Cultural Farce Became a Political Force." In *Over (T)here: Transatlantic Essays in Honor of Rob Kroes*. Edited by Kate Delaney and Ruud Janssens. Amsterdam: VU University Press, 2005.

———. "When the Cosmopolitan Was Not a Drink: World's Fairs, Wild West Shows, and the Weirs." In *A Seamless Web: Transatlantic Art in the Nineteenth Century*, 67–82. Edited by Cheryll L. May and Marian Wardle. Newcastle upon Tyne, UK: Cambridge Scholars, 2014.

Rydell, Robert W., and Rob Kroes. *Buffalo Bill in Bologna: The Americanization of the World, 1869–1922*. Chicago: University of Chicago Press, 2005.

Sartain Family Papers, 1795–1944. Archives of American Art. Smithsonian Institution.

Savine, Albert. *Roosevelt intime*. Paris: Juven, 1904.

Sbacchi, Alberto. "Italian Colonization in Ethopia: Plans and Projects, 1936-1940." *Africa: Rivista trimestrale di studi e documentazione dell'Istituto italiano per l'Africa e l'Oriente* 32, no. 4 (December 1977): 503–16.

Schivelbusch, Wolfgang. *The Railway Journey: Trains and Travel in the Nineteenth Century*. Translated by Anselm Hollo. New York: Urizen Books, 1979.

Schmidt-Nowara, Christopher. *The Conquest of History*. Pittsburg: University of Pittsburg Press, 2006.

Scott, Hugh Lenox. *Some Memories of a Soldier*. New York: The Century Co., 1928.

Scott, James Brown. "Peace Conference at The Hague, 1899: Instructions to the International (Peace) Conference at the Hague." The Avalon Project. Yale University. http://avalon.law.yale.edu/19th_century/hag99-03.asp

Scudder, Horace. "Childhood in Modern Literature and Art." *Atlantic Monthly* 56, no. 338 (December 1885): 751–68.

Sears, John. "Bierstadt, Buffalo Bill and the Wild West in Europe." In *Cultural Transmissions and Receptions*, 3–13. Edited by Robert Kroes, Robert Rydell, and D. F. J. Bosscher. Amsterdam: Virginia University Press, 1993.

Sell, Henry Blackman, and Victor Weybright. *Buffalo Bill and the Wild West*. New York: Oxford University Press, 1955.

Sharwood, Robin. "Princes and Peace Makers: The Story of The Hague Peace Conference of 1899." In *The Hague Peace Conferences of 1899 and 1907 and International Arbitration. Reports and Documents*, 447–88. Edited by Shabtai Rosenne. The Hague, Netherlands: T. M. C. Asser Press, 2001.

Sheehan, James J. *Where Have All the Soldiers Gone? The Transformation of Modern Europe*. Boston: Houghton Mifflin Company, 2008.

Shinn, Earl. "Art-Study at the Imperial School in Paris." *Nation*, April 15, 1869, 292–94.

———. "Art-Study in the Imperial School at Paris. No. V. 'Style' and 'Quality': The Routine of Work—Eugenie." *Nation*, July 22, 1869, 67–69.

Shirley, Glenn. *Pawnee Bill: A Biography of Major Gordon W. Lillie*. Albuquerque: University of New Mexico Press, 1958.

Sinnett, Gretchen R. "Envisioning Female Adolescence: Rites of Passage in Late Nineteenth- and Early Twentieth-Century American Painting." PhD Diss., University of Pennsylvania, 2006.

Slotkin, Richard. *The Fatal Environment: The Myth of the American Frontier in the Age of Industrialization, 1800–1890*. New York: Athenaeum, 1985.

———. *Regeneration through Violence: The Mythology of the American Frontier, 1600–1860.* Middletown, CT: Wesleyan University Press, 1973.

Smith, Henry Nash. *Virgin Land: The American West as Symbol and Myth.* Cambridge, MA: Harvard University Press, 1970.

Smith, Michelle J. *Empire in British Girls' Literature and Culture: Imperial Girls, 1880–1915.* Basingstoke: Palgrave Macmillan, 2011.

Smythe, Donald. *Pershing: General of the Armies.* Bloomington: Indiana University Press, 1986.

Somigli, Luca. "Fumetti." In *Encyclopedia of Italian Literary Studies*, 787–91. Edited by Gaetana Marrone and Paola Puppa. New York: Routledge, 2007.

Sorg, Eric V. *Buffalo Bill: Myth and Reality.* Albuquerque: University of New Mexico Press, 2001.

Stanton, Theodore, ed. *Reminiscences of Rosa Bonheur.* New York: Hacker Books, 1976. First published 1910 by Andrew Melrose.

Stead, William T. *The Americanization of the World, or, The Trend of the Twentieth Century.* New York: Garland Publishers, 1972. First published 1902 by William Clowes and Sons, Limited.

Stern, Georgio. *Buffalo Bill a Trieste.* Trieste: La Mongolfiera, 1994.

Susman, Warren I. *Culture as History: The Transformation of American Society in the Twentieth Century.* New York: Pantheon, 1984.

Symons, A. J. A. *Essays and Biographies.* Edited by Julian Symons. London: Cassell, 1969.

Tamarkin, Elisa. *Anglophilia: Deference, Devotion, and Antebellum America.* Chicago: University of Chicago Press, 2007.

Tedesco, Laureen. "Making a Girl into a Scout: Americanizing Scouting for Girls." In *Delinquents and Debutantes: Twentieth-Century American Girls' Cultures*, 20–21. Edited by Sherrie A. Inness. New York: New York University Press, 1998.

Testi, Arnaldo. "The Gender of Reform Politics: Theodore Roosevelt and the Culture of Masculinity." *Journal of American History* 81, no. 4 (March 1995): 1509–33.

Tickner, Lisa. *The Spectacle of Women: Imagery of the Suffrage Campaign, 1907–14.* Chicago: University of Chicago Press, 1988.

Tornos, Juan Valero de. *Cuarenta cartas: Conato de historia y descripción de la Exposición Universal de Barcelona.* Barcelona: Imp. de Pedro Ortega, 1888.

Tornsey, Cheryl B. "Translation and Transubstantiation in *The American*." *Henry James Review* 17, no. 1 (1996): 40–51.

Tortella, Gabriela. "Patterns of Economic Retardation and Recovery in South-West Europe in the 19th and 20th Centuries." *Economic History Review* 47, no. 1 (February 1994): 1–21.

Trachtenberg, Alan. *Shades of Hiawatha: Staging Indians, Making Americans, 1880–1930.* New York: Hill and Wang, 2004.

Truettner, William, ed. *The West as America: Reinterpreting Images of the Frontier, 1820–1920.* Washington, DC: National Museum of American Art, 1991.

Tucker, Paul Hayes. *Monet in the '90s: The Series Paintings*. Boston: Museum of Fine Arts, 1989.

Turner, Frederick Jackson. "The Problem of the West." 1896. Reprinted in *Rereading Frederick Jackson Turner: "The Significance of the Frontier in American History" and Other Essays*, 61–76. Edited by John Mack Faragher. New York: Henry Holt, 1994.

———. "The Significance of the Frontier in American History." 1893. Reprinted in *Rereading Frederick Jackson Turner: "The Significance of the Frontier in American History" and Other Essays*, 31–60. Edited by John Mack Faragher. New York: Henry Holt, 1994.

Tyrrell, Ian. *Transnational Nation: United States History in Global Perspective since 1789*. New York: Palgrave Macmillan, 2007.

Urban, William. "When the 'Wild West' Went to Florence." *Illinois Quarterly* 40, no. 3 (Spring 1978): 5–21.

Varigny, Charles de. *The Women of the United States*. Translated by Arabella Ward. New York: Dodd, Mead, 1895.

Vázquez, Oscar E. *Inventing the Art Collection: Patrons, Markets and the State in Nineteenth-Century Spain*. University Park: Pennsylvania State University Press, 2001.

Vincent, David. "The Progress of Literacy." *Victorian Studies* 45, no. 3 (Spring 2003): 405–31.

Vincent, Mary. *Spain 1833–2002: People and State*. New York: Oxford University Press, 2008.

Viereck, George Sylvester, ed. *As They Saw Us: Foch, Ludendorff and Other Leaders Write Our War History*. Garden City, NY: Doubleday, Doran and Company, Inc., 1929.

Voskuil, Lynn M. *Acting Naturally: Victorian Theatricality and Authenticity*. Charlottesville: University of Virginia Press, 2004.

Vuillard, Éric. *Sorrow of the Earth: Buffalo Bill, Sitting Bull, and the Tragedy of Show Business*. Translated by Ann Jefferson. London: Pushkin Press, 2016. Originally published as *Tristesse de la terre* by Arles: Actes Sud, 2014.

Wahl, Kimberly. *Dressed as in a Painting: Women and British Aestheticism in an Age of Reform*. Durham, NH: University of New Hampshire Press, 2013.

Wallace, Ernest, and E. Adamson Hoebel. *The Comanches: Lords of the Southern Plains*. Norman: University of Oklahoma Press.

Walton, Whitney. *Internationalism, National Identities, and Study Abroad: France and the United States, 1890–1970*. Stanford: Stanford University Press, 2010.

Warren, Louis S. *Buffalo Bill's America: William Cody and the Wild West Show*. New York: Alfred A. Knopf, 2005.

Watts, Sarah. *Rough Rider in the White House: Theodore Roosevelt and the Politics of Desire*. Chicago: University of Chicago Press, 2003.

Wawro, Geoffrey. *The Franco-Prussian War: The German Conquest of France in 1870–1871*. Cambridge: Cambridge University Press, 2003.

Webb, Walter Prescott. *The Great Frontier.* Boston: Houghton Mifflin, 1952.

Weber, Eugen. *France: Fin de Siècle.* Cambridge: The Belknap Press of Harvard University Press, 1986.

Weinberg, H. Barbara. *The Lure of Paris: Nineteenth-Century American Painters and Their French Teachers.* New York: Abbeville Press Publishers, 1991.

Werth, Margaret. "'A Long Entwined Effort': Colonizing Giverny." In *Impressionist Giverny: A Colony of Artists, 1885–1915*, 57–73. Edited by Katherine Bourguignon. Giverny, France: Musée d'art américain and Terra Foundation for American Art, 2007.

Westermeier, Clifford. "Buffalo Bill's Cowboys Abroad." *Colorado Magazine* 52 (Fall 1975): 277–98.

White, Richard. "Frederick Jackson Turner and Buffalo Bill." In *The Frontier in American Culture: An Exhibition at the Newberry Library, August 26, 1994–January 7, 1995*, 7–65. Edited by James R. Grossman. Berkeley: University of California Press, 1994.

———. *"It's Your Misfortune and None of My Own": A New History of the American West.* Norman: University of Oklahoma Press, 1991.

———. *Railroaded: The Transcontinentals and the Making of Modern America.* New York: W. W. Norton, 2011.

Wiener, Joel H. *The Americanization of the British Press, 1830s–1914: Speed in the Age of Transatlantic Journalism.* New York: Palgrave Macmillan, 2011.

Wiesinger, Véronique, Arthur Breton, Philippe Grunchec, and Isabelle Gournay. *Le voyage de Paris: Les américains dans les écoles d'art, 1868–1918 / Paris Bound: Americans in Art Schools, 1868–1918.* Paris: Réunion des musées nationaux, 1990.

Wilde, Oscar. "The American Invasion." *Court and Society Review* 23 March, 1887: 270–71.

———. "The English Renaissance of Art." *Oscar Wilde's Essays and Lectures.* Rockville, MD: Arc Manor, 2008.

———. *The Complete Letters of Oscar Wilde.* Edited by Merlin Holland and Rupert Hart-Davis. London: Fourth Estate, 2000.

———. *Impressions of America.* Edited by Stuart Mason. Sunderland: Keystone, 1906.

Wilder, Marshall P. *The People I've Smiled With: Recollections of a Merry Little Life.* New York: Werner, 1899.

William F. "Buffalo Bill" Cody Collection. MS 6. McCracken Research Library, Buffalo Bill Center of the West.

Wister, Owen. *The Virginian: A Horseman of the Plains.* New York: Gramercy Books, 1902.

Worcester, Donald Emmet. *The Apaches: Eagles of the Southwest.* Norman: University of Oklahoma Press, 1979.

Worster, Donald. *Rivers of Empire: Water, Aridity, and the Growth of the American West.* New York: Pantheon Books, 1985.

Wrobel, David M. "Considering Frontiers and Empires: George Kennan's Siberia and the U.S. West." *Western Historical Quarterly* 46 (Autumn 2015): 284–309.

———. *The End of American Exceptionalism: Frontier Anxiety from the Old West to the New Deal.* Lawrence: University Press of Kansas, 1993.

———. *Global West, American Frontier: Travel, Empire and Exceptionalism from Manifest Destiny to the Great Depression.* Albuquerque: University of New Mexico Press, 2013.

———. *Promised Lands: Promotion, Memory, and the Creation of the American West.* Lawrence: University Press of Kansas, 2002.

Yockelson, Mitchell A. *Borrowed Soldiers: Americans under British Command, 1918.* Norman: University of Oklahoma Press, 2008.

Young, Raymond A. "Pinckney's Treaty—A New Perspective." *Hispanic American Historical Review* 43, no. 4. (1963): 526–35.

Zaide, Gregorio F., and Sonia M. Zaide. *Jose Rizal: Life, Works, and Writings of a Genius, Writer, Scientist, and National Hero.* Quezon City, Philippines: All Nations Publishing Co., 1999.

Zaretsky, Robert. *Cock & Bull Stories: Folco de Baroncelli and the Invention of the Camargue.* Lincoln: University of Nebraska Press, 2004.

Contributors

Emily C. Burns is assistant professor of art history at Auburn University. Her research analyzes Franco-American artistic and cultural exchange in the late nineteenth and early twentieth centuries. Her projects have been supported by the Terra Foundation for American Art, the Metropolitan Museum of Art, the Smithsonian American Art Museum, the Baird Library Society of Fellows, and the Buffalo Bill Center of the West.

Frank Christianson is associate professor of English at Brigham Young University and senior editor of the Papers of William F. Cody at the Buffalo Bill Center of the West. His publications include editions of *The Life of Hon. William F. Cody* (2011) and *The Wild West in England* (2012).

Chris Dixon is assistant head of the School of Languages, Law, and Social Sciences at the Dublin Institute of Technology. He holds a PhD in American history from the University of Strathclyde, where he wrote his doctoral dissertation on Buffalo Bill's Wild West in Barcelona. His publications include editions of *Four Years in Europe with Buffalo Bill* (2010) and *Buffalo Bill from Prairie to Palace* (2012).

Jennifer R. Henneman, PhD, is assistant curator at the Petrie Institute of Western American Art at the Denver Art Museum. While undertaking her doctoral degree in nineteenth-century British and American art and visual culture at the

University of Washington, she served as a research fellow at the Amon Carter Museum of American Art, the Buffalo Bill Center of the West, and the Harry Ransom Center. Her interdisciplinary transatlantic research, which has taken her from the wilds of the American West to the cosmopolitan streets of London, reflects her own upbringing on a cattle ranch in Montana and her interest in the dominant cultural and artistic spheres of the late Victorian era.

Jamie Horrocks is assistant professor of English at Brigham Young University, where she teaches courses on Victorian literature and culture and gender studies. Her research interests center on Victorian aesthetics and the intersection of literature and art, especially in the later nineteenth century. She has published on Oscar Wilde, Vernon Lee, Virginia Woolf, the aesthetic movement, and Victorian periodical illustration.

Jeremy M. Johnston is the Hal and Naoma Tate Endowed Chair and Curator of Western History at the Buffalo Bill Center of the West and Ernest J. Goppert Curator of the Buffalo Bill Museum. He is managing editor of the Papers of William F. Cody. His work has appeared in *Annals of Wyoming*, *Colorado Heritage*, *Readings of Wyoming History*, and the magazine *Points West*. He has published photo histories of Powell, Wyoming, and an annotated version of Ernest Thompson-Seton's *The Biography of a Grizzly* (with Charles Preston). He is a past president of the Wyoming State Historical Society and has appeared on various Wyoming PBS documentaries.

Renee M. Laegreid is professor of history at the University of Wyoming. Her research focuses on women in the American West and on the transnational use of the cowboy image in the United States and Italy. She is coeditor of the anthology *Riding Pretty: Rodeo Royalty in the American West*, *Women on the North American Plains* (2006) and author of "The Legacy of the West in Twentieth Century Italy," published in the *Western Historical Quarterly*.

Monica Rico is associate professor of history at Lawrence University in Appleton, Wisconsin, where she has taught since 2001. Her research interests include early American history, environmental history, and gender history. Her publications include *Nature's Noblemen: Transatlantic Masculinities and the Nineteenth-Century American West* (2013).

Robert W. Rydell is professor of history at Montana State University. He is the author of many books and articles on world's fairs. He is also the coauthor, with Rob Kroes, of *Buffalo Bill in Bologna: The Americanization of the World, 1869–1922*.

Julia Stetler, PhD, has served as a contract historian for the Wyoming Humanities Council and the Women's Veterans Initiative and as visiting assistant professor at the University of Wyoming. She has also been associate editor for the Papers of William F. Cody since 2010. She is currently revising a book-length manuscript on the Wild West in Germany.

David Wrobel is the David L. Boren Professor and the Ward Merrick Chair in Western American History at the University of Oklahoma, where he is also the faculty director of the Western History Collections. His most recent book is *Global West, American Frontier: Travel, Empire, and Exceptionalism from Manifest Destiny to the Great Depression* (2013). In addition to articles on "the West and America" and "John Steinbeck's America," he is currently working on a textbook to be titled *We Hold These Truths: American Ideas and Ideals from the Precolonial Era to the Present.*

Index